THE GREAT GATSBY: *a study*

THE GREAT GATSBY: a study

edited, *with an introduction, by*

FREDERICK J. HOFFMAN
The University of California, Riverside

CHARLES SCRIBNER'S SONS   NEW YORK

COPYRIGHT © 1962 CHARLES SCRIBNER'S SONS

This book published simultaneously in the United States of America and in Canada— Copyright under the Berne Convention

All rights reserved. No part of this book may be reproduced in any form without the permission of Charles Scribner's Sons.

A-2.62[H]

Printed in the United States of America
Library of Congress Catalog Card Number 62-9650

NOTE TO THE READER

The Introduction and commentaries (including the headnotes and identifying footnotes) are set in oblique type to distinguish them from the selections in this book.

I have left the letters as they were originally; if Fitzgerald chose to refer to one of his distinguished contemporaries as "Hemminway," I have thought that the peculiar spelling ought to be retained. Other such errors have also been repeated, because they do not harm the meaning and add a bit of authenticity to the documents in which they are found.

I am grateful to the editorial staff at Scribners and to several kind persons, who have helped with the proofreading at crucial times. My wife, Eleanor Hoffman, is of course the most important of these, and I once again owe her an immense debt for this and many other indispensable acts of assistance.

Frederick J. Hoffman

Riverside, California
December 2, 1961

TABLE OF CONTENTS

NOTE TO THE READER vii

INTRODUCTION 1

*PART I. From THIS SIDE OF PARADISE to
THE GREAT GATSBY* 19

❇ ❇ Fitzgerald's Reputation before *Gatsby*

    F. Scott Fitzgerald   EDMUND WILSON   21
    F. Scott Fitzgerald   PAUL ROSENFELD   29

❇ ❇ Fitzgerald from 1920 to 1925

    Selected Quotations from *This Side of Paradise*   35
    Fitzgerald Chronology 1920-1925   46
    Selection from "The National Letters"   H. L. MENCKEN   48
    Preface to *The Nigger of the Narcissus*   JOSEPH CONRAD   59
    Selections from *Joseph Conrad: A Personal Remembrance*
    FORD MADOX FORD   65

❇ ❇ Anticipations of *The Great Gatsby*

    Winter Dreams   F. SCOTT FITZGERALD   89

PART II. THE GREAT GATSBY and its world 115

    The Delegate from Great Neck   EDMUND WILSON   119
    How to Live on $36,000 a Year   F. SCOTT FITZGERALD   133
    The Man Who Fixed the Series   LEO KATCHER   148

Excerpts from "Descriptions of Girls"   F. SCOTT FITZGERALD
160

PART III. THE GREAT GATSBY   163

⌘ ⌘ Critical Problems

An Introduction to *The Great Gatsby*   F. SCOTT FITZGERALD
165
Letters about *The Great Gatsby* from F. Scott Fitzgerald   169
Letters to Fitzgerald about *The Great Gatsby* and Related
Matters   173

⌘ ⌘ The Method of *The Great Gatsby*

Scenic Narration: Selected Quotations   185
The Narrator and the Narrated: Selected Quotations   196
Beyond West Egg: The End of *The Great Gatsby*   203

PART IV. The permanence of THE GREAT GATSBY   207

The Moral of Scott Fitzgerald   GLENWAY WESCOTT   209
Scott Fitzgerald—the Authority of Failure   WILLIAM
TROY   224
F. Scott Fitzgerald   LIONEL TRILLING   232
Fitzgerald's Brave New World   EDWIN FUSSELL   244
Scott Fitzgerald's Criticism of America   MARIUS BEWLEY   263
The Theme and the Narrator of 'The Great Gatsby'   THOMAS
HANZO   286
The Great Gatsby   RICHARD CHASE   297
Fitzgerald's Triumph   GALE H. CARRITHERS, JR.   303
The Untrimmed Christmas Tree: The Religious Background
of *The Great Gatsby*   HENRY DAN PIPER   321

BIBLIOGRAPHY   335

THE GREAT GATSBY: a study

INTRODUCTION

I

When The Great Gatsby first appeared, in 1925, the majority of Fitzgerald's readers and critics were surprised by its excellence. To all but a handful of the latter, Fitzgerald had seemed an amusing but superficial and undisciplined chronicler of the eccentricities of his "Jazz Age": a label he had himself given the generation of the young who had been in college during the years of World War I, and were twenty when the century was.

The Great Gatsby was a critical triumph, exceeding almost all expectations of his contemporaries, who saw in Fitzgerald's past nothing with which to compare it. The story of how he had come about the writing of it is one of the three basic approaches to the novel; the other two have to do with its method and structure and its skillful use of the milieu with which it is centrally concerned. Many things happened to Fitzgerald in the years 1920 to 1925. He became a writer, to begin with, because of the prestige and the money he thought the life might bring to him. His work came easily out of his undergraduate experiences at Princeton; and when, in 1920, the publication of This Side of Paradise quickly made him a celebrity, he thought he had the formula needed to give him fame and to sustain him in it.

When he began writing for the campus literary magazine, the

Nassau Lit, Fitzgerald's literary heroes were nineteenth-century romantics and early twentieth-century realists. The "paradise" of his first novel was an undergraduate's Eden, as he himself acknowledged in a letter to Edmund Wilson (1918): ". . . really if Scribner takes it I know I'll wake up some morning and find that the debutantes have made me famous over night. I really believe that no one else could have written so searchingly the story of the youth of our generation."[1] In the same letter, he acknowledges "traces" of Tarkington, Chesterton, Chambers, Wells, Rupert Brooke, and more than traces of Compton Mackenzie's novel Sinister Street (1913-14), an English model for the American undergraduate novel.

The point of relevance in all of this is that at the beginning of his career Fitzgerald went all out for the inclusive, accommodating, all-embracing "novel of saturation." When he wrote This Side of Paradise he was very close to his material, even intimately acquainted with it; it was difficult for him to be detached, to judge the behavior of his creatures objectively. His was a bright, spontaneous, but undisciplined talent, and he saw no reason for assuming that an attitude of sentimental attachment to the fates of his undergraduate heroes wasn't the best point of view from which to describe them.

This Side of Paradise was, therefore, "Exhibit A" of the romantic fallacy. Edmund Wilson spoke of Fitzgerald's sense of romantic action as having "all the naïve and romantic gusto of a small boy imagining himself a brave hunter of Indians. . . ."[2] The novel was topical, autobiographical, romantic, and realistic at the same time. The artist in Fitzgerald was scarcely ever separated from the sentimental enthusiast. His point of view was never clearly separated from those of his characters. Worse, it was difficult to see a point of view for either his characters or himself.

[1] The Crack-Up, ed. Edmund Wilson (New York: New Directions, 1945), p. 252.
[2] Quoted by Arthur Mizener in The Far Side of Paradise (Boston: Houghton, Mifflin and Co., 1951), p. 328.

The style erratically suggested all approaches, and none, to the novel's subject.

This Side of Paradise *seemed the work of a genius manqué—very much lacking in many of the disciplines necessary to its re-alization.* Both Wilson and Paul Rosenfeld saw the talent and hoped it would some day be fulfilled. Rosenfeld's essay, published in 1925 on the eve of The Great Gatsby and with no knowledge of it, spoke of Fitzgerald's lack of detachment: ". . . the world of his subject-matter is still too much within Fitzgerald himself for him to see it sustainedly against the universe. . . . Hence, wanting philosophy, and a little overeager like the rest of America to arrive without having really sweated, he falls victim to the favorite delusions of the society of which he is a part, tends to indulge it in its dreams of grandeur, and misses the fine flower of pathos."[3] In fact, the most consistent of criticisms had to do with Fitzgerald's failure to achieve objectivity, to separate himself from his material. "He always suffered from an extreme environmental sense," Glenway Wescott said a few weeks after Fitzgerald's death.[4] William Troy maintained in 1945 that his failure was intensified because of "his unusually high sense of vocation," to which, like Gatsby to his, he was not entirely equal.[5]

In no other modern American writer (except, perhaps, Thomas Wolfe) were the pressures of environment and ambition so strong and so difficult to control. Fitzgerald was a victim of a curious kind of mixed emotion concerning his role as artist. He wanted to "enjoy" (to be rich and profligate, to have the freedom and mobility of the wealthy), but he also wanted to pass judgment upon the excesses and carelessness and cruelty of the wealthy classes. Arthur Mizener puts the difficulty very well indeed, in one of the best biographical and critical studies in recent scholarship:

[3] "F. Scott Fitzgerald," in *Men Seen* (New York: Dial Press, 1925), p. 224. See pages 29 and 21 for the full texts of Rosenfeld's and Wilson's essays.
[4] In *The New Republic*, February 17, 1941. Reprinted in *The Crack-Up*, pp. 323-37. See page 209 for Wescott's essay.
[5] "Scott Fitzgerald: The Authority of Failure," *Accent*, Vol. 6 (Autumn, 1945), 56-70. See page 224 for Troy's essay.

. . . His nature was divided. Partly he was an enthusiastic, romantic young man. Partly he was what he called himself in the "General Plan" for *Tender Is the Night*, "a spoiled priest." This division shows itself in nearly every aspect of his life. The romantic young man was full of confidence about his own ability and the world's friendliness; the spoiled priest distrusted both himself and the world. . . .

. . . All his best work is a product of the tension between these two sides of his nature, of his ability to hold in balance the impulses "to achieve and to enjoy, to be prodigal and open-hearted, and yet ambitious and wise, to be strong and self-controlled, yet to miss nothing—to do and yet to symbolize." . . .[6]

These tensions are also communicated in his art. In This Side of Paradise *they exist in conflict, with neither dominating and in fact no clearly discernible strategy of putting them in order. Fitzgerald's history in the years 1920 to 1925 is a story of his search for a means to exploit and to order the very rich rewards of his imagination without destroying their spontaneity and their charm. James E. Miller, in a much neglected and underrated little book,* The Fictional Technique of Scott Fitzgerald[7] *has plotted his development to* The Great Gatsby *in terms of the move from "saturation" to "selectivity." I should like to offer my version of that career, with much acknowledgment of my debt to Miller.*

1. In the years before 1920, his major interest was in "the novel of saturation," as Henry James had called it: that is, in the omnibus novel, written in a number of styles and from a variety of points of view (what Wilson called, in characterizing This Side of Paradise, *the "collected works of F. Scott Fitzgerald"). This work is a mixture of realistic passages, half unconscious parodies and half imitations of nineteenth-century romanticism, and romantically entangled commitments to the attitudes of youth (that is, people of his age or a very few years younger than he).*

2. Partly because of the scorn with which This Side of Paradise *was visited (by Wilson, John Peale Bishop, Heywood Broun, and*

[6] *The Far Side of Paradise*, pp. 60-61.
[7] The Hague: Martinus Nijhoff, 1957.

others), partly because he himself saw the need to improve, Fitzgerald moved as far as he could away from the limitations of This Side of Paradise in the years between it and the publication of The Beautiful and Damned (1922). But the change was only partial and not entirely successful. He was, for one thing, unwilling to give up the hold H. G. Wells had upon him, but merely shifted from him to H. L. Mencken. The extent of the shift was to move from a "quest" book, or a sentimental, "world weary" bildungsroman, to the kind of objectivity and social judgment contained in Mencken's Prejudices and in The Smart Set (the magazine which published Fitzgerald's first story). The Beautiful and Damned and his play, The Vegetable (1923) are informed by Mencken's kind of "objectivity," which is not objective at all but depends upon the use of a sure aim against an easy target. This development meant at least that Fitzgerald had halfway succeeded in dissociating himself from his characters; it meant also that Mencken's attack upon gentility in American fiction had had its effect upon what Fitzgerald thought a novel's progress should be. Anthony Patch, hero of The Beautiful and Damned, is as much a victim of Mencken's misreading of Dostoevsky as he is of his own inner weaknesses.

3. Nevertheless, in the five years after This Side of Paradise, Fitzgerald showed himself again and again interested in new models and exemplars. He continued to raise his sights; he read intelligently and with a professional interest those discussions and applications of point of view which directly concerned his own problem. That problem was to find a point of vantage from which his very exciting and real contemporary world might be examined and represented without damage or confusion. He was extraordinarily sensitive to his times; he had that "extreme environmental sense" to which Glenway Wescott has referred. He needed to stand off from them, to measure and examine them, and above all to find the aesthetic convention according to which they might be most brilliantly recorded and judged.

II

What went into The Great Gatsby, therefore, was the result of five years of erratic but earnest search and experiment. In the years following This Side of Paradise, his occasional reviews of novels mention again and again the need of "selectivity," of taking a firm grasp upon character and scene, of recording ideas and "plot" through scenes. More than that, he gradually dismisses his earlier literary heroes and finds new ones; he wants to be "the champion" and needs better sparring partners. It is not only that such writers as Joseph Conrad are better artists than Wells and Mackenzie; they are also concerned with the specific problems that, Fitzgerald sensed (or that Wilson and Bishop sensed for him), he needed to solve.

It was a question of where the author stood with respect to his subject and his material. It was also a question of how: by what means could a set of details and circumstances be presented without losing the reader altogether in them or confusing him about point of view and judgment. It is obvious that Conrad was a major tutor in these years. Fitzgerald himself admitted later that this was the case; speaking of the circumstances surrounding the writing of Gatsby, he says "I had just re-read Conrad's preface to The Nigger, and I had recently been kidded half haywire by critics who felt that my material was such as to preclude all dealing with mature persons in a mature world."[8] "My task," Conrad had said in that Preface, "is, by the power of the written word to make you hear, to make you feel—it is, before all, to make you see . . . ."[9] This made a good and useful motto, but Fitzgerald had to go elsewhere for precise directions. He was probably the most sensitive of all readers of fiction in these years—and at the same time the

[8] Introduction to The Great Gatsby, The Modern Library Edition (New York: Random House, 1934). See page 165 for the full text of the Introduction.
[9] Joseph Conrad, "Preface to The Nigger of the Narcissus," in Conrad's Prefaces to His Works (London: J. M. Dent & Sons Ltd., 1937), p. 52. See page 59 for the full text of the "Preface."

most erratic of practitioners of the art, throwing good stories after bad, accumulating and discharging both literary and financial debts in a reckless and frantic succession of maneuvers.

The obvious sources of help were Conrad's *Lord Jim* and *The Heart of Darkness*, whose Marlow served the limited but significant role Nick Carraway was to serve in Gatsby. But other works also interested him. Joyce's *Ulysses* impressed him as a novel preeminently worked out from what Wilson called a "precise technical plan." Surely *Ulysses* impressed him as a masterful warning of the need of careful attention to technique, though there is no specific indebtedness in Gatsby. James was another master of technique to whom Fitzgerald might have turned, but there is not even any indication that he had gone beyond *Daisy Miller* and *The American* by the time he had written Gatsby, if indeed he had read that far. But James's uses of point of view, his scenic maneuvers, his care for the refashioning of dialogue (to make it precisely adequate), are not in any way inimical to Fitzgerald's thinking and practice. Perhaps Willa Cather was more nearly contemporary and intelligible. Miller points out the similarities of *My Ántonia* and *A Lost Lady* to Fitzgerald's interest, but then quite properly discounts the former and asks that the parallel of the latter with Gatsby not be pressed too far. The truth is that Fitzgerald needed to borrow not a subject (which he had uniquely and in abundance), but a method and a technique; and these he worked out from whatever sources were available: Conrad, James, Cather, Ford Madox Ford. In Ford's *Personal Remembrance of Conrad* (first published in 1924 in his *transatlantic review*) the problems of scenic representation and point of view are carefully worked out, in such a manner as could have helped Fitzgerald immensely.[10]

III

The problems associated with the study of The Great Gatsby are clearly a product of the history of its composition. Fitzgerald

[10] Ford Madox Ford, *Joseph Conrad: A Personal Remembrance* (London: Duckworth, 1924). See page 65 for excerpts.

had come upon a most remarkable and a most profitable means of representing contemporary society (or at least a significant part of it). Gatsby is linked to the 1920's world itself, but he is also historically associated with the "American dream," with the progress of American wealth and ambition from the very dawn of New World aspirations. In many ways, Gatsby is a marvel of symbolically compressed cultural history: of the original promise, seen in the "fresh, green breast of the new world" (Gatsby, p. 182)[11]; of the growth and decline of that promise as the history of American money-getting moved into the twentieth century; of the vulgarization and venality of the privilege conferred by wealth; but above all, of its association with a romantic view of time and the past. This romantic "illusion" is at the core of Gatsby's characterization as a figure of tragedy or pathos. At one point he cries out to Nick Carraway, "Can't repeat the past? . . . Why of course you can" (Gatsby, p. 111). He wishes not only to repeat the past but to fix it forever; and the means of fixing time, of ruling out history, is to move quickly toward the possession of wealth and to its use, in matching and exceeding the advantages wealth has given Tom Buchanan.

This role of money in The Great Gatsby involves one, by implication and indirection, in three major cultural symbols: that of the social role of wealth, which became a moral and aesthetic convention in James and Howells; that of the Manhattan underworld, the source of Gatsby's fortune; and that of the world of appearances, especially of young and privileged love. All three of these are present in Fitzgerald's other works; all of them receive masterful treatment in The Great Gatsby. Perhaps for the first time Fitzgerald saw the world of his subject clearly and with a moderate objectivity. The pathos of Gatsby's vulgarity is evident not only in the glare of his parties but also in the obscenity and tragic indifference with which his invitations are used and received. But it is a

[11] F. Scott Fitzgerald, The Great Gatsby, the Scribner Library Edition (New York: Charles Scribner's Sons, 1960). All page references in this Introduction are to this edition.

most complex symbol, involving not only Gatsby and his indifferent guests, but the Buchanans from across the bay, and Carraway
himself (who is learning the bond business and is twice offered a
special "deal" by Gatsby). Most of all, the social value of money
serves as the means of testing and measuring the vitality and the
integrity of human impulses and desires: the network of contrasts
and confusions involved in Tom Buchanan's two women and in
Gatsby's being mixed up with both, sets up the basic uses of wealth
in the novel. These uses are revealed in the four scenes of residence
(the three houses on East and West Egg, the apartment on 158th
Street), in which the arrangements of space are brilliant clues to
taste, moral discretion, human arrogance and humility, and romantic impulse.

William Rose Benét, reviewing Gatsby for the Saturday Review
of Literature, said that "For the first time Fitzgerald surveys the
Babylonian captivity of this era unblinded by the bright lights."[12]
There are many reasons for this central truth: the use of Nick
Carraway as a narrator who plays several roles, as a man who articu-
lates, is skeptical of, judges, and eventually accepts Gatsby's aspirations and his illusion; the skill of "scenic narration," in which
objects and their arrangements speak much in little space; the
great and successful use of symbolic devices (the "valley of ashes,"
the eyes of Doctor T. J. Eckleburg, the green light at the end of
the Buchanan dock, the many-leveled and many-angled Rolls-Royce
of Gatsby), and of the imagery of sounds, sight, and atmosphere
which serve to weave these into a pattern; the great fitness of the
minutiae of style in dialogue, transition, and forms of narration.

Above all, Gatsby is successful because it is presented and not
merely "told." The succession of "party" chapters, 1, 2, and 3,
provide as good an opening as there is in modern fiction. The
places are suggestively given before the full significance is known
of those who inhabit them. In each case, the place and the man-

---

[12] *Saturday Review of Literature*, May 9, 1925, p. 740. Quoted in *The Fictional
Technique of Scott Fitzgerald*, p. 90.

ners of those who move in and about them leave something of a mystery, that needs to be both defined and solved in the action that follows. Fitzgerald maneuvers present and past in a succession of scenic records: Louisville, Long Island, Minnesota, Europe are all seen, whether in memory or in the impact of present action.

This interweaving of present and past is especially important, in the light of Nick Carraway's role as narrator. The real triumph of The Great Gatsby lies in its combining two principal strands of emotional and intellectual development: Carraway moves toward an understanding of Gatsby (he must "solve the mystery" of what appears at first to be a "purposeless splendor"); but he also comes to accept Gatsby, as the mystery recedes and the "young roughneck" vulgarity is discounted, for the "romantic readiness for hope" that transcends it.

These are the major means of the novel. It is, therefore, a novel with both Gatsby and Carraway as heroes. Only Carraway grows in the novel; but that is because Gatsby had very early in his life decided his destinies and in his case it is circumstance rather than personal inadequacy that affects it. Carraway's virtue is one of limitation; Gatsby's greatness comes from his having impulsively, anxiously, and absolutely committed himself to an illusion that transcended all limit. The two qualities are the polarities of American "promise," as Fitzgerald saw it. Gatsby has gone "all the way" before we have even seen him; Carraway must go much of the way toward him. They meet "on Gatsby's side, and alone" (Gatsby, p. 165), but Carraway's sense of restraint is sufficient to make him stop short of Gatsby's absurdity, the uncomprehending vulgarity of his means, and to cause him to appreciate the romantic purity of Gatsby's ends without submitting to its almost ludicrous and pathetic moral chaos of means.

The Great Gatsby, because of its posing its two heroes against one another and because of its moving them toward one another, economically provides for a remarkable range of representation, of every nuance and detail of wealth in the contemporary American scene. In Carraway's interpretation of him, Gatsby offers an almost disembodied symbol of its romantic impulse. "The truth was," he says of Gatsby midway in the novel, "that Jay Gatsby of West Egg, Long Island, sprang from his Platonic conception of himself. He was a son of God—a phrase which, if it means anything, means just that—and he must be about His Father's business, the service of a vast, vulgar, and meretricious beauty" (Gatsby, p. 99). In its purest form, Gatsby's "conception" has nothing to do with money in itself, but rather with the realization of an ideal "promise," somehow transcending both person and setting. This is in its most ideal form the absolute synthesis of the American ideal, which is briefly glimpsed at the novel's end, when (as the moonlight dissolves the "inessential houses") the green light and the "green breast of the new world" become one, as they once were "for Dutch sailors' eyes" (Gatsby, p. 182).

This impression might easily have led to the worst kind of sentimental indulgence, except for Fitzgerald's method, which helps to introduce this aspect of Gatsby gradually, and almost apologetically, so that we know him at first as a "mystery character," then as an absurd one, then a pathetic soul, finally an admirable exception to the whole "rotten crowd" (Gatsby, p. 154). Three perspectives play upon the novel's central subjects: Gatsby's in the extreme sense, as Carraway describes it at the beginning of chapter 6; Carraway's Midwestern, "pastoral," "slow-thinking," moderate and moderating view; and that of the actual world, which is indifferent to either the virtue of restraint or the ideal of an ambition transcending gain. Several persons, or groups of persons, play among these three. The Buchanans are of course a part of the third; they are careless and cruel and selfish and wayward. But Daisy alternates between Gatsby's and Tom's fundamental views of "civilization." She is not equal to Gatsby's, but she finds Tom's wholly unsatisfactory. She is above all frightened by Gatsby, both by the intensity of his vision and by the confusion and uncertainty of the means he has taken to realize it. The Wilsons, and their place, serve as "Waste Land" variations upon the first and the third perspective. Both express a pathetic remnant of the vision, which in their cases is seen in a vital despair and a sense of apocalyptic vision. The death of Gatsby comes ironically from George Wilson's having totally misunderstood the world of Tom Buchanan and of Myrtle. The eyes of Dr. Eckleburg, brooding over the valley of ashes, become what is left of the "son of God" Gatsby has imagined himself to be. In the end, Tom Buchanan belongs to the crowd of people who attend, uninvited, Gatsby's parties, whose names Carraway once jotted down on the empty spaces of an old railway time-table (Gatsby, p. 61-63).

IV

The problems worthy of discussion in The Great Gatsby have to do first of all with a consideration of Fitzgerald's immense advance from his earliest work. Are there evidences in that work of his ability to achieve so successful a form as he does in Gatsby? What are the specific weaknesses of such novels as This Side of Paradise and The Beautiful and Damned, as they compare with The Great Gatsby: overloading of characters, confusion of styles, rhetorical interference by the author with his materials and his subject? What theories and practices in modern literature served most to help Fitzgerald see his way to a solution of these problems?

When we come to Gatsby itself, there are several kinds of questions. The subject-matter would itself seem to suffer from two inadequacies: it is inchoate and it is inarticulate. That is, the "world" of Gatsby and his parties is confused, available to no recognizable or useful standards of order; it needs to be interpreted from a point of view outside itself, whether the author himself or a narrator specially designated by him for the task. Further, no one within that world is capable of articulating the meaning of its story: Gatsby's vocabulary is limited, and there is a symbolic value in his failure to penetrate beneath the surface of the life he has chosen (that is, his inarticulateness is necessary to the novel's meaning); Wolfsheim is obviously not suited to speak for himself or even of himself; and the others are indifferent to the point of moral paralysis.

In order to communicate the meaning of The Great Gatsby, Fitzgerald had to find a narrator whose presence on the scene is acceptable, who does not find the scene so alien and forbidding that he is incapable of doing it justice, but who is also able (partly because of his separation, but also because of his involvement) to define and describe its meaning and to judge it unobnoxiously. This character is Nick Carraway. We must first of all be sure of his acceptability as a character in this role. He tells us from the start that he is "inclined to reserve all judgments" (Gatsby, p. 1), that he is "slow-thinking and full of interior rules that act as brakes on [his] desires . . ." (Gatsby, p. 59); but he also admits to great admiration for the kind of "extraordinary gift for hope, a romantic readiness . . ." (Gatsby, p. 2) which he sees in Gatsby. Carraway's background is sketched in sufficiently to enable us to see the sources of his point of view. It is Midwestern, traditional, contained; most important is its stability, which comes from his family's having lived in the same place, even the same house, for several generations (Gatsby, pp. 2-3). Extreme mobility, in both Gatsby's and Buchanan's case, is a moral liability.

These conditions, stated quite arbitrarily and matter-of-factly, would seem to make Carraway ideally suited to the tasks of narrating and judging Gatsby's story. If anything, they might have made him less than ideally useful to an understanding of it (from sheer distaste for it), were it not for two facts: Carraway is involved in the Gatsby story, through his relation to the Buchanans and the affair with Jordan Baker; he is also, very significantly, ready to accept the vigor of Gatsby's drive and will, because of his love of the "romantic will" as he sees it in others. The two qualities (stability of moral position, appreciation of the romantic impulse) must appear to be ideally balanced in his final estimate of Gatsby and in his commitment to him. One may say that Carraway's moral sense is educated, even that it is brought to life, through its contact with Gatsby's more powerful and less inhibited romantic

will: that Carraway therefore emerges in possession of a new and
a wholly revitalized moral knowledge.

Is this entirely true? To put the question another way, are Carraway's moral judgments reliable, or is the fact of his making them
acceptable to us? One way of answering this question is to say
that if we cannot accept Carraway, the novel is a chaos: that is,
that the chaos of Gatsby's world requires some kind of judgment
from a set of standards we can accept, or the novel is meaningless.
Does Carraway betray his standards? Mr. Robert W. Stallman
would like us to believe that he does, in the essay "Gatsby and the
Hole in Time."[13] There is the affair with Jordan Baker, in which
he seems to conduct himself dishonestly, permitting himself her
standards and apparently dismissing his own for the duration.
There are other affairs, imagined or just barely begun, in which
he seems to have been involved from time to time. Isn't it therefore an act of deceitful arrogance for him to say, "Every one suspects himself of at least one of the cardinal virtues, and this is
mine: I am one of the few honest people that I have ever known"
(Gatsby, p. 60)?

Carraway is, after all, neither saint nor prig. There is nothing
in his statement of position that requires of him that he be strait-
laced or pure moralist. In fact, if he were to meet Stallman's impossible standards, his presence at West Egg would itself have
been an intolerable imposture. I think we can grant Nick Carraway's sins as understandable deviations from what would otherwise
have been an insufferable excellence. As Thomas Hanzo has put it
in the best answer so far given to Stallman's strange tirade,
". . . Nick's irregularities of behavior, his carelessness, do not escape his judgment; he does not grow more confused but learns to
see more clearly what Eastern society and morality are and how
he has been corrupted by them."[14]

[13] In *Modern Fiction Studies*, I (November, 1955), 2-16.
[14] "The Theme and the Narrator of 'The Great Gatsby'," *Modern Fiction
Studies*, II (Winter, 1956-57), 185. See page 286 for the full text of Hanzo's
essay.

If we may accept Nick Carraway as narrator and judge of the Gatsby story, we need to look further, into the apparently intended analogy with American history. In Carraway's mind at least, the Gatsby dream has been defiled. He decides to return to the West, not because of Gatsby, but because of "what preyed on Gatsby, what foul dust floated in the wake of his dreams . . ." (Gatsby, p. 2). The "foul dust" has many equivalents, personal and impersonal, in the novel. Perhaps the most affecting of these occurs near the end of chapter 6, when Gatsby vigorously asserts that "of course you can" repeat the past: "He broke off and began to walk up and down a desolate path of fruit rinds and discarded favors and crushed flowers" (Gatsby, p. 111). The fruit rinds and discarded favors and related images are combined in a single detail at the novel's end: on the night before his departure, Carraway pays one last visit to Gatsby's mansion and there discovers an obscene word scratched on one of the stone steps: "On the white steps an obscene word, scrawled by some boy with a piece of brick, stood out clearly in the moonlight, and I erased it, drawing my shoe raspingly along the stone . . ." (Gatsby, p. 181).

The question raised by the suggestions of analogy is twofold: is Gatsby's illusion (this "Platonic conception of himself") competent to be judged analogically; and, is Carraway competent to so judge it? As for the first, we can only say that Fitzgerald, through Carraway, has intended that it be so extended, and has provided the means of its extension (the matter of Dan Cody and Meyer Wolfsheim in the line of succession as heirs of the "American dream"; the fact that Gatsby's own "dream" is supported by the vulgarities and the power provided by Wolfsheim). It is important that many of Gatsby's claims to gentility and worth are in themselves pathetic, if they are not pure fabrication; the irony which enforces the pathos is that Gatsby, with a powerful romantic will is nevertheless entirely innocent of pretension, indeed of taste of any kind: the smile that "faced—or seemed to face—the whole eternal world for an instant, and then concentrated on you with an *irresistible prejudice in your favor . . ."* fades, leaving "an elegant young roughneck, a year or two over thirty, whose elaborate formality of speech just missed being absurd" (*Gatsby*, p. 48).

One may, I think, reasonably conclude not only that Gatsby is deserving of his fate and of the sympathy accorded him because of it, but also that he is quite appropriately situated in the world that makes him suffer it. He is neither blessed by the refinements of an aristocracy of wealth (he is infinitely more vulgar than James's Christopher Newman, himself the master naïf of James's fiction), nor cursed by the cruelty and carelessness of a Tom Buchanan.

As for the second of these questions, whether Carraway is competent to suggest the analogy, perhaps Thomas Hanzo provides the best answer to it: "Nick's discovery is that the power of will without the direction of intelligence is a destructive power, that there must be some real end beyond the satisfaction of private desire—however desire may be exalted—to justify the expenditure of life. But he believes too that, except for the anachronistic and fatal instance of Gatsby, the time when such ends could have existed is now done. . . ."[15] Within his own limits, of which he is thoroughly aware, it is possible for Carraway to withdraw from Gatsby's manner, even to be frightened by it; it is possible also for him to admire the purity and consistency of Gatsby's romantic will (especially since Carraway is himself not capable of sustaining it); finally, he can, in the light of Gatsby's death and especially of the conspiracy of silence and indifference which attends his funeral, recognize that conditions no longer permit that such a will be realized. Carraway's insights into Gatsby are the major rewards, among many, of Fitzgerald's having so carefully selected and persisted in his narrative point of view.

Many other questions deserve at least to be stated. Some of these have to do with the sequence of narration, the alternation of Gatsby's past with the present action, which James Miller has so

[15] *Ibid.*, p. 189.

neatly discussed.[16] Narration combines most successfully with scenic presentation, to develop the substance of the tale; this is especially true of the opening chapters, in which present facts are edged by suggestions of past causes but do not give away the crucial meaning until all of the pieces, past and present, are fitted together. Fitzgerald's skill in maneuvering both symbol and supporting image deserves exhaustive analysis: these range from the description of Gatsby's cream-colored Rolls-Royce and its subsequent involvement in the death of Myrtle Wilson (consider, for example, how the "mistake" expresses Gatsby's being "trapped" in the Buchanan world), to the elaborate "ash décor" of the Valley of Ashes, which penetrates the lives of all West Egg and East Egg personages.

Above all, the question of Gatsby's success comes from Fitzgerald's having skillfully counterpointed his characters within a single framework of interpretation. Carraway's "understanding" of Gatsby is of course the central narrative line; but within this relationship all other characters are somehow drawn. Perhaps this intricate pattern is best seen in chapter five, and especially in the passage that describes Gatsby's tour of his house with Daisy and Nick (Gatsby, pp. 91-97), a masterful fusion of significant image and idiom, dialogue, and interpretation. The shadings of belief, conviction, and meaning, from Gatsby's pure will down to the marginal pathos of Klipspringer's "performance" at the piano, are representative of the deep involvement found throughout the novel. Carraway and Gatsby, in their fundamental natures, direct and qualify our views of the other characters. They are judged and placed somewhere along the line described by Carraway's narrative move toward Gatsby's death and its consequences.

Of the great values of The Great Gatsby there can be little doubt. There may be differences concerning the proper weighting of these values, or the exact margin of success in any given instance. The materials offered in this collection are designed for

[16] See The Fictional Technique of Scott Fitzgerald, pp. 96-97.

two ends: to describe the course Fitzgerald took from his first novel to his masterpiece; and to present as many perspectives upon The Great Gatsby as may be usefully seen. It is designed to document Fitzgerald's career, but also critically and variously to assess the worth of its greatest achievement.

From THIS SIDE OF PARADISE
to THE GREAT GATSBY

part *1*

FITZGERALD'S REPUTATION BEFORE *GATSBY*

F. SCOTT FITZGERALD*

Edmund Wilson

This essay was originally published in the Bookman (March, 1922) pp. 20-25. It was also later published in Wilson's collection, The Shores of Light (New York: Farrar, Straus, and Young, 1952) pp. 27-35, and in Alfred Kazin's selection, F. Scott Fitzgerald (Cleveland: World, 1951), pp. 77-83.

It has been said by a celebrated person that to meet F. Scott Fitzgerald is to think of a stupid old woman with whom some one has left a diamond; she is extremely proud of the diamond and shows it to every one who comes by, and everybody is surprised that such an ignorant old woman should possess so valuable a jewel; for in nothing does she appear so stupid as in the remarks she makes about the diamond.

The person who invented this simile did not know Scott Fitzgerald very well and can have seen him only, I think, in particularly uninteresting moods. The reader must not suppose that there is any literal truth in the image. Scott Fitzgerald, as anybody will recognize almost immediately upon meeting him, is not a stupid old woman but a good-looking young man of not undistinguished

* Edmund Wilson, from "F. Scott Fitzgerald," The Literary Spotlight, ed. John Farrar (New York: Doran, 1924), pp. 125-34. Reprinted with the permission of the author.

21

appearance and ingenuous charm, who far from being stupid is extremely entertaining. But there is, none the less, a symbolic truth in the description quoted above: it is true that Fitzgerald has been left with a jewel which he doesn't know quite what to do with. For he has been given imagination without intellectual control of it; he has been given a desire for beauty without an aesthetic ideal; and he has been given a gift for expression without many ideas to express.

Consider, for example, the novel with which he founded his reputation, "This Side of Paradise." It has almost every fault and deficiency that a novel can possibly have. It is not only highly imitative but it is imitated from a bad novel. Fitzgerald, when he wrote it, was drunk with Compton Mackenzie, and the book sounds like an American attempt to rewrite "Sinister Street." Now Mackenzie, despite his extraordinary gift for picturesque and comic invention and the capacity for pretty writing which he says that he learned from Keats, lacks both the intellectual force and the emotional imagination to give body and outline to the material which he secretes in such enormous abundance. With the seeds he took from Keats's garden (one of the best kept gardens in the world) he exfloreated so profusely that he blotted out the path of his own. Michael Fane, the hero of "Sinister Street," was swamped in the forest of description; he was smothered by columbine. From the time he went up to Oxford, his personality disappeared and when last seen (at Belgrade) he was no longer recognizable as anybody in particular. As a consequence, Amory Blaine, the hero of "This Side of Paradise," had a very poor chance of coherence: he had more emotional life, it is true, than the phantom Michael Fane, who, like most of Mackenzie's creations, had practically none at all; but he was quite as much an uncertain quantity in a phantasmagoria of incident which had no dominating intention to endow it with unity and force. In short, one of the chief weaknesses of "This Side of Paradise" is that it is really not *about* anything: intellectually it amounts to little more than a gesture—a gesture of indefinite revolt. For another thing, "This Side of Paradise" is very immaturely imagined: it is always just verging on the ludicrous. And, finally, it is one of the most illiterate books of any merit ever published (a fault which the publisher's proofreader apparently made no effort to correct). It is not only ornamented with bogus ideas and faked literary references but it is full of English words misused with the most reckless abandon.

I have said that "This Side of Paradise" commits almost every sin that a novel can possibly commit: it is true that it does commit every sin except the unpardonable sin: it does not fail to live. The whole preposterous farrago is animated with life. It is, to be sure, rather a fluttering and mercurial sort of life: its emotions do not move you profoundly; its drama does not make you hold your breath; but its gaiety and color and movement gave it a distinction for a literary criticism long accustomed to heaviness and dinginess in serious American fiction. If one recalls the sort of gritty fodder of which Ernest Poole's "The Harbor" is an example, one understands the extravagant enthusiasm with which "This Side of Paradise" was hailed.

For another thing, it was well written—well written, *quand même*. It is true, as I have said above, that Fitzgerald misuses words; his works are full of malapropisms of the most disconcerting kind: you will find—"Whatever your flare (*sic*) proves to be—religion, architecture, literature," "the Juvenalia of my collected editions," "There were nice things in it (the room) . . . offsprings of a vicarious (vagarious?), impatient taste acting in stray moments," "a mind like his, lucrative in intelligence, intuition, and lightning decision," etc., etc. It reminds one rather of

> *Agib, who could readily, at sight,*
> *Strum a march upon the loud Theodolite.*
> *He would diligently play*
> *On the Zoetrope all day,*
> *And blow the gay Pantechnicon all night.*

It is true that Fitzgerald plays the language entirely by ear. But, for all that, his flute is no mean one. He has an instinct for graceful and vivid prose which some of his more serious fellows might envy.

In regard to the man himself, there are perhaps two things worth knowing for the influence they have had on his work. In the first place, he comes from the middle west—from St. Paul, Minnesota. Fitzgerald is as much of the middle west of large cities and country clubs as Lewis is of the middle west of the prairies and little towns. What we find in him is much what we find in the prosperous strata of these cities: sensitivity and eagerness for life without a sound base of culture and taste; a brilliant structure of hotels and exhilarating social activities built not on the eighteenth century but simply on the prairie. And it seems to me a great pity that he has not written more of the west: it is perhaps the only milieu that he thoroughly understands; when he approaches the east, he brings to it the standards of the wealthy west—the preoccupation with display, the love of magnificence and jazz, the vigorous social atmosphere of amiable flappers and youths comparatively unpoisoned as yet by the snobbery of the east. In "The Beautiful and Damned," for example, we feel that he is moving in a vacuum; the characters have no convincing connection with the background to which they are assigned; they are not part of the organism of New York as the characters in, say, "Bernice Bobs Her Hair" are a part of the organism of St. Paul. Surely Fitzgerald should do for Summit Avenue what Lewis has done for Main Street.

But you are not to suppose from all this that Fitzgerald is merely a typical middle westerner, with correct clothes and clear skin, who has been sent east to college. The second thing one should understand about him is the fact that he is part Irish and that he brings to the writing of fiction some qualities rarely found in America. For, like the Irish, he is romantic, but is also cynical about romance; he is ecstatic and bitter; lyrical and sharp. He is bound to represent himself as a playboy, yet he mocks incessantly at the playboy. He is vain, a little malicious, of quick intelligence and wit and with a gift for turning language into something iridescent and surprising. In fact, he often reminds one of the description which a great Irishman has written of the Irish:

> An Irishman's imagination never lets him alone, never convinces him, never satisfies him; but it makes him that he can't face reality nor deal with it nor handle it nor conquer it: He can only sneer at them that do . . . and imagination's such a torture that you can't bear it without whisky. . . . And all the while there goes on a horrible, senseless, mischievous laughter.

For the rest, he is a rather childlike fellow, very much wrapped up in his dream of himself and his projection of it on paper. For a person of his intellectual nimbleness he is extraordinarily little occupied with the general affairs of the world: like a woman, he is not much given to abstract or impersonal thought. Conversations about politics or criticism have a way of snapping back to Fitzgerald. But he seldom makes you angry in this way; he does it usually without pompousness or airs. He is utterly devoid of affectation and takes the curse off his relentless egoism by his readiness to laugh at himself and his boyish uncertainty of his abilities. And he possesses, both personally and in his writings, a quality exceedingly rare among even the young American writers of the day: he is almost the only one among them who has any real light-hearted gayety. Where Sinclair Lewis would stew "the Problem of Salesmanship" in acrid rancorous fumes, Fitzgerald, in "The Beautiful and Damned," has turned it into hilarious farce. His characters—and himself—are actors in an elfin harlequinade; they are as nimble, as gay and as lovely—and as hard-hearted—as fairies: Columbine elopes with Harlequin on a rope ladder from the Ritz and both go morris-dancing amuck on a case of bootleg liquor; Pantaloon is pinked with an epigram that withers him up like a leaf; the Policeman is tripped by Harlequin and falls into the Pulitzer Fountain. In the end, Harlequin puts on false whiskers and pretends he is Bernard Shaw; he gives an elaborate interview to the newspapers on politics, history, and religion; a hundred thousand readers read it and are enormously impressed; Columbine nearly dies laughing; Harlequin buys another case of gin.

Let me quote a characteristic incident in connection with "The Beautiful and Damned," which will give a better idea of Fitzgerald than any number of adjectives could do.

Since writing "This Side of Paradise"—on the inspiration of Wells and Mackenzie—Fitzgerald has become acquainted with another school of fiction: the ironical-pessimistic. In college, he had supposed that the thing to do was to write biographical novels with a burst of ideas toward the close; since his advent into the literary world, he has discovered that there is another genre in favor: the kind which makes much of the tragedy and "the meaninglessness of life." Hitherto, he had supposed that the thing to do was to discover a meaning in life; but he now set bravely about to produce a sufficiently desolating tragedy which should be, also, 100 per cent meaningless. As a result of this determination, the first version of "The Beautiful and Damned" culminated in a carnival of disaster for which the reader was imperfectly prepared: Fitzgerald ruined his characters wholesale with a set of catastrophes so arbitrary that beside them, the worst perversities of Hardy were like the working of natural laws. The heroine loses her beauty at a prematurely early age and her character, though it is hard to see why, goes incontinently with it; Richard Caramel, a writer of promise, loses all his literary ideals and becomes a prostitute of popular taste; and the hero, Anthony Patch, who has formerly been very rich, not only loses all his money but, unable to make a living by himself, succumbs to inertia and drink, and eventually goes mad. But the bitterest moment of the story comes at the very end, when Anthony is wandering the streets of New York in an attempt to borrow some money. After several humiliating failures, he finally approaches an old friend whom he sees with an elegant lady just getting into a cab. It is Maury Noble, the most brilliant of all his friends, a cynic, an intellectual, and a man of genuine parts. But Maury fails to recognize Anthony; he cuts him dead; and drives away in the taxi. "But," the author explains, "he really had not seen Anthony. For Maury had indulged his appetite for alcoholic beverage once too often: he was now stone-blind!"

But the point of my story is this: though he had written the passage in all seriousness, as soon as he heard other people laughing at it, he began laughing at it himself, and with as much gayety and surprise as if he had just read it in Max Beerbohm. And he began to improvise a burlesque which ran somewhat as follows: "It seemed to Anthony that Maury's eyes had a fixed glassy stare; his legs moved stiffly as he walked and when he spoke his voice seemed to have no life in it. When Anthony came nearer, he saw that Maury was dead!"

To conclude, it would be unfair to submit Fitzgerald already to a rigorous critical overhauling while he is still only in his twenties and has presumably most of his work before him. His restless imagination may yet precipitate as something durably brilliant. For the present, however, this imagination is certainly not seen to very good advantage: it suffers badly from lack of discipline and poverty of aesthetic ideas. Fitzgerald is a dazzling extemporizer but his stories have a way of petering out: he seems never to have planned them thoroughly or to have thought them out from the beginning. This is true even of some of his most successful fantasies, such as "The Diamond as Big as the Ritz" or his comedy, "The Vegetable." On the other hand, "The Beautiful and Damned," imperfect as it was, marked an advance over "This Side of Paradise": the style is more nearly mature and the subject more solidly unified, and certain scenes in it are probably the most convincing he has ever invented.

And in any case, in spite of all I have said, Fitzgerald has his intellectual importance. In his very moral anarchy, in the very confusion of his revolt, he is typical of the generation of the war— the generation described on the last page of "This Side of Paradise" as "grown up to find all gods dead, all wars fought, all faiths in men shaken." There is a profounder truth in "The Beautiful and Damned" than the author perhaps intended to convey: the hero and heroine are strange creatures without purpose or method, who give themselves up to wild debaucheries and do not, from beginning to end of the book, perform a single serious act: but you somehow get the impression that, in spite of their madness, they are the most rational people in the book: wherever they touch the common life, the institutions of men are made to appear a contemptible farce of the futile and the absurd; the world of finance, the army, and, finally, the world of business are successively and casually exposed as completely without dignity or point. The inference is that, in such a civilization, the sanest and most creditable thing is to live for the jazz of the moment and forget the activities of men. And it is not altogether a personal confusion which has produced the confusion of such a book. It may be that we must not expect too much intellectual balance of young men who write books in the year 1921: we must remember that their environment and their chief source of stimulation have been the wars, the society, and the commerce of the Age of Confusion itself.

F. SCOTT FITZGERALD*

Paul Rosenfeld

This essay was first published in Men Seen: *Twenty-Four Modern Authors (New York: Dial, 1925), pp. 215-224. It was written just before the publication of* The Great Gatsby *(April 10, 1925). It has also been printed in Alfred Kazin's selection,* F. Scott Fitzgerald *(Cleveland: World, 1951), pp. 71-76.*

The utmost that can be charged against F. Scott Fitzgerald is that too oftentimes his good material eludes him. Of the ultimate values of said material there is no dispute. Certain racehorses run for the pure joy of running, and the author of *The Beautiful and Damned* and *Tales of the Jazz Age* is such an animal. He is a born writer, amusing himself with tales and pictures; and eventually nothing is interesting except the natural bent. Salty and insipid, exaggeratedly poetical and bitterly parodistic, his writing pours exuberantly out of him. Flat paragraphs are redeemed by brilliant metaphors, and conventional descriptions by witty, penetrating turns. Ideas of diamond are somewhat indiscriminately mixed with ideas of rhinestone and ideas of window glass; yet purest rays serene are present in veritable abundance. They must come to this bannerman of the slickers and flappers in a sort of dream, un-

*Paul Rosenfeld, from "F. Scott Fitzgerald," The Crack-Up, ed. Edmund Wilson (New York: New Directions, 1945), pp. 317-22. Reprinted with the permission of Edna Bryner.

expectedly out of some arcana where they have been concealing themselves, and surprise him by smiling up at him from underneath his pen. For so they startle the reader, unprepared to encounter, in writing as carelessly undertaken, ideas so mature and poignant and worthy of fine settings.

Not a contemporary American senses as thoroughly in every fiber the tempo of privileged post-adolescent America. Of that life, in all its hardness and equally curious softness, its external clatter, movement and boldness, he is a part; and what he writes reflects the environment not so much in its superficial aspects as in its pitch and beat. He knows how talk sounds, how the dances feel, how the crap-games look. Unimportant detail shows how perfect the unconscious attunement: the vignette of a boy drawing gasolene out of an automobile tank during a dance so that a girl can clean her satin shoe; the vignette of a young fellow sitting in his B.V.D.'s after a bath running his hand down his naked skin in indolent satisfaction; the vignette of two bucks from a pump-and-slipper dance throwing hash by the handful around Childs' at six A.M. Not another has gotten flashes from the psyches of the golden young intimate as those which amaze throughout *The Beautiful and Damned*. And not another has fixed as mercilessly the quality of brutishness, of dull indirection and degraded sensibility running through American life of the hour.

Taken as things, nevertheless, both the novels of Fitzgerald, and the majority of his tales as well, lie on a plane inferior to the one upon which his best material extends. He has the stuff for pathos, and this fact he fairly consistently ignores. Certain preoccupations seem to intrude between him and his material, spoiling his power to correctly appreciate it. Hence, instead of the veritable stories he has to tell, there appear smart social romanzas and unhappy happy endings. Of Fitzgerald's preconceptions, the chief sinner appears to be the illusion that the field of his vision is essentially the field of "youth." Now, it would be insanity to deny the author's almost constant preoccupation with exquisite creatures in chiffon and their slender snappy companions, or to deny the jolly subjects of his observations vivacity and frankness of spirit, and perfect elegance of texture. There is a place where an eternal dance proceeds, and this place for the while they occupy, filling it with their proper motions and gestures. And whatever the quality of these, who can for even an instant maintain that it is inferior to that of the dreadful motions and gestures which filled it a generation, or two or three generations ago? What one does affirm, however, and affirm with passion, is that the author of *This Side of Paradise* and of the jazzy stories does not sustainedly perceive his girls and men for what they are, and tends to invest them with precisely the glamour with which they in pathetic assurance rather childishly invest themselves. At the time of the appearance of Fitzgerald's first book, it was evident that to an extent he was indebted to Compton Mackenzie for the feeling with which he regarded the "dreaming spires" of Princeton; and since then it has become apparent that he tends a trifle overmuch to view everything which he sees in the light of Europe's past experiences. His protagonists he observes through the enchanted eyes of a perpetual Maytime, perceiving among the motors and crap-games a wave of cool spring flowers, a flutter of white and yellow ephemeridae. Even when he marks the cruel and shabby side, the decay and ignobility of his objective, he tends to overplay the general attractiveness more than the detail warrants. The couple in *The Beautiful and Damned*, charming and comely enough and yet portrayed at length in the horrible effort to perpetuate a state of narcissistic irresponsibility, we are begged to perceive as iridescently wonderful bodies and souls.

And it is fresh, juicy and spontaneous that the American juveniles of the class described by Fitzgerald exactly are not. Superficially, perhaps. But was not the forest green which Europe called by the name of youth somewhat more a thing of courage? And the number of us willing to face the world without the panoply of elaborate material protections is not overwhelming. It is claimed that in the American South virgins are carefully trained to inquire out the income and prospects of suitors, and nip in the bud any passion which threatens to direct itself upon an unworthy object. But it does not seem probable there is any truth in the report. For such maneuvers can scarcely be necessary. It is undoubtedly physically impossible for any really nice American girl South or North to respond to the desires of a male who does not make the spiritual gesture paralleling the Woolworth Building's. Through either external persuasion or inherent idealism, and which it is we know not, and undoubtedly it is both, the selfrespecting damsels early acquire the conviction that splendidly complete orientation onto the business of material increase is the primary characteristic of maleness, and that any offer of love unaccompanied by the tautness for money is the profoundest of insults to the psyche seated in the tender depths of them. And the strapping, college-bred, Brooks-clad youths no less than they share this beautiful innate belief. They too seem unable to face life without having at the back of them the immense upholstery of wealth. Nothing which they might be or do, were they relieved of the necessity of being a worldly success, appears to them capable of making good to the lady the absence of the fur garment and the foreign roadster, and the presence of inevitable suffering. Thus the spirit of the business world is established well before the advent of puberty; and the spirit of business is compromise, which is not exactly it would seem the spirit of youth.

And even the lightest, least satirical of Fitzgerald's pages bear testimonial to the prevalence of the condition. A moralist could gather evidence for a most terrible condemnation of bourgeois America from the books of this protagonist of youth. And yet, *Lieb Vaterland, magst ruhig sein.*[1] It is not a state of immorality in the general sense of the word that might be uncovered. If by morality we mean obedience to the *mores* of the tribal, then Fitzgerald's diverting flappers and slickers are in no sense licentious.

[1] Dear Fatherland, remain at peace (don't be upset).

By means of necking parties and booze fights of the sort he describes the republic is maintained. Business rests on them. But immorality may be taken to signify a falling away from the ideal spirit of life, and in that sense America is proven the breeding ground of a kind of decay. In all unconsciousness Fitzgerald shows us types of poor golden young too shallow to feel, vainly attitudinizing in the effort to achieve sensation: girls who know they cannot live without riches and men perpetually sucking the bottle for solace. The people aren't young: they are merely narcissistic. Knowledge of life is gotten from books, and the naïveté is not quite lovely. That is all very well; one has no fault to find with it; it is quite sanitary and not at all messy as passion usually is; but why call it spring? And occasionally Fitzgerald drops the light guitar and with cool ferocity speaks the veritable name. *May Day*, perhaps the most mature of all his tales, brings the bitter brackish dry taste of decay fully to the mouth. With an air of almost glacial impersonality Fitzgerald gives a curious atmosphere of mixed luxury and rottenness of the heart. Through the entire story there seems to run the brutishness of the two soldiers hiding among pails and mops in the dust closet waiting for some stolen liquor to be handed in to them. And in the fantasia *The Diamond as Big as the Ritz*, Fitzgerald strikes perhaps quite undeliberately further notes of satire: Mr. Braddock Washington, the richest and most profoundly unsympathetic man in the world, looks dangerously like a jazz-age portrait of the father of the country.

But the world of his subject-matter is still too much within Fitzgerald himself for him to see it sustainedly against the universe. Its values obtain too strongly over him, and for that reason he cannot set them against those of high civilization, and calmly judge them so. Hence, wanting philosophy, and a little overeager like the rest of America to arrive without having really sweated, he falls victim to the favorite delusions of the society of which he is a part, tends to indulge it in its dreams of grandeur, and misses the fine flower of pathos. He seems to set out writing under the compulsion of vague feelings, and when his wonderfully revelatory passages appear, they come rather like volcanic islands thrown to the surface of a sea of fantasy. By every law *The Beautiful and Damned* should have been a tragedy, the victims damned indeed; yet at the conclusion Fitzgerald welched, and permitted his pitiful pair to have the alleviations of some thirty millions of dollars, and his hero tell the readers he had won out. To be sure, a steady growth has been going on within this interesting author. The amusing insolence of his earlier manner of writing has persistently given way before a bolder, sharper stroke less personal in reference. The descriptions in *May Day*: the sight of the avenue, the drinking scene in Delmonico's, the adventures of Mr. In and Out, are done with quiet virtuosity. A very genuine gift of fantasy arrives in *Benjamin Button*. There are even Lawrence-like strong moments in *The Beautiful and Damned*. And still, in spite of *May Day*, Fitzgerald has not yet crossed the line that bounds the field of art. He has seen his material from its own point of view, and he has seen it completely from without. But he has never done what the artist does: seen it simultaneously from within and without; and loved it and judged it, too. For *May Day* lacks a focal point, and merely juxtaposes a number of small pieces. Should Fitzgerald finally break his mold, and free himself of the compulsions of the civilization in which he grew, it might go badly with his popularity. It will be a pathetic story he will have to tell, the legend of a moon which never rose; and that is precisely the story a certain America does not wish to hear. Nevertheless, we would like hugely to hear him tell it. And Fitzgerald might scarcely miss his following.

FITZGERALD FROM 1920 TO 1925

SELECTED QUOTATIONS FROM
*THIS SIDE OF PARADISE**

F. Scott Fitzgerald

This novel was Fitzgerald's first. He had written an earlier version of it (called The Romantic Egotist; the title is retained as Book One of the published novel) at Princeton and during the war in an Alabama army camp. In a letter to Wilson (1918), Fitzgerald described it in this way: "There are twenty-three chapters, all but five are written and it is poetry, prose, vers libre and every mood of a temperamental temperature. . . . It rather damns much of Princeton but its nothing to what it thinks of men and human nature in general. . . ."

Of the final version, Wilson said (in a letter, November 21, 1919): ". . . as an intellectual Amory is a fake of the first water and I read his views on art, politics, religion and society with more riotous mirth than I should care to have you know . . ." and went on to advise Fitzgerald: "Cultivate a universal irony and do read something other than contemporary British novelists. . . ." Though the novel was praised by some reviewers and it proved to be a best

* F. Scott Fitzgerald, This Side of Paradise (New York: Charles Scribner's Sons, 1920), pp. 36, 76-77, 98, 113-14, 182-84, 199, 209-10, 282-84, 298-300, 304-305. Copyright 1920 Charles Scribner's Sons; renewal copyright 1948 Zelda Fitzgerald. Reprinted by permission of Charles Scribner's Sons. The currently available edition (1960) of This Side of Paradise is the source for the pages herein quoted.

seller, it was also knocked about rather consistently by persons for whom Fitzgerald had some respect, with the result that he took a more serious view of his talent and his limitations, and started on the long road to The Great Gatsby.

The following quotations are designed (a) to give some suggestion of the novel's quality, and (b) to show the features of it that made Fitzgerald a "Jazz Age" celebrity. They ought to be seen as demonstrations of the errors of style and conception to which Edmund Wilson and Paul Rosenfeld refer in the previous essays; and they may also be compared and contrasted with Fitzgerald's mature treatment of similar details in Gatsby.

[At St. Regis prep school, Amory Blaine] read voluminously all spring, the beginning of his eighteenth year: "The Gentleman from Indiana," "The New Arabian Nights," "The Morals of Marcus Ordeyne," "The Man Who Was Thursday," which he liked without understanding; "Stover at Yale," that became somewhat of a text-book; "Dombey and Son," because he thought he really should read better stuff; Robert Chambers, David Graham Phillips, and E. Phillips Oppenheim complete, and a scattering of Tennyson and Kipling. Of all his class work only "L'Allegro" and some quality of rigid clarity in solid geometry stirred his languid interest. [33]

"Isabelle," he whispered. "You know I'm mad about you. You do give a darn about me."

"Yes."

"How much do you care—do you like any one better?"

"No." He could scarcely hear her, although he bent so near that he felt her breath against his cheek.

"Isabelle, I'm going back to college for six long months, and why shouldn't we—if I could only just have one thing to remember you by—"

"Close the door. . . ." Her voice had just stirred so that he half wondered whether she had spoken at all. As he swung the door swiftly shut, the music seemed quivering just outside.

> *"Moonlight is bright,*
> *Kiss me good night."*

What a wonderful song, she thought—everything was wonderful to-night, most of all this romantic scene in the den, with their hands clinging and the inevitable looming charmingly close. The future vista of her life seemed an unending succession of scenes like this: under moonlight and pale starlight, and in the backs of warm limousines and in low, cosey roadsters stopped under sheltering trees—only the boy might change, and this one was *so* nice. He took her hand softly. With a sudden movement he turned it and, holding it to his lips, kissed the palm. [69-70]

Then at six they arrived at the Borgés' summer place on Long Island, and Amory rushed up-stairs to change into a dinner coat. As he put in his studs he realized that he was enjoying life as he would probably never enjoy it again. Everything was hallowed by the haze of his own youth. He had arrived, abreast of the best in his generation at Princeton. He was in love and his love was returned. Turning on all the lights, he looked at himself in the mirror, trying to find in his own face the qualities that made him see clearer than the great crowd of people, that made him decide firmly, and able to influence and follow his own will. There was little in his life now that he would have changed. . . . Oxford might have been a bigger field.

Silently he admired himself. How conveniently well he looked, and how well a dinner coat became him. He stepped into the hall and then waited at the top of the stairs, for he heard footsteps coming. It was Isabelle, and from the top of her shining hair to her little golden slippers she had never seemed so beautiful.

"Isabelle!" he cried, half involuntarily, and held out his arms. As in the story-books, she ran into them, and on that half-minute, as their lips first touched, rested the high point of vanity, the crest of his young egotism. [88-89]

Monsignor Darcy, who speaks in the following passage, is Amory Blaine's confidant and advisor, one of a few whom he trusts. The model for him is Father Sigourney Fay, to whom This Side of Paradise is dedicated.

"A personality is what you thought you were, what this Kerry and Sloane you tell me of evidently are. Personality is a physical matter almost entirely; it lowers the people it acts on—I've seen it vanish in a long sickness. But while a personality is active, it overrides 'the next thing.' Now a personage, on the other hand, gathers. He is never thought of apart from what he's done. He's a bar on which a thousand things have been hung—glittering things sometimes, as ours are; but he uses those things with a cold mentality back of them." [104]

Rosalind Connage is Amory's most serious "affair." The following quotations suggest an early treatment of the privileges of wealth and the disasters of poverty. They recall (and probably draw upon) his own near calamity when Zelda refused him because he was poor. In "Handle with Care" (Esquire, March, 1936), Fitzgerald described that affair as follows: "During a long summer of despair I wrote a novel instead of letters, so it came out all right, but it came out all right for a different person. The man with the jingle of money in his pocket who married the girl a year later would always cherish an abiding distrust, an animosity, toward the leisure class— not the conviction of a revolutionist but the smouldering hatred of a peasant. In the years since then I have never been able to stop wondering where my friends' money came from, nor to stop thinking that at one time a sort of droit de seigneur might have been exercised to give one of them my girl."

(And now ROSALIND *enters.** ROSALIND *is—utterly* ROSALIND.

* This excerpt is reproduced in italics as it is in the original.

She is one of those girls who need never make the slightest effort to have men fall in love with them. Two types of men seldom do: dull men are usually afraid of her cleverness and intellectual men are usually afraid of her beauty. All others are hers by natural prerogative.

If ROSALIND *could be spoiled the process would have been complete by this time, and as a matter of fact, her disposition is not all it should be; she wants what she wants when she wants it and she is prone to make every one around her pretty miserable when she doesn't get it—but in the true sense she is not spoiled. Her fresh enthusiasm, her will to grow and learn, her endless faith in the inexhaustibility of romance, her courage and fundamental honesty—these things are not spoiled.*

There are long periods when she cordially loathes her whole family. She is quite unprincipled; her philosophy is carpe diem for herself and laissez-faire for others. She loves shocking stories: she has that coarse streak that usually goes with natures that are both fine and big. She wants people to like her, but if they do not it never worries her.

She is by no means a model character.

The education of all beautiful women is the knowledge of men. ROSALIND *had been disappointed in man after man as individuals, but she had great faith in man as a sex. Women she detested. They represented qualities that she felt and despised in herself —incipient meanness, conceit, cowardice, and petty dishonesty. She once told a roomful of her mother's friends that the only excuse for women was the necessity for a disturbing element among men. She danced exceptionally well, drew cleverly but hastily, and had a startling facility with words, which she used only in love-letters.*

But all criticism of ROSALIND *ends in her beauty. There was that shade of glorious yellow hair, the desire to imitate which supports the dye industry. There was the eternal kissable mouth, small, slightly sensual, and utterly disturbing. There were gray*

*eyes and an unimpeachable skin with two spots of vanishing
color. She was slender and athletic, without underdevelopment,
and it was a delight to watch her move about a room, walk
along a street, swing a golf club, or turn a "cart-wheel."* [170-171]

Within two weeks Amory and Rosalind were deeply and passionately in love. The critical qualities which had spoiled for each
of them a dozen romances were dulled by the great wave of emotion that washed over them.

"It may be an insane love-affair," she told her anxious mother,
"but it's not inane."

The wave swept Amory into an advertising agency early in
March, where he alternated between astonishing bursts of rather
exceptional work and wild dreams of becoming suddenly rich and
touring Italy with Rosalind.

They were together constantly, for lunch, for dinner, and nearly
every evening—always in a sort of breathless hush, as if they feared
that any minute the spell would break and drop them out of this
paradise of rose and flame. But the spell became a trance, seemed
to increase from day to day; they began to talk of marrying in July
—in June. All life was transmitted into terms of their love, all experience, all desires, all ambitions, were nullified—their senses of
humor crawled into corners to sleep; their former love-affairs
seemed faintly laughable and scarcely regretted juvenalia.

For the second time in his life Amory had had a complete
bouleversement and was hurrying into line with his generation.
[186]

ROSALIND: Amory, I'm yours—you know it. There have been
times in the last month I'd have been completely yours if you'd
said so. But I can't marry you and ruin both our lives.

AMORY: We've got to take our chance for happiness.

ROSALIND: Dawson says I'd learn to love him.

(AMORY *with his head sunk in his hands does not move. The
life seems suddenly gone out of him.*)

ROSALIND: Lover! Lover! I can't do with you, and I can't imagine life without you.

AMORY: Rosalind, we're on each other's nerves. It's just that we're both high-strung, and this week—

(*His voice is curiously old. She crosses to him and taking his face in her hands, kisses him.*)

ROSALIND: I can't Amory. I can't be shut away from the trees and flowers, cooped up in a little flat, waiting for you. You'd hate me in a narrow atmosphere. I'd make you hate me.

(*Again she is blinded by sudden uncontrolled tears.*)

AMORY: Rosalind—

ROSALIND: Oh, darling, go—Don't make it harder! I can't stand it—

AMORY: (*His face drawn, his voice strained*) Do you know what you're saying? Do you mean forever?

(*There is a difference somehow in the quality of their suffering.*)

ROSALIND: Can't you see—

AMORY: I'm afraid I can't if you love me. You're afraid of taking two years' knocks with me.

ROSALIND: I wouldn't be the Rosalind you love.

AMORY: (*A little hysterically*) I can't give you up! I can't, that's all! I've got to have you!

ROSALIND: (*A hard note in her voice*) You're being a baby now.

AMORY: (*Wildly*) I don't care! You're spoiling our lives!

ROSALIND: I'm doing the wise thing, the only thing.

AMORY: Are you going to marry Dawson Ryder?

ROSALIND: Oh, don't ask me. You know I'm old in some ways—in others—well, I'm just a little girl. I like sunshine and pretty things and cheerfulness—and I dread responsibility. I don't want to think about pots and kitchens and brooms. I want to worry whether my legs will get slick and brown when I swim in the summer. [195-196]

*After Amory has been rejected by Rosalind, for reasons of his an-
nounced inability to support her, he goes the round of Manhattan
bars, then becomes "serious," cultivates his role as a young intellectual wise before his time. The following quotations show him
in this role and culminate in the affirmation of disillusioned will
that helped so much in improving the sales of This Side of
Paradise. The dialogue in the second selection takes place between
Amory and a businessman who has given him a ride on the way to
Princeton.*

There were no more wise men; there were no more heroes;
Burne Holiday was sunk from sight as though he had never lived:
Monsignor was dead. Amory had grown up to a thousand books, a
thousand lies; he had listened eagerly to people who pretended to
know, who knew nothing. The mystical reveries of saints that had
once filled him with awe in the still hours of night, now vaguely
repelled him. The Byrons and Brookes who had defied life from
mountain tops were in the end but flaneurs and poseurs, as best
mistaking the shadow of courage for the substance of wisdom. The
pageantry of his disillusion took shape in a world-old procession
of Prophets, Athenians, Martyrs, Saints, Scientists, Don Juans,
Jesuits, Puritans, Fausts, Poets, Pacifists; like costumed alumni at
a college reunion they streamed before him as their dreams, personalities, and creeds had in turn thrown colored lights on his
soul; each had tried to express the glory of life and the tremendous
significance of man; each had boasted of synchronizing what had
gone before into his own rickety generalities; each had depended
after all on the set stage and the convention of the theatre, which
is that man in his hunger for faith will feed his mind with the
nearest and most convenient food.

Women—of whom he had expected so much; whose beauty he
had hoped to transmute into modes of art; whose unfathomable
instincts, marvellously incoherent and inarticulate, he had thought
to perpetuate in terms of experience—had become merely con-

secrations to their own posterity. Isabelle, Clara, Rosalind, Eleanor, were all removed by their very beauty, around which men had swarmed, from the possibility of contributing anything but a sick heart and a page of puzzled words to write.

Amory based his loss of faith in help from others on several sweeping syllogisms. Granted that his generation, however bruised and decimated from this Victorian war, were the heirs of progress. Waving aside petty differences of conclusions which, although they might occasionally cause the deaths of several millions of young men, might be explained away—supposing that after all Bernard Shaw and Bernhardi, Bonar Law and Bethmann-Hollweg were mutual heirs of progress if only in agreeing against the ducking of witches—waiving the antitheses and approaching individually these men who seemed to be the leaders, he was repelled by the discrepancies and contradictions in the men themselves. [262-263]

"I am both interested and amused," said the big man. "You are very young."

"Which may only mean that I have neither been corrupted nor made timid by contemporary experience. I possess the most valuable experience, the experience of the race, for in spite of going to college I've managed to pick up a good education."

"You talk glibly."

"It's not all rubbish," cried Amory passionately. "This is the first time in my life I've argued Socialism. It's the only panacea I know. I'm restless. My whole generation is restless. I'm sick of a system where the richest man gets the most beautiful girl if he wants her, where the artist without an income has to sell his talents to a button manufacturer. Even if I had no talents I'd not be content to work ten years, condemned either to celibacy or a furtive indulgence, to give some man's son an automobile."

"But, if you're not sure—"

"That doesn't matter," exclaimed Amory. "My position couldn't be worse. A social revolution might land me on top. Of course I'm selfish. It seems to me I've been a fish out of water in too many outworn systems. I was probably one of the two dozen men in my class at college who got a decent education; still they'd let any well-tutored flathead play football and *I* was ineligible, because some silly old men thought we should *all* profit by conic sections. I loathed the army. I loathed business. I'm in love with change and I've killed my conscience—

"So you'll go along crying that we must go faster."

"That, at least, is true," Amory insisted. "Reform won't catch up to the needs of civilization unless it's made to. A laissez-faire policy is like spoiling a child by saying he'll turn out all right in the end. He will—if he's made to."

"But you don't believe all this Socialist patter you talk."

"I don't know. Until I talked to you I hadn't thought seriously about it. I wasn't sure of half of what I said."

"You puzzle me," said the big man, "but you're all alike. They say Bernard Shaw, in spite of his doctrines, is the most exacting of all dramatists about his royalties. To the last farthing."

"Well," said Amory, "I simply state that I'm a product of a versatile mind in a restless generation—with every reason to throw my mind and pen in with the radicals. Even if, deep in my heart, I thought we were all blind atoms in a world as limited as a stroke of a pendulum, I and my sort would struggle against tradition; try, at least, to displace old cants with new ones. I've thought I was right about life at various times, but faith is difficult. One thing I know. If living isn't a seeking for the grail it may be a damned amusing game." [277-278]

Long after midnight the towers and spires of Princeton were visible, with here and there a late-burning light—and suddenly out of the clear darkness the sound of bells. As an endless dream it went on; the spirit of the past brooding over a new generation, the chosen youth from the muddled, unchastened world, still fed romantically on the mistakes and half-forgotten dreams of dead statesmen and poets. Here was a new generation, shouting the old cries, learning the old creeds, through a revery of long days and nights; destined finally to go out into that dirty gray turmoil to follow love and pride; a new generation dedicated more than the last to the fear of poverty and the worship of success; grown up to find all Gods dead, all wars fought, all faiths in man shaken. . . .

Amory, sorry for them, was still not sorry for himself—art, politics, religion, whatever his medium should be, he knew he was safe now, free from all hysteria—he could accept what was acceptable, roam, grow, rebel, sleep deep through many nights. . . .

There was no God in his heart, he knew; his ideas were still in riot; there was ever the pain of memory; the regret for his lost youth—yet the waters of disillusion had left a deposit on his soul, responsibility and a love of life, the faint stirring of old ambitions and unrealized dreams. But oh, Rosalind! Rosalind! . . .

"It's all a poor substitute at best," he said sadly.

And he could not tell why the struggle was worth while, why he had determined to use to the utmost himself and his heritage from the personalities he had passed. . . .

He stretched out his arms to the crystalline, radiant sky.

"I know myself," he cried, "but that is all." [282]

FITZGERALD CHRONOLOGY 1920-1925

The information in the following brief chronology is based upon Arthur Mizener's admirable biography, The Far Side of Paradise (Boston: Houghton, Mifflin, 1951). The chronology does not include publications of separate stories or journalistic pieces. For detailed information regarding Fitzgerald's activities in these five crucial years, see Mizener, chapters five to eight, pp. 96-168, and James E. Miller, Jr., The Fictional Technique of Scott Fitzgerald (The Hague: Martinus Nijhoff, 1957).

1920 March 26	This Side of Paradise published by Scribner's in New York.
Spring	Scott and Zelda travel to Montgomery, Alabama, home of Zelda's parents.
1920-21 Winter	Fitzgeralds back in New York, where Scott is at work on The Beautiful and Damned.
1921 May	Trip to Europe; to France, where Scott meets James Joyce in Paris.
July	Back in Montgomery, Alabama.
1921-22 July	Return to Saint Paul, Fitzgerald's birthplace (from August, 1921, to October, 1922).
1921 October 26	Daughter (Frances Scott) born, Saint Paul.
1922 March 3	The Beautiful and Damned published by Scribner's in New York.
March—April	To New York, for party lasting two weeks.

September   Tales of the Jazz Age, short stories, published by Scribner's in New York.

October   Return to New York, residence at Great Neck, Long Island. Era of many parties.

November   Production of Fitzgerald's play, The Vegetable, Apollo Theatre, Atlantic City: a failure.

1922-23   Fitzgerald, in debt for $5000, writes eleven
November—   stories for income of $17,000 (Great Neck,
April   Long Island).

1923 May   Abortive attempt to attract attention of Joseph Conrad, who is visiting America (See Mizener, p. 158). Friendship with Ring Lardner begins.

October   Because of debts (which need short stories to discharge), temporarily abandons plans for writing The Great Gatsby.

1924 April   Return to plans for Gatsby. Move to Southeastern France, the Riviera.

June   Fitzgeralds settle down in St. Raphael, France. Quarrel over Zelda's flirtations.

November   Manuscript of Gatsby sent to Maxwell Perkins, editor at Scribner's.

1924-25 Winter   Fitzgeralds in Rome, result of Zelda's having read Henry James's Roderick Hudson.

1925 January   Meeting, at Capri, with Compton Mackenzie, idol of Fitzgerald's early years.

April 10   The Great Gatsby published by Scribner's in New York.

May   In Paris.

August   Antibes, French Riviera, with Gerald Murphy and friends (source material of Tender Is the Night).

SELECTION FROM "THE NATIONAL LETTERS"*

H. L. Mencken

In the early years after This Side of Paradise, *Fitzgerald was much interested in Mencken's kind of literary and social criticism, and especially in his contrast of American with European fiction. Both the novel* The Beautiful and Damned *(1922) and the play* The Vegetable *(1923) reflect Mencken's views of American life and mores. A passage like this, from* The Beautiful and Damned, *demonstrates his alliance with Mencken:*

> [At the age of 57, after an attack of sclerosis, Adam J. Patch determined] to consecrate the remainder of his life to the moral regeneration of the world. He became a reformer among reformers. Emulating the magnificent efforts of Anthony Comstock, after whom his grandson was named, he levelled a varied assortment of uppercuts and body-blows at liquor, literature, vice, art, patent medicines, and Sunday theatres. His mind, under the influence of that insidious mildew which eventually forms on all but the few, gave itself up furiously to every indignation of the age. . . . (p. 4)

But the influence of Mencken did not last long. Fitzgerald did not really respect his very limited literary judgment, and in any case he was becoming interested in more substantial literary minds like Conrad and Ford Madox Ford. In a 1924 interview with

*H. L. Mencken, "The National Letters," Prejudices: Second Series (New York: Alfred A. Knopf, 1920), pp. 39-54. Reprinted by permission of Alfred A. Knopf, Inc. Copyright 1920, 1948 by Alfred A. Knopf, Inc.

48

Charles C. Baldwin (published in The Men Who Make Our Novels, New York: Dodd, Mead), he speaks of Mencken as one of a few in America who provide "an intelligent body of opinion" concerning fiction; but later, in a Bookman essay, "How to Waste Material" (1926), he accused Mencken of lacking aesthetic judgment and of actually doing harm to the literary promise of the 1920s. With his "family of hammer and tongs men," Fitzgerald said, who were "insensitive, suspicious of glamour, preoccupied exclusively with the external, the contemptible, the 'national' and the drab," Mencken mistook "incoherence for vitality, chaos for vitality." It is obvious that Mencken's type of criticism did not have a lasting effect on Fitzgerald; but for a short while they saw eye to eye on the matter of the special role of fiction.

The following passage from "The National Letters" is the one most relevant to Fitzgerald's interest.

Underlying causes

Here is one of the fundamental defects of American fiction— perhaps the one character that sets it off sharply from all other known kinds of contemporary fiction. It habitually exhibits, not a man of delicate organization in revolt against the inexplicable tragedy of existence, but a man of low sensibilities and elemental desires yielding himself gladly to his environment, and so achieving what, under a third-rate civilization, passes for success. To get on: this is the aim. To weigh and reflect, to doubt and rebel: this is the thing to be avoided. I describe the optimistic, the inspirational, the Authors' League, the popular magazine, the peculiarly American school. In character creation its masterpiece is the advertising agent who, by devising some new and super-imbecile boob-trap, puts his hook-and-eye factory "on the map," ruins all other factories, marries the daughter of his boss, and so ends as an eminent man. Obviously, the drama underlying such fiction— what Mr. Beach would call its John Henry Plot—is false drama, Sunday-school drama, puerile and disgusting drama. It is the sort of thing that awakens a response only in men who are essentially unimaginative, timorous and degraded—in brief, in democrats, bagmen, yahoos. The man of reflective habit cannot conceivably take any passionate interest in the conflicts it deals with. He doesn't want to marry the daughter of the owner of the hook-and-eye factory; he would probably burn down the factory itself if it ever came into his hands. What interests this man is the far more poignant and significant conflict between a salient individual and the harsh and meaningless fiats of destiny, the unintelligible mandates and vagaries of God. His hero is not one who yields and wins, but one who resists and fails.

Most of these conflicts, of course, are internal, and hence do not make themselves visible in the overt melodrama of the Beaches, Davises and Chamberses. A superior man's struggle in the world is not with exterior lions, trusts, margraves, policemen, rivals in love, German spies, radicals and tornadoes, but with the obscure, atavistic impulses within him—the impulses, weaknesses and limitations that war with his notion of what life should be. Nine times out of ten he succumbs. Nine times out of ten he must yield to the dead hand. Nine times out of ten his aspiration is almost infinitely above his achievement. The result is that we see him sliding downhill—his ideals breaking up, his hope petering out, his character in decay. Character in decay is thus the theme of the great bulk of superior fiction. One has it in Dostoievsky, in Balzac, in Hardy, in Conrad, in Flaubert, in Zola, in Turgenieff, in Goethe, in Sudermann, in Bennett, and, to come home, in Dreiser. In nearly all first-rate novels the hero is defeated. In perhaps a majority he is completely destroyed. The hero of the inferior—i.e., the typically American—novel engages in no such doomed and fateful combat. His conflict is not with the inexplicable ukases of destiny, the limitations of his own strength, the dead hand upon him, but simply with the superficial desires of his elemental fellow men. He thus has a fair chance of winning—and in bad fiction that chance is always converted into a certainty. So he marries the daughter of the owner of the factory and eventually gobbles the factory itself. His success gives thrills to persons who can imagine no higher aspiration. He embodies their optimism, as the other hero embodies the pessimism of more introspective and idealistic men. He is the protagonist of that great majority which is so inferior that it is quite unconscious of its inferiority.

It is this superficiality of the inferior man, it seems to me, that is the chief hallmark of the American novel. Whenever one encounters a novel that rises superior to it the thing takes on a subtle but unmistakable air of foreignness—for example, Frank Norris' "Vandover and the Brute," Hergesheimer's "The Lay Anthony" and Miss Cather's "My Ántonia," or, to drop to short stories, Stephen Crane's "The Blue Hotel" and Mrs. Wharton's "Ethan Frome." The short story is commonly regarded, at least by American critics, as a preëminently American form; there are even patriots who argue that Bret Harte invented it. It meets very accurately, in fact, certain characteristic demands of the American temperament: it is simple, economical and brilliantly effective. Yet the same hollowness that marks the American novel also marks the American short story. Its great masters, in late years, have been such cheesemongers as Davis, with his servant-girl romanticism, and O. Henry, with his smoke-room and variety show smartness. In the whole canon of O. Henry's work you will not find a single recognizable human character; his people are unanimously marionettes; he makes Mexican brigands, Texas cowmen and New York cracksmen talk the same highly ornate Broadwayese. The successive volumes of Edward J. O'Brien's "Best Short-Story" series throw a vivid light upon the feeble estate of the art in the land. O'Brien, though his aesthetic judgments are ludicrous, at least selects stories that are thoroughly representative; his books are trade successes because the crowd is undoubtedly with him. He has yet to discover a single story that even the most naïve professor would venture to mention in the same breath with Joseph Conrad's "Heart of Darkness," or Andrieff's "Silence," or Sudermann's "Das

Sterbelied," or the least considerable tale by Anatole France. In many of the current American makers of magazine short stories—for example, Gouverneur Morris—one observes, as I have said, a truly admirable technical skill. They have mastered the externals of the form. They know how to get their effects. But in content their work is as hollow as a jug. Such stuff has no imaginable relation to life as men live it in the world. It is as artificial as the heroic strut and romantic eyes of a moving-picture actor.

I have spoken of the air of foreignness that clings to certain exceptional American compositions. In part it is based upon a psychological trick—upon the surprise which must inevitably seize upon any one who encounters a decent piece of writing in so vast a desert of mere literacy. But in part it is grounded soundly enough on the facts. The native author of any genuine force and originality is almost invariably found to be under strong foreign influences, either English or Continental. It was so in the earliest days. Freneau, the poet of the Revolution, was thoroughly French in blood and traditions. Irving, as H. R. Haweis has said, "took to England as a duck takes to water," and was in exile seventeen years. Cooper, with the great success of "The Last of the Mohicans" behind him, left the country in disgust and was gone for seven years. Emerson, Bryant, Lowell, Hawthorne and even Longfellow kept their eyes turned across the water; Emerson, in fact, was little more than an importer and popularizer of German and French ideas. Bancroft studied in Germany; Prescott, like Irving, was enchanted by Spain. Poe, unable to follow the fashion, invented mythical travels to save his face—to France, to Germany, to the Greek isles. The Civil War revived the national consciousness enormously, but it did not halt the movement of émigrés. Henry James, in the seventies, went to England, Bierce and Bret Harte followed him, and even Mark Twain, absolutely American though he was, was forever pulling up stakes and setting out for Vienna, Florence or London. Only poverty tied Whitman to the soil; his andience, for many years was chiefly beyond the water, and there, too, he often longed to be. This distaste for the national scene is often based upon a genuine alienness. The more, indeed, one investigates the ancestry of Americans who have won distinction in the fine arts, the more one discovers tempting game for the critical Know Nothings. Whitman was half Dutch, Harte was half Jew, Poe was partly German, James had an Irish grandfather, Howells was largely Irish and German, Dreiser is German, and Hergesheimer is Pennsylvania Dutch. Fully a half of the painters discussed in John C. van Dyke's "American Painting and Its Tradition" were of mixed blood, with the Anglo-Saxon plainly recessive. And of the five poets singled out for encomium by Miss Lowell in "Tendencies in Modern American Poetry" one is a Swede, two are partly German, one was educated in the German language, and three of the five exiled themselves to England as soon as they got out of their nonage. The exiles are of all sorts: Frank Harris, Vincent O'Sullivan, Ezra Pound, Herman Scheffauer, T. S. Eliot, Henry B. Fuller, Stuart Merrill, Edith Wharton. They go to England, France, Germany, Italy—anywhere to escape. Even at home the literatus is perceptibly foreign in his mien. If he lies under the New England tradition he is furiously colonial— more English than the English. If he turns to revolt, he is apt to put on a French hat and a Russian red blouse. *The Little Review*, the organ of the extreme wing of *révoltés*, is so violently exotic that several years ago, during the plupatriotic days of the war, some of its readers protested. With characteristic lack of humor it replied with an American number—and two of the stars of that number bore the fine old Anglo-Saxon names of Ben Hecht and Elsa von Freytag-Loringhoven.

This tendency of American literature, the moment it begins to show enterprise, novelty and significance, to radiate an alien smell is not an isolated phenomenon. The same smell accompanies practically all other sorts of intellectual activity in the republic. Whenever one hears that a new political theory is in circulation, or a scientific heresy, or a movement toward rationalism in religion, it is always safe to guess that some discontented stranger or other has a hand in it. In the newspapers and on the floor of Congress a new heterodoxy is always denounced forthwith as a product of foreign plotting, and here public opinion undoubtedly supports both the press and the politicians, and with good reason. The native culture of the country—that is, the culture of the low caste Anglo-Saxons who preserve the national tradition—is almost completely incapable of producing ideas. It is a culture that roughly corresponds to what the culture of England would be if there were no universities over there, and no caste of intellectual individualists and no landed aristocracy—in other words, if the tone of the national thinking were set by the nonconformist industrials, the camorra of Welsh and Scotch political scoundrels, and the town and country mobs. As we shall see, the United States has not yet produced anything properly describable as an aristocracy, and so there is no impediment to the domination of the inferior orders. Worse, the Anglo-Saxon strain, second-rate at the start, has tended to degenerate steadily to lower levels—in New England, very markedly. The result is that there is not only a great dearth of ideas in the land, but also an active and relentless hostility to ideas. The chronic suspiciousness of the inferior man here has full play; never in modern history has there been another civilization showing so vast a body of prohibitions and repressions, in both conduct and thought. The second result is that intellectual experimentation is chiefly left to the immigrants of the later migrations, and to the small sections of the native population that have been enriched with their blood. For such a pure Anglo-Saxon as Cabell to disport himself in the field of ideas is a rarity in the United States—and no exception to the rule that I have just mentioned, for Cabell belongs to an aristocracy that is now almost extinct, and has no more in common with the general population than a Baltic baron has with the indigenous herd of Letts and Esthonians. All the arts in America are thoroughly exotic. Music is almost wholly German or Italian, painting is French, literature may be anything from English to Russian, architecture (save when it becomes a mere branch of engineering) is a maddening phantasmagoria of borrowings. Even so elemental an art as that of cookery shows no native development, and is greatly disesteemed by Americans of the Anglo-Saxon majority; any decent restaurant that one blunders upon in the land is likely to be French, and if not French, then Italian or German or Chinese. So with the sciences: they have scarcely any native development. Organized scientific research began in the country with the founding of the Johns Hopkins University, a bald imitation of the German universities, and long held suspect by native opinion. Even after its great success, indeed, there was rancorous hostility to its scheme of things on chauvinistic grounds, and some years ago efforts were begun to Americanize it, with the result that it is now sunk to the level of Princeton, Amherst and other such glorified high-schools, and is dominated by native savants who would be laughed at in any Continental university. Science, oppressed by such assaults from below, moves out of the academic grove into the freer air of the great foundations, where the pursuit of the shy fact is uncontaminated by football and social pushing. The greatest of these foundations is the Rockefeller Institute. Its salient men are such investigators as Flexner, Loeb and Carrell—all of them Continental Jews.

Thus the battle of ideas in the United States is largely carried on under strange flags, and even the stray natives on the side of free inquiry have to sacrifice some of their nationality when they enlist. The effects of this curious condition of affairs are both good and evil. The good ones are easily apparent. The racial division gives the struggle a certain desperate earnestness, and even bitterness, and so makes it the more inviting to lively minds. It was a benefit to the late D. C. Gilman rather than a disadvantage that national opinion opposed his traffic with Huxley and the German professors in the early days of the Johns Hopkins; the stupidity of the opposition stimulated him, and made him resolute, and his resolution, in the long run, was of inestimable cultural value. Scientific research in America, indeed, was thus set securely upon its legs precisely because the great majority of right-thinking Americans were violently opposed to it. In the same way it must be obvious that Dreiser got something valuable out of the grotesque war that was carried on against him during the greater war overseas because of his German name—a *jehad* fundamentally responsible for the suppression of "The 'Genius.' " The chief danger that he ran six or seven years ago was the danger that he might be accepted, explained away, and so seduced downward to the common level. The attack of professional patriots saved him from that calamity. More, it filled him with a keen sense of his isolation, and stirred up the vanity that was in him as it is in all of us, and so made him cling with new tenacity to the very peculiarities that differentiate him from his inferiors. Finally, it is not to be forgotten that, without this rebellion of immigrant iconoclasts, the whole body of the national literature would tend to sink to the 100% American level of such patriotic literary business men as the president of the Authors' League. In other words, we must put up with the aesthetic Bolshevism of the Europeans and Asiatics who rage in the land, for without them we might not have any literature at all.

But the evils of the situation are not to be gainsaid. One of them I have already alluded to: the tendency of the beginning literatus, once he becomes fully conscious of his foreign affiliations, to desert the republic forthwith, and thereafter view it from afar, and as an actual foreigner. More solid and various cultures lure him; he finds himself uncomfortable at home. Sometimes, as in the case of Henry James, he becomes a downright expatriate, and a more or less active agent of anti-American feeling; more often, he goes over to the outlanders without yielding up his theoretical citizenship, as in the cases of Irving, Harris, Pound and O'Sullivan. But all this, of course, works relatively light damage, for not many native authors are footloose enough to indulge in any such physical desertion of the soil. Of much more evil importance is the tendency of the cultural alienism that I have described to fortify the uncontaminated native in his bilious suspicion of all the arts, and particularly of all artists. The news that the latest poet to flutter the dovecotes is a Jew, or that the last novelist mauled by comstockery has a German or Scandinavian or Russian name, or that the critic newly taken in sacrilege is a partisan of Viennese farce or of the French moral code or of English literary theory—this news, among a people so ill-informed, so horribly well-trained in flight from bugaboos, and so savagely suspicious of the unfamiliar in ideas, has the inevitable effect of stirring up opposition that quickly ceases to be purely aesthetic objection, and so becomes increasingly difficult to combat. If Dreiser's name were Tompkins or Simpson, there is no doubt whatever that he would affright the professors a good deal less, and appear less of a hobgloblin to the *intelligentsia* of the women's clubs. If Oppenheim were less palpably levantine, he would come much nearer to the popularity of Edwin Markham and Walt Mason. And if Cabell kept to the patriotic business of a Southern gentlemen, to wit, the praise of General Robert E. Lee, instead of prowling the strange and terrible fields of mediaeval Provençe, it is a safe wager that he would be sold openly over the counter instead of stealthily behind the door.

In a previous work I have discussed this tendency in America to estimate the artist in terms of his secular character. During the war, when all of the national defects in intelligence were enormously accentuated, it went to ludicrous lengths. There were then only authors who were vociferous patriots and thus geniuses, and authors who kept their dignity and were thus suspect and without virtue. By this gauge Chambers became the superior of Dreiser and Cabell, and Joyce Kilmer and Amy Lowell were set above Sandburg and Oppenheim. The test was even extended to foreigners: by it H.G. Wells took precedence of Shaw, and Blasco Ibáñez became a greater artist than Romain Rolland. But the thing is not peculiar to war times; when peace is densest it is to be observed. The man of letters, pure and simple, is a rarity in America. Almost always he is something else—and that something else commonly determines his public eminence. Mark Twain, with only his books to recommend him, would probably have passed into obscurity in middle age; it was in the character of a public entertainer, not unrelated to Coxey, Dr. Mary Walker and Citizen George Francis Train, that he wooed and won his country. The official criticism of the land denied him any solid literary virtue to the day of his death, and even to-day the campus critics and their journalistic valets stand aghast before "The Mysterious Stranger" and "What is Man?" Emerson passed through almost the same experience. It was not as a man of letters that he was chiefly thought of in his time, but as the prophet of a new cult, half religious, half philosophical, and wholly unintelligible to nine-tenths of those who discussed it. The first author of a hand-book of American literature to sweep away the codfish Moses and expose the literary artist was the Polish Jew, Leon Kellner, of Czernowitz. So with Whitman and Poe—both hobgoblins far more than artists. So, even, with Howells: it was as the exponent of a dying culture that he was venerated, not as the practitioner of an art. Few actually read his books. His celebrity, of course, was real enough, but it somehow differed materially from that of a pure man of letters—say Shelley, Conrad, Hauptmann, Hardy or Synge. That he was himself keenly aware of the national tendency to judge an artist in terms of the citizen was made plain at the time of the Gorky scandal, when he joined Clemens in an ignominious desertion of Gorky, scared out of his wits by the danger of being manhandled for a violation of the national pecksniffery. Howells also refused to sign the Dreiser Protest. The case of Frank Harris is one eloquently in point. Harris has written, among other books, perhaps the best biography ever done by an American. Yet his politics keep him in a sort of Coventry and the average American critic would no more think of praising him than of granting Treitschke any merit as an historian.

PREFACE TO *THE NIGGER OF THE NARCISSUS**

Joseph Conrad

This and the following piece are good examples of the approach to fiction Fitzgerald grew more and more to appreciate in the early years of the 1920s. The Conrad he definitely read; the Ford he very well might have read, on the way to The Great Gatsby. As for Conrad's Preface, he quotes it in a Saturday Evening Post article (March 4, 1933); and in his Introduction (p. 167) to the 1934 Modern Library edition of Gatsby, he mentions having re-read it while he was writing his novel.

A work that aspires, however humbly, to the condition of art should carry its justification in every line. And art itself may be defined as a single-minded attempt to render the highest kind of justice to the visible universe, by bringing to light the truth, manifold and one, underlying its every aspect. It is an attempt to find in its forms, in its colours, in its light, in its shadows, in the aspects of matter, and in the facts of life what of each is fundamental, what is enduring and essential—their one illuminating and convincing quality—the very truth of their existence. The artist, then,

* Joseph Conrad, Preface to The Nigger of the Narcissus (1897), in Conrad's Prefaces to His Works, ed. Edward Garnett (London: J. M. Dent, 1937), pp. 49-54. Conrad originally published this preface in the last installment of the serialized novel, in the New Review, December, 1897. Reprinted by permission of J. M. Dent & Sons Ltd.

59

like the thinker or the scientist, seeks the truth and makes his appeal. Impressed by the aspect of the world the thinker plunges into ideas, the scientist into facts—whence, presently, emerging they make their appeal to those qualities of our being that fit us best for the hazardous enterprise of living. They speak authoritatively to our common sense, to our intelligence, to our desire of peace, or to our desire of unrest; not seldom to our prejudices, sometimes to our fears, often to our egoism—but always to our credulity. And their words are heard with reverence, for their concern is with weighty matters: with the cultivation of our minds and the proper care of our bodies, with the attainment of our ambitions, with the perfection of the means and the glorification of our precious aims.

It is otherwise with the artist.

Confronted by the same enigmatical spectacle the artist descends within himself, and in that lonely region of stress and strife, if he be deserving and fortunate, he finds the terms of his appeal. His appeal is made to our less obvious capacities: to that part of our nature which, because of the warlike conditions of existence, is necessarily kept out of sight within the more resisting and hard qualities—like the vulnerable body within a steel armour. His appeal is less loud, more profound, less distinct, more stirring—and sooner forgotten. Yet its effect endures forever. The changing wisdom of successive generations discards ideas, questions facts, demolishes theories. But the artist appeals to that part of our being which is not dependent on wisdom; to that in us which is a gift and not an acquisition—and, therefore, more permanently enduring. He speaks to our capacity for delight and wonder, to the sense of mystery surrounding our lives; to our sense of pity, and beauty, and pain; to the latent feeling of fellowship with all creation—and to the subtle but invincible conviction of solidarity that knits together the loneliness of innumerable hearts, to the solidarity in dreams, in joy, in sorrow, in aspirations, in illusions, in hope, in fear, which binds men to each other, which binds together all humanity—the dead to the living and the living to the unborn.

It is only some such train of thought, or rather of feeling, that can in a measure explain the aim of the attempt, made in the tale which follows, to present an unrestful episode in the obscure lives of a few individuals out of all the disregarded multitude of the bewildered, the simple, and the voiceless. For, if any part of truth dwells in the belief confessed above, it becomes evident that there is not a place of splendour or a dark corner of the earth that does not deserve, if only a passing glance of wonder and pity. The motive, then, may be held to justify the matter of the work; but this preface, which is simply an avowal of endeavour, cannot end here—for the avowal is not yet complete.

Fiction—if it at all aspires to be art—appeals to temperament. And in truth it must be, like painting, like music, like all art, the appeal of one temperament to all the other innumerable temperaments whose subtle and resistless power endows passing events with their true meaning, and creates the moral, the emotional atmosphere of the place and time. Such an appeal to be effective must be an impression conveyed through the senses; and, in fact, it cannot be made in any other way, because temperament, whether individual or collective, is not amenable to persuasion. All art, therefore, appeals primarily to the senses, and the artistic aim when expressing itself in written words must also make its appeal through the senses, if its high desire is to reach the secret spring of responsive emotions. It must strenuously aspire to the plasticity of sculpture, to the colour of painting, and to the magic suggestiveness of music—which is the art of arts. And it is only through complete, unswerving devotion to the perfect blending of form and substance; it is only through an unremitting never-discouraged care for the shape and ring of sentences that an approach can be made to plasticity, to colour, and that the light of magic suggestiveness may be brought to play for an evanescent instant over the commonplace surface of words: or the old, old words, worn thin, defaced by ages of careless usage.

The sincere endeavour to accomplish that creative task, to go as far on that road as his strength will carry him, to go undeterred by faltering, weariness, or reproach, is the only valid justification for the worker in prose. And if his conscience is clear, his answer to those who, in the fullness of a wisdom which looks for immediate profit, demand specifically to be edified, consoled, amused; who demand to be promptly improved, or encouraged, or frightened, or shocked, or charmed, must run thus: My task which I am trying to achieve is, by the power of the written word to make you hear, to make you feel—it is, before all, to make you *see*. That —and no more, and it is everything. If I succeed, you shall find there according to your deserts: encouragement, consolation, fear, charm—all you demand—and, perhaps, also that glimpse of truth for which you have forgotten to ask.

To snatch in a moment of courage, from the remorseless rush of time, a passing phase of life, is only the beginning of the task. The task approached in tenderness and faith is to hold up unquestioningly, without choice and without fear, the rescued fragment before all eyes in the light of a sincere mood. It is to show its vibration, its colour, its form; and through its movement, its form, and its colour, reveal the substance of its truth—disclose its inspiring secret: the stress and passion within the core of each convincing moment. In a single-minded attempt of that kind, if one be deserving and fortunate, one may perchance attain to such clearness of sincerity that at last the presented vision of regret or pity, of terror or mirth, shall awaken in the hearts of the beholders that feeling of unavoidable solidarity; of the solidarity in mysterious origin, in toil, in joy, in hope, in uncertain fate, which binds men to each other and all mankind to the visible world.

It is evident that he who, rightly or wrongly, holds by the convictions expressed above cannot be faithful to any one of the temporary formulas of his craft. The enduring part of them—

the truth which each only imperfectly veils—should abide with him as the most precious of his possessions, but they all: Realism, Romanticism, Naturalism, even the unofficial sentimentalism (which, like the poor, is exceedingly difficult to get rid of), all these gods must, after a short period of fellowship, abandon him —even on the very threshold of the temple—to the stammerings of his conscience and to the outspoken consciousness of the difficulties of his work. In that uneasy solitude the supreme cry of Art for Art, itself, loses the exciting ring of its apparent immorality. It sounds far off. It has ceased to be a cry, and is heard only as a whisper, often incomprehensible, but at times and faintly encouraging.

Sometimes, stretched at ease in the shade of a roadside tree, we watch the motions of a labourer in a distant field, and after a time, begin to wonder languidly as to what the fellow may be at. We watch the movements of his body, the waving of his arms, we see him bend down, stand up, hesitate, begin again. It may add to the charm of an idle hour to be told the purpose of his exertions. If we know he is trying to lift a stone, to dig a ditch, to uproot a stump, we look with a more real interest at his efforts; we are disposed to condone the jar of his agitation upon the restfulness of the landscape; and even, if in a brotherly frame of mind, we may bring ourselves to forgive his failure. We understood his object, and, after all, the fellow has tried, and perhaps he had not the strength—and perhaps he had not the knowledge. We forgive, go on our way—and forget.

And so it is with the workman of art. Art is long and life is short, and success is very far off. And thus, doubtful of strength to travel so far, we talk a little about the aim—the aim of art, which, like life itself, is inspiring, difficult—obscured by mists. It is not in the unveiling of one of those heartless secrets which are called the Laws of Nature. It is not less great, but only more difficult.

To arrest, for the space of a breath, the hands busy about the work of the earth, and compel men entranced by the sight of distant goals to glance for a moment at the surrounding vision of form and colour, of sunshine and shadows; to make them pause for a look, for a sigh, for a smile—such is the aim, difficult and evanescent, and reserved only for a very few to achieve. But sometimes, by the deserving and the fortunate, even that task is accomplished. And when it is accomplished—behold!—all the truth of life is there: a moment of vision, a sigh, a smile—and the return to an eternal rest.

SELECTION FROM *JOSEPH CONRAD:*
*A PERSONAL REMEMBRANCE**

Ford Madox Ford

There is no proof that Fitzgerald read this memoir of Ford's experiences in collaborating with Conrad (which originally appeared in Ford's transatlantic review in 1924), but it concerns the very problems of technique and method that are suggested in Conrad's Preface to The Nigger of the Narcissus.

General effect

We agreed that the general effect of a novel must be the general effect that life makes on mankind. A novel must therefore not be a narration, a report. Life does not say to you: In 1914 my next door neighbour, Mr. Slack, erected a greenhouse and painted it with Cox's green aluminum paint. . . . If you think about the matter you will remember, in various unordered pictures, how one day Mr. Slack appeared in his garden and contemplated the wall of his house. You will then try to remember the year of that occurrence and you will fix it as August 1914 because having had the foresight to bear the municipal stock of the city of Liège you were able to afford a first-class season ticket for

* Ford Madox Ford, Joseph Conrad: A Personal Remembrance (London: Duckworth, 1924), pp. 180-215. Reprinted by permission of Mrs. Janice Biala and David Higham Associates, Ltd.

the first time in your life. You will remember Mr. Slack—then much thinner because it was before he found out where to buy that cheap Burgundy of which he has since drunk an inordinate quantity though whisky you think would be much better for him! Mr. Slack again came into his garden, this time with a pale, weaselly-faced fellow, who touched his cap from time to time. Mr. Slack will point to his house-wall several times at different points, the weaselly fellow touching his cap at each pointing. Some days after, coming back from business you will have observed against Mr. Slack's wall. . . . At this point you will remember that you were then the manager of the fresh-fish branch of Messrs. Catlin and Clovis in Fenchurch Street. . . . What a change since then! Millicent had not yet put her hair up. . . . You will remember how Millicent's hair looked, rather pale and burnished in plaits. You will remember how it now looks, henna'd: and you will see in one corner of your mind's eye a little picture of Mr. Mills the vicar talking—oh, very kindly—to Millicent after she has come back from Brighton. . . . But perhaps you had better not risk that. You remember some of the things said by means of which Millicent has made you cringe—and her expression! . . . Cox's Aluminium Paint! You remember the half empty tin that Mr. Slack showed you—he had a most undignified cold—with the name in a horse-shoe over a blue circle that contained a red lion asleep in front of a real-gold sun. . . .

And, if that is how the building of your neighbour's greenhouse comes back to you, just imagine how it will be with your love-affairs that are so much more complicated. . . .

Impressionism

We accepted without much protest the stigma: "Impressionists" that was thrown at us. In those days Impressionists were still considered to be bad people: Atheists, Reds, wearing red ties with which to frighten householders. But we accepted the name because Life appearing to us much as the building of Mr. Slack's greenhouse comes back to you, we saw that Life did not narrate, but made impressions on our brains. We in turn, if we wished to produce on you an effect of life, must not narrate but render . . . impressions.

Selection

We agreed that the whole of Art consists in selection. To render your remembrance of your career as a fish-salesman might enhance the story of Mr. Slack's greenhouse, or it might *not*. A little image of iridescent, blue-striped, black-striped, white fish on a white marble slab with water trickling down to them round a huge mass of orange salmon-roe; a vivid description of a horrible smell caused by a cat having stolen and hidden in the thick of your pelargoniums a cod's head that you had brought back as a perquisite, you having subsequently killed the cat with a hammer, but long, long before you had rediscovered her fishy booty. . . . Such little impressions might be useful as contributing to illustrate your character—one should not kill a cat with a hammer! They might illustrate your sense of the beautiful—or your fortitude under affliction—or the disagreeableness of Mr. Slack, who had a delicate sense of smell—or the point of view of your only daughter Millicent.

We should then have to consider whether your sense of the beautiful or your fortitude could in our rendering carry the story forward or interest the reader. If it did we should include it; if in our opinion it was not likely to, we should leave it out. Or the story of the cat might in itself seem sufficiently amusing to be inserted as a purposed *longueur*, so as to give the idea of the passage of time. . . . It may be more amusing to read the story of a cat with your missing dinner than to read: "A fortnight elapsed. . . ." Or it might be better after all to write boldly: "Mr. Slack, after a fortnight had elapsed, remarked one day very querulously: 'That smell seems to get worse instead of better.'"

Selection (Speeches)

That last would be compromise, for it would be narration instead of rendering: it would be far *better* to give an idea of the passage of time by picturing a cat with a cod's head, but the length of the story must be considered. Sometimes to render anything at all in a given space will take up too much room—even to render the effect and delivery of a speech. Then just boldly and remorselessly you must relate and *risk* the introduction of yourself as author, with the danger that you may destroy all the illusion of the story.

Conrad and the writer would have agreed that the ideal rendering of Mr. Slack's emotions would be as follows:

"A scrawny, dark-brown neck, with an immense Adam's apple quivering over the blue stripes of a collar erected itself between the sunflower stems above the thin oaken flats of the dividing fence. An unbelievably long, thin gap of a mouth opened itself beneath a black-spotted handkerchief, to say that the unspeakable odour was sufficient to slay all the porters in Covent Garden. Last week it was only bad enough to drive a regiment of dragoons into a faint. The night before the people whom he had had to supper—I wondered who could eat any supper with any appetite under the gaze of those yellow eyes—people, mind you, to whom he had hoped to sell a little bit of property in the neighbourhood. Good people. With more than a little bit in the bank. People whose residence would give the whole neighborhood a lift. They had asked if he liked going out alone at night with so many undiscovered murders about. . . . 'Undiscovered murders!' he went on repeating as if the words gave him an intimate sense of relief. He concluded with the phrase: 'I *don't* think!' "

That would be a very fair *rendering* of part of an eipsode: it would have the use of getting quite a lot of Mr. Slack in; but you might want to get on towards recounting how you had the lucky idea of purchasing shares in a newspaper against which Mr. Slack had counselled you. . . . And you might have got Mr. Slack in already!

The rendering in fact of speeches gave Conrad and the writer more trouble than any other department of the novel whatever. It introduced at once the whole immense subject of under what convention the novel is to be written. For whether you tell it direct and as author—which is the more difficult way—or whether you put it into the mouth of a character—which is easier by far but much more cumbersome—the question of reporting or rendering speeches has to be faced. To pretend that any character or any author writing directly can remember whole speeches with all their words for a matter of twenty-four hours, let alone twenty-four years, is absurd. The most that the normal person carries away of a conversation after even a couple of hours is just a salient or characteristic phrase or two, and a mannerism of the speaker. Yet, if the reader stops to think at all, or has any acuteness whatever, to render Mr. Slack's speech directly: "Thet there odour is enough to do all the porters in Common Gorden in. Lorst week it wouldn' no more 'n 'v sent a ole squad of tinwiskets barmy on the crumpet. . . ." and so on through an entire monologue of a page and a half, must set the reader at some point or other wondering, how the author or the narrator can possibly, even if they were present, have remembered every word of Mr. Slack's long speech. Yet the object of the novelist is to keep the reader entirely oblivious of the fact that the author exists—even of the fact that he is reading a book. This is of course not possible to the bitter end, but a reader *can* be rendered very engrossed, and the nearer you can come to making him entirely insensitive to his surroundings, the more you will have succeeded.

Then again, directly reported speeches in a book do move very slowly; by the use of indirect locutions, together with the rendering of the effects of other portions of speech, you can get a great deal more into a given space. There is a type of reader that likes what is called conversations—but that type is rather the reader in an undeveloped state than the reader who has read much. So, wherever practicable, we used to arrange speeches much as in the paragraph devoted to Mr. Slack above. But quite often we compromised and gave passages of direct enough speech.

This was one of the matters as to which the writer was more uncompromising than was Conrad. In the novel which he did at last begin on his forty-first birthday there will be found to be hardly any direct speech at all, and probably none that is more than a couple of lines in length. Conrad indeed later arrived at the conclusion that, a novel being in the end a matter of convention—and in the beginning too for the matter of that, since what are type, paper, bindings and all the rest, but matters of agreement and convenience—you might as well stretch convention a little farther, and postulate that your author or your narrator is a person of a prodigious memory for the spoken. He had one minute passion with regard to conversations: he could not bear the repetition of 'he said's' and 'she said's,' and would spend agitated hours in chasing those locutions out of his or our pages and substituting: 'he replied,' 'she ejaculated,' 'answered Mr. Verloc' and the like. The writer was less moved by this consideration: it seemed to him that you could employ the words 'he said' as often as you like, accepting them as being unnoticeable, like 'a,' 'the,' 'his,' 'her,' or 'very.'

Conversations

One unalterable rule that we had for the rendering of conversations—for genuine conversations that are an exchange of thought, not interrogatories or statements of fact—was that no speech of one character should ever answer the speech that goes before it. This is almost invariably the case in real life where few people listen, because they are always preparing their own next speeches. When, of a Saturday evening, you are conversing over the fence with your friend Mr. Slack, you hardly notice that he tells you he has seen an incredibly coloured petunia at a market-gardener's, because you are dying to tell him that you have determined to turn author to the extent of writing a letter on local politics to the newspaper of which, against his advice, you have become a large shareholder.

He says: "Right down extraordinary that petunia was—"
You say: "What would you think now of my . . ."
He says: "Diamond-shaped stripes it had, blue-black and salmon. . . ."
You say: "I've always thought I had a bit of a gift. . . ."
Your daughter Millicent interrupts: "Julia Gower has got a pair of snake-skin shoes. She bought them at Wiston and Willocks's."

You miss Mr. Slack's next two speeches in wondering where Millicent got that bangle on her wrist. You will have to tell her more carefully than ever that she must *not* accept presents from Tom, Dick and Harry. By the time you have come out of that reverie Mr. Slack is remarking:

"I said to him use turpentine and sweet oil, three parts to two. What do you think?"

Surprise

We agreed that the one quality that gave interest to Art was the quality of surprise. That is very well illustrated in the snatch of conversation just given. If you reported a long speech of Mr. Slack's to the effect that he was going to enter some of his petunias for the local flower show and those, with his hydrangeas and ornamental sugar-beet, might well give him the Howard Cup for the third time, in which case it would become his property out and out. He would then buy two silver and cut-glass epergnes one to stand on each side of the Cup on his sideboard. He always did think that a touch of silver and cut glass. . . . If, after that you gave a long speech of your own: after, naturally, you had added a few commonplaces as a politeness to Mr. Slack: if you gave a long speech in which with modesty you dwelt on the powers of observation and of the pen that you had always considered yourself to possess, and in which you announced that you certainly meant to write a letter to the paper in which you had shares—

on the statuary in the façade of the new town hall which was an offence to public decency. . . . And if in addition to that you added a soliloquy from your daughter Millicent to the effect that she intended to obtain on credit from your bootmakers, charging them to your account, a pair of scarlet morocco shoes with two-inch heels with which to go joy-riding on the Sunday with a young actor who played under the name of Hildebrand Hare and who had had his portrait in your paper. . . . If you gave all these long speeches one after the other you might be aware of a certain dullness when you re-read that *compte rendu*. . . . But if you carefully broke up petunias, statuary, and flower-show motives and put them down in little shreds one contrasting with the other, you would arrive at something much more coloured, animated, life-like and interesting and you would convey a profoundly significant lesson as to the self-engrossment of humanity. Into that live scene you could then drop the piece of news that you wanted to convey and so you would carry the chapter a good many stages forward.

Here, again, compromise must necessarily come in: there must come a point in the dramatic working up of every scene in which the characters do directly answer each other, for a speech or for two or three speeches. It was in this department, as has already been pointed out, that Conrad was matchless and the writer very deficient. Or, again, a point may come in which it is necessary—in which at least it is to take the line of least resistance—to report directly a whole tremendous effort of eloquence as ebullient as an oration by Mr. Lloyd George on the hymns of the Welsh nation. For there are times when the paraphernalia of indirect speech, interruptions and the rest retard your action too much. Then they must go: the sense of reality must stand down before the necessity to get on.

But, on the whole, the indirect, interrupted method of handling interviews is invaluable for giving a sense of the complexity, the tantalisation, the shimmering, the haze, that life is. In the pre-war period the English novel began at the beginning of a hero's life and went straight on to his marriage without pausing to look aside. This was all very well in its way, but the very great objection could be offered against it that such a story was too confined to its characters and, too self-centredly, went on, *in vacuo*. If you are so set on the affair of your daughter Millicent with the young actor that you forget that there *are* flower shows and town halls with nude statuary your intellect will appear a thing much more circumscribed than it should be. Or, to take a larger matter. A great many novelists have treated of the late war in terms solely of the war: in terms of pip-squeaks, trench-coats, wire-aprons, shells, mud, dust, and sending the bayonet home with a grunt. For that reason interest in the late war is said to have died. But, had you taken part actually in those hostilities, you would know how infinitely little part the actual fighting itself took in your mentality. You would be lying on your stomach, in a beast of a funk, with an immense, horrid German barrage going on all over and round you and with hell and all let loose. But, apart from the occasional, petulant question: "When the deuce will our fellows get going and shut 'em up?" your thoughts were really concentrated on something quite distant: on your daughter Millicent's hair, on the fall of the Asquith Ministry, on your financial predicament, on why your regimental ferrets kept on dying, on whether Latin is really necessary to an education, or in what way really *ought* the Authorities to deal with certain diseases. . . . You were there, but great shafts of thought from the outside, distant and unattainable world infinitely for the greater part occupied your mind.

It was that effect then, that Conrad and the writer sought to get into their work, that being Impressionism.

But these two writers were not unaware that there are other methods: they were not rigid in their own methods: they were sensible to the fact that compromise is at all times necessary in the execution of every work of art.

Style

We agreed on this axiom:

The first business of Style is to make work interesting: the

second business of Style is to make work interesting: the third business of Style is to make work interesting: the fourth business of Style is to make work interesting: the fifth business of Style. . . .
Style, then, has no other business.

A style interests when it carries the reader along: it is then a good style. A style ceases to interest when by reason of disjointed sentences, over-used words, monotonous or jog-trot cadences, it fatigues the reader's mind. *Too* startling words, however apt, *too* just images, too great displays of cleverness are apt in the long run to be as fatiguing as the most over-used words or the most jog-trot cadences. That a face resembles a Dutch clock has been too often said; to say that it resembles a ham is inexact and conveys nothing; to say that it has the mournfulness of an old, squashed-in meat tin, cast away on a waste building lot, would be smart—but too much of that sort of thing would become a nuisance. To say that a face was cramoisy is undesirable: few people nowadays know what the word means. Its employment will make the reader marvel at the user's erudition: in thus marvelling he ceases to consider the story and an impression of vagueness or length is produced on his mind. A succession of impressions of vagueness and length render a book in the end unbearable.

There are, of course, pieces of writing intended to convey the sense of the author's cleverness, knowledge of obsolete words or power of inventing similes: with such exercises Conrad and the writer never concerned themselves.

We used to say: the first lesson that an author has to learn is that of humility. Blessed are the humble because they do not get between the reader's legs. Before everything the author must learn to suppress himself: he must learn that the first thing he has to consider is his story and the last thing that he has to consider is his story, and in between that he will consider his story.

We used to say that a passage of good style began with a fresh, usual word, and continued with fresh, usual words to the end: there was nothing more to it. When we felt that we had really got hold of the reader, with a great deal of caution we would introduce a word not common to a very limited vernacular, but that only very occasionally. Very occasionally indeed: practically never. Yet it is in that way that a language grows and keeps alive. People get tired of hearing the same words over and over again. . . . It is again a matter for compromise.

Our chief masters in style were Flaubert and Maupassant: Flaubert in the greater degree, Maupassant in the less. In about the proportion of a sensible man's whisky and soda. We stood as it were on those hills and thence regarded the world. We remembered long passages of Flaubert: elaborated long passages in his spirit and with his cadences and then translated them into passages of English as simple as the subject under treatment would bear. We remembered short, staccato passages of Maupassant: invented short staccato passages in his spirit and then translated them into English as simple as the subject would bear. Differing subjects bear differing degrees of simplicity: To apply exactly the same timbre of language to a dreadful interview between a father and a daughter as to the description of a child's bedroom at night is impracticable because it is unnatural. In thinking of the frightful scene with your daughter Millicent which ruined your life, town councillor and parliamentary candidate though you had become, you will find that your mind employs a verbiage quite different from that which occurs when you remember Millicent asleep, her little mouth just slightly opened, her toys beside the shaded night-light.

Our vocabulary, then, was as simple as was practicable. But there are degrees of simplicity. We employed as a rule in writing the language that we employed in talking the one to the other. When we used French in speaking we tried mentally to render in English the least literary equivalent of the phrase. We were, however, apt to employ in our conversation words and periphrases that are not in use by, say, financiers. This was involuntary, we imagining that we talked simply enough. But later a body of younger

men with whom the writer spent some years would say, after dinner: "Talk like a book, H. . . . Do talk like a book!" The writer
would utter some speeches in the language that he employed
when talking with Conrad: but he never could utter more than
a sentence or two at a time. The whole mess would roar with
laughter and, for some minutes, would render his voice inaudible.

If you will reflect on the language you then employed—and the
writer—you will find that it was something like: "Cheerio, old
bean. The beastly Adjutant's Parade is at five ack emma. Will you
take my Johnnie's and let me get a real good fug in my downy
bug walk? I'm fair blind to the wide to-night." That was the
current language then and, in the earlier days of our conversations,
some equivalent with which we were unacquainted must normally
have prevailed. That we could hardly have used in our books,
since within a very short time such languages become incomprehensible. Even to-day the locution 'ack emma' is no longer used
and the expression 'blind to the wide' is incomprehensible—the
very state is unfamiliar—to more than half the English-speaking
populations of the globe.

So we talked and wrote a Middle-High-English of as unaffected
a sort as would express our thoughts. And that was all that there
really was to our 'style.' Our greatest admiration for a stylist in
any language was given to W.H. Hudson of whom Conrad said
that his writing was like the grass that the good God made to
grow and when it was there you could not tell how it came.

Carefully examined a good—an interesting—style will be found
to consist in a constant succession of tiny, unobservable surprises.
If you write: "His range of subject was very wide and his conversation very varied and unusual; he could rouse you with his per-
orations or lull you with his periods; therefore his conversation met
with great appreciation and he made several fast friends"—you
will not find the world very apt to be engrossed by what you have
set down. The results will be different if you put it: "He had the
power to charm or frighten rudimentary souls into an aggravated

witch-dance; he could also fill the small souls of the pilgrims with bitter misgivings: he had one devoted friend at least, and he had conquered one soul in the world that was neither rudimentary nor tainted with self-seeking."

Or, let us put the matter in another way. The catalogue of an ironmonger's store is uninteresting as literature because things in it are all classified and thus obvious: the catalogue of a farm sale is more interesting because things in it are contrasted. No one would for long read: Nails, drawn wire, ½ inch, per lb. . . .; nails do., ¾ inch, per lb. . . .; nails, do., inch, per lb. . . . But it is often not disagreeable to read desultorily "Lot 267, Pair rabbit gins. *Lot* 268, Antique powder flask. *Lot* 269, Malay Kris. *Lot* 270, Set of six sporting prints by Herring. *Lot* 271, Silver caudle cup . . . " for that, as far as it goes, has the quality of surprise.

That is, perhaps, enough about Style. This is not a technical manual, and at about this point we arrive at a region in which the writer's memory is not absolutely clear as to the points on which he and Conrad were agreed. We made in addition an infinite number of experiments, together and separately in points of style and cadence. The writer, as has been said, wrote one immense book entirely in sentences of not more than ten syllables. He read the book over. He found it read immensely long. He went through it all again. He joined short sentences: he introduced relative clauses: he wrote in long sentences that had a gentle sonority and ended with a dying fall. The book read less long. Much less long.

Conrad also made experiments, but not on such a great scale since he could always have the benefit of the writer's performances of that sort. The writer only remembers specifically one instance of an exercise on Conrad's part. He was interested in blank verse at the moment—though he took no interest in English verse as a rule—and the writer happening to observe that whole passages of *Heart of Darkness* were not very far off blank verse Conrad tried for a short time to turn a paragraph into decasyllabic lines. The writer remembers the paragraph quite well. It is the one which begins:

"She walked with measured steps, draped in striped and fringed cloths, treading the earth proudly with a slight jingle and flash of barbarous ornaments. . . ."

But he cannot remember what Conrad added or took away. There come back vaguely to him a line or two like:

> She carried high her head, her hair was done
> In the shape of a helmet; she had greaves of brass
> To the knee; gauntlets of brass to th' elbow.
> A crimson spot. . . .

That, however, may just as well be the writer's contrivance as Conrad's: it happened too long ago for the memory to be sure. A little later, the writer occupying himself with writing French rhymed *vers libre*, Conrad tried his hand at that too. He produced:

> Riez toujours! La vie n'est pas si gaie,
> Ces tristes jours quand à travers la haie
> Tombe le long rayon
> Dernier
> De mon soleil qui gagne
> Les sommets, la montagne,
> De l'horizon. . . .

There was a line or two more that the writer has forgotten.

That was Conrad's solitary attempt to write verse.

We may as well put the rest of this matter under a separate heading:

Cadence

This was the one subject upon which we never came to any agreement. It was the writer's view that everyone has a natural cadence of his own from which in the end he cannot escape. Conrad held that a habit of good cadence could be acquired by the study of models. His own he held came to him from constant reading of Flaubert. He did himself probably an injustice.

But questions of cadence and accentuation as of prosody in general we were chary of discussing. They were matters as to which Conrad was very touchy. His ear was singularly faulty for one who was a great writer of elaborated prose so that at times the writer used to wonder how the deuce he *did* produce his effects of polyphonic closings to paragraphs. In speaking English he had practically no idea of accentuation whatever, and indeed no particular habits. He would talk of Mr. Cunninghame Graham's book *Success* alternately as *Suc*cess and Suc*cess* half a dozen times in the course of a conversation about the works of that very wonderful writer. Over French he was not much better. He became quite enraged when told that if the first line of his verse quoted above was to be regarded as decasyllabic—and it *must* by English people be regarded as decasyllabic—then the word 'vie' must be a monosyllable in spite of its termination in e. He had the second line quite correctly allowed for '*tristes*' as being two syllables, and '*tombe*' in the third. In the clash of French verse-theories of those days he might be correct or incorrect without committing a solecism, but he could not be incorrect in the first line and formal in the others. Conrad's face would cloud over. He would snatch up a volume of Racine and read half a dozen lines. He would exclaim contemptuously: "Do you mean to say that each of those verses *cons*ists of ten syllables?" . . . Yet he would have read the verse impeccably. . . . He would flush up to the eyes. He would cry: "Did you ever hear a Frenchman say vee-yeh when he meant vee? You never did! *Jamais de la vie!*" And with fury he would read his verse aloud, making, with a slight stammer, 'vie' a monosyllable and, with impetus, two syllables each out of *tristes* and *tombe*. He would begin to gesticulate, his eyes flashing. . . .

One would change the subject of discussion to the unfailing topic of the rottenness of French as a medium for poetry, finding perfect harmony again in the thought that French was as rotten for verse-poetry as was English for any sort of prose. . . .

The curious thing was that when he read his prose aloud his

accentuation was absolutely faultless. So that it always seemed to the writer that Conrad's marvellous gift of language was, in the end, dramatic. When he talked his sense of phonetics was dormant, but the moment it came to any kind of performance the excitement would quicken the brain centres that governed his articulation. It was, indeed, the same with his French. When conversing desultorily with the writer, he had much of the accent and the negligence of an aristocratic, meridional lounger of the seventies. . . . But when at Lamb House, Rye, he addressed compliments to Mr. Henry James, you could imagine, if you closed your eyes, that it was the senior actor of the Théâtre Français, addressing an eulogium to the bust of Molière. . . .

Probably the mere thought of reading aloud subconsciously aroused memories of once-heard orations of Mr. Gladstone or John Bright: so, in writing, even to himself he would accentuate and pronounce his words as had done those now long defunct orators. . . . And it is to be remembered that, during all those years, the writer wrote every word that he wrote, with the idea of reading aloud to Conrad, and that during all those years Conrad wrote what he wrote with the idea of reading it aloud to this writer.

Structure

That gets rid, as far as is necessary in order to give a pretty fair idea of Conrad's methods, of the questions that concern the texture of a book. More official or more learned writers who shall not be novelists shall treat of this author's prose with less lightness —but assuredly too with less love. . . . Questions then of vocabulary, selection of incident, style, cadence and the rest concern themselves with the colour and texture of prose and, since this writer, again, will leave to more suitable pens the profounder appraisements of Conrad's morality, philosophy and the rest, there remains only to say a word or two on the subject of form.

Conrad then, never wrote a true short story, a matter of two or three pages of minutely considered words, ending with a smack . . . with what the French call a *coup de canon*. His stories were always what for lack of a better phrase one has to call 'long-short' stories. For these the form is practically the same as that of the novel. Or, to avoid the implication of saying that there is only one form for the novel, it would be better to put it that the form of long-short stories may vary as much as may the form for novels. The short story of Maupassant, of Tchekhov or even of the late O. Henry is practically stereotyped—the introduction of a character in a word or two, a word or two for atmosphere, a few paragraphs for story, and then, click! a sharp sentence that flashes the illumination of the idea over the whole.

This Conrad—and for the matter of that, the writer—never so much as attempted, either apart or in collaboration. The reason for this lies in all that is behind the mystic word 'justification.' Before everything a story must convey a sense of inevitability: that which happens in it must seem to be the only thing that could have happened. Of course a character may cry: "If I had then acted differently how different everything would now be." The problem of the author is to make his then action the only action that character could have taken. It must be inevitable, because of his character, because of his ancestry, because of past illness or on account of the gradual coming together of the thousand small circumstances by which Destiny, who is inscrutable and august, will push us into one certain predicament. Let us illustrate:

In the rendering of your long friendship with, and ultimate bitter hostility towards, your neighbour Mr. Slack who had a greenhouse painted with Cox's aluminium paint you will, if you wish to get yourself in with the scrupulousness of a Conrad, have to provide yourself, in the first place, with an ancestry at least as far back as your grandparents. To account for your own stability of character and physical robustness you will have to give yourself two dear old grandparents in a lodge at the gates of a great nobleman: if necessary you will have to give them a brightly polished copper kettle simmering on a spotless hob, with silhouettes on each side of the mantel: in order to account for the lamentable procedure of your daughter Millicent you must provide yourself with an actress- or gipsy-grandmother. Or at least with a French one. This grandmother will have lived, unfortunately unmarried, with someone of eloquence—possibly with the great Earl-Prime Minister at whose gates is situated the humble abode of your other grandparents—at any rate she will have lived with someone from whom you will have inherited your eloquence. From her will have descended the artistic gifts to which the reader will owe your admirable autobiographic novel. If you have any physical weakness, to counterbalance the robustness of your other grandparents, you will provide your mother, shortly before your birth, with an attack of typhoid fever, due to a visit to Venice in company with your father, who was a gentleman's courier in the family in which your mother was a lady's maid. Your father, in order to be a courier, will have had, owing to his illegitimacy, to live abroad in very poor circumstances. The very poor circumstances will illustrate the avarice of his statesman father—an avarice which will have descended to you in the shape of that carefulness in money matters that, reacting on the detrimental tendencies inherited by Millicent from her actress-grandmother, so lamentably influences your daughter's destiny.

And of course there will have to be a great deal more than that, always supposing you to be as scrupulous as was Conrad in this matter of justification. For Conrad—and for the matter of that the writer—was never satisfied that he had really and sufficiently got his characters in: he was never convinced that he had convinced the reader, this accounting for the great lengths of some of his books. He never introduced a character, however subsidiary, without providing that character with ancestry and hereditary characteristics, or at least with home surroundings—always supposing that character had any influence on the inevitability of the story. Any policeman who arrested any character must be 'justified' because the manner in which he effected the arrest, his mannerisms, his vocabulary and his voice, might have a permanent effect on the psychology of the prisoner. The writer remembers Conrad using almost those very words during the discussion of the plot of *The Secret Agent*.

This method, unless it is very carefully handled, is apt to have the grave defect of holding a story back very considerably. You must as a rule bring the biography of a character in only after you have introduced the character: yet, if you introduce a policeman to make an arrest the rendering of his biography might well retard the action of an exciting point in the story. . . . It becomes then your job to arrange that the very arresting of the action is an incitement of interest in the reader, just as, if you serialise a novel, you take care to let the words *"to be continued in our next"* come in at as harrowing a moment as you can contrive.

And of course the introducing of the biography of a character may have the great use of giving contrast to the tone of the rest of the book. . . . Supposing that in your history of your affair with Mr. Slack you think that the note of your orderly middle-class home is growing a little monotonous, it would be very handy if you could discover that Mr. Slack had a secret, dipsomaniacal wife, confined in a country cottage under the care of a rather criminal old couple: with a few pages of biography of that old couple you could give a very pleasant relief to the sameness of your narrative. In that way the sense of reality is procured.

Philosophy, etc.

We agreed that the novel is absolutely the only vehicle for the thought of our day. With the novel you can do anything: you can inquire into every department of life, you can explore every department of the world of thought. The one thing that you can not do is to propagandise, as author, for any cause. You must not, as author, utter any views: above all you must not fake any events.

You must not, however humanitarian you may be, over-elaborate the fear felt by a coursed rabbit.

It is obviously best if you can contrive to be without views at all: your business with the world is rendering, not alteration. You have to render life with such exactitude that more specialised beings than you, learning from you what are the secret needs of humanity, may judge how many white-tiled bathrooms are, or to what extent parliamentary representation is, necessary for the happiness of men and women. If, however, your yearning to amend the human race is so great that you cannot possibly keep your fingers out of the watchsprings there is a device that you can adopt.

Let us suppose that you feel tremendously strong views as to sexual immorality or temperance. You feel that you must express these, yet you know that, like, say, M. Anatole France, who is also a propagandist, you are a supreme novelist. You must then invent, justify, and set going in your novel a character who can convincingly express your views. If you are a gentleman you will also invent, justify and set going characters to express views opposite to those you hold. . . .

You have reached the climax of your long relationship with Mr. Slack; you have been invited and are just going to address a deputation that has come to invite you to represent your native city in the legislature of your country. The deputation is just due. Five minutes before it arrives to present you with the proudest emotion of your life, you learn that your daughter Millicent is going to have a child by Mr. Slack (Him, of course, you will have already 'justified' as the likely seducer of a young lady whose cupidity in the matter of bangles and shoes you by your pecuniary carefulness have kept perpetually on the stretch.) Mr. Slack has a dipsomaniacal wife, so there is no chance of his making the matter good. . . .

You thus have an admirable opportunity of expressing quite a number of views through the mouth of the character whom you have so carefully 'justified' as yourself. Quite a number of views!

That then was, cursorily stated, the technique that we evolved at the Pent. It will be found to be nowadays pretty generally accepted as the normal way of handling the novel. It is founded on common sense and some of its maxims may therefore stand permanently. Or they may not.

Progression d'effet

There is just one other point. In writing a novel we agreed that every word set on paper—*every* word set on paper—must carry the story forward and, that as the story progressed, the story must be carried forward faster and faster and with more and more intensity. That is called *progression d'effet*, words for which there is no English equivalent.

One might go on to further technicalities, such as how to squeeze the last drop out of a subject. The writer has, however, given an instance of this in describing how we piled perils of the hangman's rope on the unfortunate John Kemp. To go deeper into the matter would be to be too technical. Besides enough has been said in this chapter to show you what was the character, the scrupulousness and the common sense of our hero.

There remains to add once more:

But these two writers were not unaware—were not unaware—that there are other methods of writing novels. They were not rigid even in their own methods. They were sensible to the fact that compromise is at all times necessary to the execution of a work of art.

The lay reader will be astonished at this repetition and at these italics. They are inserted for the benefit of gentlemen and ladies who comment on books in the Press.

Language

It would be disingenuous to avoid the subject of language. This is the only matter on which the writer ever differed fundamentally from Conrad. It was one upon which the writer felt so deeply that, for several years, he avoided his friend's society. The pain of approaching the question is thus very great.

Conrad's dislike for the English language, then, was during all the years of our association extreme, his contempt for his medium, unrivalled. Again and again during the writing of, say, *Nostromo* he expressed passionate regret that it was then too late to hope to make a living by writing in French, and as late as 1916 he expressed to the writer an almost equally passionate envy of the writer who was in a position to write in French, propaganda for the government of the French Republic. . . . And Conrad's contempt for English as a prose language was not as in the writer's case mitigated by love for English as the language for verse-poetry. For, to the writer, English is as much superior to French in the one particular as French to English in the other.

Conrad, however, knew nothing of, and cared less for, English verse—and his hatred for English as a prose medium reached such terrible heights that during the writing of *Nostromo* the continual weight of Conrad's depression broke the writer down. We had then published *Romance* and Conrad, breaking, in the interests of that work, his eremitic habits, decided that we ought to show ourselves in Town. The writer therefore took a very large, absurd house on Campden Hill and proceeded to 'entertain.' Conrad had lodgings also on Campden Hill. At this time *Nostromo* had begun to run as a serial in a very popular journal, and on the placards of that journal Conrad's name appeared on every hoarding in London. This publicity caused Conrad an unbelievable agony, he conceiving himself forever dishonoured by such vicarious pandering to popularity.

It was the most terrible period of Conrad's life and of the writer's. Conrad at that time considered himself completely unsuccessful; ignored by the public; ill-treated by the critics; [he was certainly at that date being treated with unusual stupidity by the critics] he was convinced that he would never make a decent living. And he was convinced that he would never master

English. He used to declare that English was a language in which it was impossible to write a direct statement. That was true enough. He used to declare that to make a direct statement in English is like trying to kill a mosquito with a forty-foot stock-whip when you have never before handled a stock-whip. One evening he made, in French, to the writer, the impassioned declaration which will be found in French at the end of this volume. On the following afternoon he made a really terrible scene at the writer's house. . . .

The writer was at the time very much harassed. The expense of keeping up a rather portentous establishment made it absolutely necessary that he should add considerably to his income with his pen—a predicament with which he had not yet been faced. There was nothing in that except that it was almost impossible to find time to write. An epidemic of influenza running through the house crippled its domestic staff so that all sorts of household tasks had of necessity to be performed by the writer: there were, in addition, social duties—and the absolute necessity of carrying Conrad every afternoon through a certain quantum of work without which he must miss his weekly instalments in the popular journal. . . .

Conrad's indictment of the English language was this, that no English word is a word: that all English words are instruments for exciting blurred emotions. "Oaken" in French means 'made of oak wood'—nothing more. 'Oaken' in English connotes innumerable moral attributes: it will connote stolidity, resolution, honesty, blond features, relative unbreakableness, absolute unbendableness —also, made of oak. . . . The consequence is, that no English word has clean edges: a reader is always, for a fraction of a second, uncertain as to which meaning of the word the writer may intend. Thus, all English prose is blurred. Conrad desired to write a prose of extreme limpidity. . . .

We may let it go at that. In later years Conrad achieved a certain fluency and a great limpidity of language—the result being *The Rover*, which strikes the writer as being a very serene and beautiful work. Conrad then regretted that, for him, all the romance of writing was gone. In between the two he made tributes to the glory of the English language by implication contemning the tongue that Flaubert used. This at the time struck the writer, at that time in a state of exhaused depression, as unforgivable— as the very betrayal of Dain by Tom Lingard. . . . Perhaps it was. If it were Conrad faced the fact in that book. There are predicaments that beset great Adventurers, in dark hours, in the shallows: the overtired nerve will fail. . . . We may well let it go at that. . . .

> "For it would be delightful to catch the echo of the desperate and funny quarrels that enlivened these old days. The pity of it is that there comes a time when all the fun of one's life must be looked for in the past. . . ."

Those were Conrad's last words on all the matters of our collaborations here treated of. They were, too, almost his last words. . . . For those who can catch them here then are the echoes. . . .

ANTICIPATIONS OF *THE GREAT GATSBY*

WINTER DREAMS*

F. Scott Fitzgerald

There are several stories which suggest themes or ideas or even basic plots similar to those in Gatsby. Fitzgerald thought of the story "Absolution" at first as a "prologue" to the novel. "The Rich Boy" and "The Diamond as Big as the Ritz" treat the phenomenon of wealth in very different ways, but with suggestions useful to a discussion of Gatsby (for a discussion of the latter story, see Marius Bewley, The Eccentric Design, Columbia University Press, 1959, pp. 259-70). But "Winter Dreams" is apparently a preliminary draft of the story of Gatsby's relationship with Daisy. For an excellent discussion of the story and a comparison with Gatsby, see James E. Miller, The Fictional Technique of Scott Fitzgerald (The Hague: Martinus Nijhoff, 1957), pp. 83-87.

"Winter Dreams" was first published in the Metropolitan Magazine for December, 1922.

Some of the caddies were poor as sin and lived in one-room houses with a neurasthenic cow in the front yard, but Dexter Green's

* F. Scott Fitzgerald, "Winter Dreams," All the Sad Young Men (New York: Charles Scribner's Sons, 1926), pp. 57-90. Copyright 1922 Frances Scott Fitzgerald Lanahan; renewal copyright 1950. Reprinted by permission of the publishers. The Scribner Library Edition of Babylon Revisited and Other Stories (New York: Charles Scribner's Sons, 1960) is the current source of this story.

father owned the second best grocery-store in Black Bear—the best one was "The Hub," patronized by the wealthy people from Sherry Island—and Dexter caddied only for pocket-money.

In the fall when the days became crisp and gray, and the long Minnesota winter shut down like the white lid of a box, Dexter's skis moved over the snow that hid the fairways of the golf course. At these times the country gave him a feeling of profound melancholy—it offended him that the links should lie in enforced fallowness, haunted by ragged sparrows for the long season. It was dreary, too, that on the tees where the gay colors fluttered in summer there were now only the desolate sand-boxes knee-deep in crusted ice. When he crossed the hills the wind blew cold as misery, and if the sun was out he tramped with his eyes squinted up against the hard dimensionless glare.

In April the winter ceased abruptly. The snow ran down into Black Bear Lake scarcely tarrying for the early golfers to brave the season with red and black balls. Without elation, without an interval of moist glory, the cold was gone.

Dexter knew that there was something dismal about this Northern spring, just as he knew there was something gorgeous about the fall. Fall made him clinch his hands and tremble and repeat idiotic sentences to himself, and make brisk abrupt gestures of command to imaginary audiences and armies. October filled him with hope which November raised to a sort of ecstatic triumph, and in this mood the fleeting brilliant impressions of the summer at Sherry Island were ready grist to his mill. He became a golf champion and defeated Mr. T. A. Hedrick in a marvellous match played a hundred times over the fairways of his imagination, a match each detail of which he changed about untiringly—sometimes he won with almost laughable ease, sometimes he came up magnificently from behind. Again, stepping from a Pierce-Arrow automobile, like Mr. Mortimer Jones, he strolled frigidly into the lounge of the Sherry Island Golf Club—or perhaps, surrounded by an admiring crowd, he gave an exhibition of fancy diving from the springboard of the club raft. . . . Among those who watched him in open-mouthed wonder was Mr. Mortimer Jones.

And one day it came to pass that Mr. Jones—himself and not his ghost—came up to Dexter with tears in his eyes and said that Dexter was the — — best caddy in the club, and wouldn't he decide not to quit if Mr. Jones made it worth his while, because every other — — caddy in the club lost one ball a hole for him—regularly——

"No, sir," said Dexter decisively, "I don't want to caddy any more." Then, after a pause: "I'm too old."

"You're not more than fourteen. Why the devil did you decide just this morning that you wanted to quit? You promised that next week you'd go over to the state tournament with me."

"I decided I was too old."

Dexter handed in his "A Class" badge, collected what money was due him from the caddy master, and walked home to Black Bear Village.

"The best — — caddy I ever saw," shouted Mr. Mortimer Jones over a drink that afternoon. "Never lost a ball! Willing! Intelligent! Quiet! Honest! Grateful!"

The little girl who had done this was eleven—beautifully ugly as little girls are apt to be who are destined after a few years to be inexpressibly lovely and bring no end of misery to a great number of men. The spark, however, was perceptible. There was a general ungodliness in the way her lips twisted down at the corners when she smiled, and in the—Heaven help us!—in the almost passionate quality of her eyes. Vitality is born early in such women. It was utterly in evidence now, shining through her thin frame in a sort of glow.

She had come eagerly out on to the course at nine o'clock with a white linen nurse and five small new golf-clubs in a white canvas bag which the nurse was carrying. When Dexter first saw her she was standing by the caddy house, rather ill at ease and trying to conceal the fact by engaging her nurse in an obviously unnatural conversation graced by startling and irrelevant grimaces from herself.

"Well, it's certainly a nice day, Hilda," Dexter heard her say. She drew down the corners of her mouth, smiled, and glanced furtively around, her eyes in transit falling for an instant on Dexter.

Then to the nurse:

"Well, I guess there aren't very many people out here this morning, are there?"

The smile again—radiant, blatantly artificial—convincing.

"I don't know what we're supposed to do now," said the nurse, looking nowhere in particular.

"Oh, that's all right. I'll fix it up."

Dexter stood perfectly still, his mouth slightly ajar. He knew that if he moved forward a step his stare would be in her line of vision —if he moved backward he would lose his full view of her face. For a moment he had not realized how young she was. Now he remembered having seen her several times the year before—in bloomers.

Suddenly, involuntarily, he laughed, a short abrupt laugh—then, startled by himself, he turned and began to walk quickly away.

"Boy!"

Dexter stopped.

"Boy——"

Beyond question he was addressed. Not only that, but he was treated to that absurd smile, that preposterous smile—the memory of which at least a dozen men were to carry into middle age.

"Boy, do you know where the golf teacher is?"

"He's giving a lesson."

"Well, do you know where the caddy-master is?"

"He isn't here yet this morning."

"Oh." For a moment this baffled her. She stood alternately on her right and left foot.

"We'd like to get a caddy," said the nurse. "Mrs. Mortimer Jones sent us out to play golf, and we don't know how without we get a caddy."

Here she was stopped by an ominous glance from Miss Jones, followed immediately by the smile.

"There aren't any caddies here except me," said Dexter to the nurse, "and I got to stay here in charge until the caddy-master gets here."

"Oh."

Miss Jones and her retinue now withdrew, and at a proper distance from Dexter became involved in a heated conversation, which was concluded by Miss Jones taking one of the clubs and hitting it on the ground with violence. For further emphasis she raised it again and was about to bring it down smartly upon the nurse's bosom, when the nurse seized the club and twisted it from her hands.

"You damn little mean old *thing!*" cried Miss Jones wildly.

Another argument ensued. Realizing that the elements of the comedy were implied in the scene, Dexter several times began to laugh, but each time restrained the laugh before it reached audibility. He could not resist the monstrous conviction that the little girl was justified in beating the nurse.

The situation was resolved by the fortuitous appearance of the caddy-master, who was appealed to immediately by the nurse.

"Miss Jones is to have a little caddy, and this one says he can't go."

"Mr. McKenna said I was to wait here till you came," said Dexter quickly.

"Well, he's here now." Miss Jones smiled cheerfully at the caddy-master. Then she dropped her bag and set off at a haughty mince toward the first tee.

"Well?" The caddy-master turned to Dexter. "What you standing there like a dummy for? Go pick up the young lady's clubs."

"I don't think I'll go out to-day," said Dexter.

"You don't——"

"I think I'll quit."

The enormity of his decision frightened him. He was a favorite caddy, and the thirty dollars a month he earned through the summer were not to be made elsewhere around the lake. But he had received a strong emotional shock, and his perturbation required a violent and immediate outlet.

It is not so simple as that, either. As so frequently would be the case in the future, Dexter was unconsciously dictated to by his winter dreams.

II

Now, of course, the quality and the seasonability of these winter dreams varied, but the stuff of them remained. They persuaded Dexter several years later to pass up a business course at the State university—his father, prospering now, would have paid his way—for the precarious advantage of attending an older and more famous university in the East, where he was bothered by his scanty funds. But do not get the impression, because his winter dreams happened to be concerned at first with musings on the rich, that there was anything merely snobbish in the boy. He wanted not association with glittering things and glittering people —he wanted the glittering things themselves. Often he reached out for the best without knowing why he wanted it—and sometimes he ran up against the mysterious denials and prohibitions in which life indulges. It is with one of those denials and not with his career as a whole that this story deals.

He made money. It was rather amazing. After college he went to the city from which Black Bear Lake draws its wealthy patrons. When he was only twenty-three and had been there not quite two years, there were already people who liked to say: "Now *there's* a boy—" All about him rich men's sons were peddling bonds precariously, or investing patrimonies precariously, or plodding through the two dozen volumes of the "George Washington Commercial Course," but Dexter borrowed a thousand dollars on his college degree and his confident mouth, and bought a partnership in a laundry.

It was a small laundry when he went into it, but Dexter made a specialty of learning how the English washed fine woolen golf-stockings without shrinking them, and within a year he was cater-ing to the trade that wore knickerbockers. Men were insisting that their Shetland hose and sweaters go to his laundry, just as they had insisted on a caddy who could find golf-balls. A little later he was doing their wives' lingerie as well—and running five branches in different parts of the city. Before he was twenty-seven he owned the largest string of laundries in his section of the country. It was then that he sold out and went to New York. But the part of his story that concerns us goes back to the days when he was making his first big success.

When he was twenty-three Mr. Hart—one of the gray-haired men who like to say "Now there's a boy"—gave him a guest card to the Sherry Island Golf Club for a week-end. So he signed his name one day on the register, and that afternoon played golf in a foursome with Mr. Hart and Mr. Sandwood and Mr. T. A. Hedrick. He did not consider it necessary to remark that he had once carried Mr. Hart's bag over this same links, and that he knew every trap and gully with his eyes shut—but he found him-self glancing at the four caddies who trailed them, trying to catch a gleam or gesture that would remind him of himself, that would lessen the gap which lay betwen his present and his past.

It was a curious day, slashed abruptly with fleeting, familiar im-pressions. One minute he had the sense of being a trespasser—in the next he was impressed by the tremendous superiority he felt toward Mr. T. A. Hedrick, who was a bore and not even a good golfer any more.

Then, because of a ball Mr. Hart lost near the fifteenth green, an enormous thing happened. While they were searching the stiff grasses of the rough there was a clear call of "Fore!" from behind a hill in their rear. And as they all turned abruptly from their search a bright new ball sliced abruptly over the hill and caught Mr. T. A. Hedrick in the abdomen.

"By Gad!" cried Mr. T. A. Hedrick, "they ought to put some of these crazy women off the course. It's getting to be outrageous."

A head and a voice came up together over the hill:

"Do you mind if we go through?"

"You hit me in the stomach!" declared Mr. Hedrick wildly.

"Did I?" The girl approached the group of men. "I'm sorry. I yelled 'Fore!'"

Her glance fell casually on each of the men—then scanned the fairway for her ball.

"Did I bounce into the rough?"

It was impossible to determine whether this question was ingenuous or malicious. In a moment, however, she left no doubt, for as her partner came up over the hill she called cheerfully:

"Here I am! I'd have gone on the green except that I hit something."

As she took her stance for a short mashie shot, Dexter looked at her closely. She wore a blue gingham dress, rimmed at throat and shoulders with a white edging that accentuated her tan. The quality of exaggeration, of thinness, which had made her passionate eyes and down-turning mouth absurd at eleven, was gone now. She was arrestingly beautiful. The color in her cheeks was centered like the color in a picture—it was not a "high" color, but a sort of fluctuating and feverish warmth, so shaded that it seemed at any moment it would recede and disappear. This color and the mobility of her mouth gave a continual impression of flux, of intense life, of passionate vitality—balanced only partially by the sad luxury of her eyes.

She swung her mashie impatiently and without interest, pitching the ball into a sand-pit on the other side of the green. With a quick, insincere smile and a careless "Thank you!" she went on after it.

"That Judy Jones!" remarked Mr. Hedrick on the next tee, as they waited—some moments—for her to play on ahead. "All she needs is to be turned up and spanked for six months and then to be married off to an old-fashioned cavalry captain."

"My God, she's good-looking!" said Mr. Sandwood, who was just over thirty.

"Good-looking!" cried Mr. Hedrick contemptuously. "She always looks as if she wanted to be kissed! Turning those big cow-eyes on every calf in town!"

It was doubtful if Mr. Hedrick intended a reference to the maternal instinct.

"She'd play pretty good golf if she'd try," said Mr. Sandwood.

"She has no form," said Mr. Hedrick solemnly.

"She has a nice figure," said Mr. Sandwood.

"Better thank the Lord she doesn't drive a swifter ball," said Mr. Hart, winking at Dexter.

Later in the afternoon the sun went down with a riotous swirl of gold and varying blues and scarlets, and left the dry, rustling night of Western summer. Dexter watched from the veranda of the Golf Club, watched the even overlap of the waters in the little wind, silver molasses under the harvest-moon. Then the moon held a finger to her lips and the lake became a clear pool, pale and quiet. Dexter put on his bathing-suit and swam out to the farthest raft, where he stretched dripping on the wet canvas of the springboard.

There was a fish jumping and a star shining and the lights around the lake were gleaming. Over on a dark peninsula a piano was playing the songs of last summer and of summers before that —songs from "Chin-Chin" and "The Count of Luxemburg" and "The Chocolate Soldier"—and because the sound of a piano over a stretch of water had always seemed beautiful to Dexter he lay perfectly quiet and listened.

The tune the piano was playing at that moment had been gay and new five years before when Dexter was a sophomore at college. They had played it at a prom once when he could not afford the luxury of proms, and he had stood outside the gymnasium and listened. The sound of the tune precipitated in him a sort of ecstasy and it was with that ecstasy he viewed what happened to him now. It was a mood of intense appreciation, a sense that, for

once, he was magnificently attuned to life and that everything about
him was radiating a brightness and a glamour he might never
know again.

A low, pale oblong detached itself suddenly from the darkness of
the Island, spitting forth the reverberate sound of a racing motor-
boat. Two white streamers of cleft water rolled themselves out
behind it and almost immediately the boat was beside him, drown-
ing out the hot tinkle of the piano in the drone of its spray. Dexter
raising himself on his arms was aware of a figure standing at the
wheel, of two dark eyes regarding him over the lengthening space
of water—then the boat had gone by and was sweeping in an immense and purposeless circle of spray round and round in the
middle of the lake. With equal eccentricity one of the circles
flattened out and headed back toward the raft.

"Who's that?" she called, shutting off her motor. She was so
near now that Dexter could see her bathing-suit, which consisted
apparently of pink rompers.

The nose of the boat bumped the raft, and as the latter tilted
rakishly he was precipitated toward her. With different degrees
of interest they recognized each other.

"Aren't you one of those men we played through this afternoon?" she demanded.

He was.

"Well, do you know how to drive a motor-boat? Because if you
do I wish you'd drive this one so I can ride on the surf-board behind. My name is Judy Jones"—she favored him with an absurd
smirk—rather, what tried to be a smirk, for, twist her mouth as
she might, it was not grotesque, it was merely beautiful—"and I
live in a house over there on the Island, and in that house there
is a man waiting for me. When he drove up at the door I drove
out of the dock because he says I'm his ideal."

There was a fish jumping and a star shining and the lights
around the lake were gleaming. Dexter sat beside Judy Jones and
she explained how her boat was driven. Then she was in the water,

swimming to the floating surf-board with a sinuous crawl. Watching her was without effort to the eye, watching a branch waving or a sea-gull flying. Her arms, burned to butternut, moved sinuously among the dull platinum ripples, elbow appearing first, casting the forearm back with a cadence of falling water, then reaching out and down, stabbing a path ahead.

They moved out into the lake; turning, Dexter saw that she was kneeling on the low rear of the now uptilted surf-board.

"Go faster," she called, "fast as it'll go."

Obediently he jammed the lever forward and the white spray mounted at the bow. When he looked around again the girl was standing up on the rushing board, her arms spread wide, her eyes lifted toward the moon.

"It's awful cold," she shouted. "What's your name?"

He told her.

"Well, why don't you come to dinner to-morrow night?"

His heart turned over like the fly-wheel of the boat, and, for the second time, her casual whim gave a new direction to his life.

III

Next evening while he waited for her to come down-stairs, Dexter peopled the soft deep summer room and the sun-porch that opened from it with the men who had already loved Judy Jones. He knew the sort of men they were—the men who when he first went to college had entered from the great prep schools with graceful clothes and the deep tan of healthy summers. He had seen that, in one sense, he was better than these men. He was newer and stronger. Yet in acknowledging to himself that he wished his children to be like them he was admitting that he was but the rough, strong stuff from which they eternally sprang.

When the time had come for him to wear good clothes, he had known who were the best tailors in America, and the best tailors in America had made him the suit he wore this evening. He had acquired that particular reserve peculiar to his university, that set it off from other universities. He recognized the value to him of such a mannerism and he had adopted it; he knew that to be careless in dress and manner required more confidence than to be careful. But carelessness was for his children. His mother's name had been Krimslich. She was a Bohemian of the peasant class and she had talked broken English to the end of her days. Her son must keep to the set patterns.

At a little after seven Judy Jones came down-stairs. She wore a blue silk afternoon dress, and he was disappointed at first that she had not put on something more elaborate. This feeling was accentuated when, after a brief greeting, she went to the door of a butler's pantry and pushing it open called: "You can serve dinner, Martha." He had rather expected that a butler would announce dinner, that there would be a cocktail. Then he put these thoughts behind him as they sat down side by side on a lounge and looked at each other.

"Father and mother won't be here," she said thoughtfully.

He remembered the last time he had seen her father, and he was glad the parents were not to be here to-night—they might wonder who he was. He had been born in Keeble, a Minnesota village fifty miles farther north, and he always gave Keeble as his home instead of Black Bear Village. Country towns were well enough to come from if they weren't inconveniently in sight and used as footstools by fashionable lakes.

They talked of his university, which she had visited frequently during the past two years, and of the near-by city which supplied Sherry Island with its patrons, and whither Dexter would return next day to his prospering laundries.

During dinner she slipped into a moody depression which gave Dexter a feeling of uneasiness. Whatever petulance she uttered in her throaty voice worried him. Whatever she smiled at—at him, at a chicken liver, at nothing—it disturbed him that her smile could have no root in mirth, or even in amusement. When the scarlet corners of her lips curved down, it was less a smile than an invitation to a kiss.

Then, after dinner, she led him out on the dark sun-porch and deliberately changed the atmosphere.

"Do you mind if I weep a little?" she said.

"I'm afraid I'm boring you," he responded quickly.

"You're not. I like you. But I've just had a terrible afternoon. There was a man I cared about, and this afternoon he told me out of a clear sky that he was poor as a church-mouse. He'd never even hinted it before. Does this sound horribly mundane?"

"Perhaps he was afraid to tell you."

Suppose he was," she answered. "He didn't start right. You see, if I'd thought of him as poor—well, I've been mad about loads of poor men, and fully intended to marry them all. But in this case, I hadn't thought of him that way, and my interest in him wasn't strong enough to survive the shock. As if a girl calmly informed her fiancé that she was a widow. He might not object to widows, but——

"Let's start right," she interrupted herself suddenly. "Who are you, anyway?"

For a moment Dexter hesitated. Then:

"I'm nobody," he announced. "My career is largely a matter of futures."

"Are you poor?"

"No," he said frankly, "I'm probably making more money than any man my age in the Northwest. I know that's an obnoxious remark, but you advised me to start right."

There was a pause. Then she smiled and the corners of her mouth drooped and an almost imperceptible sway brought her closer to him, looking up into his eyes. A lump rose in Dexter's throat, and he waited breathless for the experiment, facing the unpredictable compound that would form mysteriously from the elements of their lips. Then he saw—she communicated her excitement to him, lavishly, deeply, with kisses that were not a promise but a fulfilment. They aroused in him not hunger demanding renewal but surfeit that would demand more surfeit . . . kisses that were like charity, creating want by holding back nothing at all.

It did not take him many hours to decide that he had wanted
Judy Jones ever since he was a proud, desirous little boy.

IV

It began like that—and continued, with varying shades of intensity, on such a note right up to the dénouement. Dexter sur-
rendered a part of himself to the most direct and unprincipled
personality with which he had ever come in contact. Whatever
Judy wanted, she went after with the full pressure of her charm.
There was no divergence of method, no jockeying for position or
premeditation of effects—there was a very little mental side to
any of her affairs. She simply made men conscious to the highest
degree of her physical loveliness. Dexter had no desire to change
her. Her deficiencies were knit up with a passionate energy that
transcended and justified them.

When, as Judy's head lay against his shoulder that first night,
she whispered, "I don't know what's the matter with me. Last
night I thought I was in love with a man and to-night I think I'm
in love with you——"—it seemed to him a beautiful and romantic
thing to say. It was the exquisite excitability that for the moment
he controlled and owned. But a week later he was compelled to
view this same quality in a different light. She took him in her
roadster to a picnic supper, and after supper she disappeared, like-
wise in her roadster, with another man. Dexter became enormously
upset and was scarcely able to be decently civil to the other people
present. When she assured him that she had not kissed the other
man, he knew she was lying—yet he was glad that she had taken
the trouble to lie to him.

He was, as he found before the summer ended, one of a varying
dozen who circulated about her. Each of them had at one time
been favored above all others—about half of them still basked in
the solace of occasional sentimental revivals. Whenever one
showed signs of dropping out through long neglect, she granted
him a brief honeyed hour, which encouraged him to tag along for

a year or so longer. Judy made these forays upon the helpless and defeated without malice, indeed half unconscious that there was anything mischievous in what she did.

When a new man came to town every one dropped out—dates were automatically cancelled.

The helpless part of trying to do anything about it was that she did it all herself. She was not a girl who could be "won" in the kinetic sense—she was proof against cleverness, she was proof against charm; if any of these assailed her too strongly she would immediately resolve the affair to a physical basis, and under the magic of her physical splendor the strong as well as the brilliant played her game and not their own. She was entertained only by the gratification of her desires and by the direct exercise of her own charm. Perhaps from so much youthful love, so many youthful lovers, she had come, in self-defense, to nourish herself wholly from within.

Succeeding Dexter's first exhilaration came restlessness and dissatisfaction. The helpless ecstasy of losing himself in her was opiate rather than tonic. It was fortunate for his work during the winter that those moments of ecstasy came infrequently. Early in their acquaintance it had semed for a while that there was a deep and spontaneous mutual attraction—that first August, for example —three days of long evenings on her dusky veranda, of strange wan kisses through the late afternoon, in shadowy alcoves or behind the protecting trellises of the garden arbors, of mornings when she was fresh as a dream and almost shy at meeting him in the clarity of the rising day. There was all the ecstasy of an engagement about it, sharpened by his realization that there was no engagement. It was during those three days that, for the first time, he had asked her to marry him. She said "maybe some day," she said "kiss me," she said "I'd like to marry you," she said "I love you"—she said—nothing.

The three days were interrupted by the arrival of a New York man who visited at her house for half September. To Dexter's agony, rumor engaged them. The man was the son of the president of a great trust company. But at the end of a month it was reported that Judy was yawning. At a dance one night she sat all evening in a motor-boat with a local beau, while the New Yorker searched the club for her frantically. She told the local beau that she was bored with her visitor, and two days later he left. She was seen with him at the station, and it was reported that he looked very mournful indeed.

On this note the summer ended. Dexter was twenty-four, and he found himself increasingly in a position to do as he wished. He joined two clubs in the city and lived at one of them. Though he was by no means an integral part of the stag-lines at these clubs, he managed to be on hand at dances where Judy Jones was likely to appear. He could have gone out socially as much as he liked— he was an eligible young man, now, and popular with down-town fathers. His confessed devotion to Judy Jones had rather solidified his position. But he had no social aspirations and rather despised the dancing men who were always on tap for the Thursday or Saturday parties and who filled in at dinners with the younger married set. Already he was playing with the idea of going East to New York. He wanted to take Judy Jones with him. No disillusion as to the world in which she had grown up could cure his illusion as to her desirability.

Remember that—for only in the light of it can what he did for her be understood.

Eighteen months after he first met Judy Jones he became engaged to another girl. Her name was Irene Scheerer, and her father was one of the men who had always believed in Dexter. Irene was light-haired and sweet and honorable, and a little stout, and she had two suitors whom she pleasantly relinquished when Dexter formally asked her to marry him.

Summer, fall, winter, spring, another summer, another fall—so much he had given of his active life to the incorrigible lips of Judy Jones. She had treated him with interest, with encouragement, with malice, with indifference, with contempt. She had inflicted on him the innumerable little slights and indignities possible in such a case—as if in revenge for having ever cared for him at all. She had beckoned him and yawned at him and beckoned him again and he had responded often with bitterness and narrowed eyes. She had brought him ecstatic happiness and intolerable agony of spirit. She had caused him untold inconvenience and not a little trouble. She had insulted him, and she had ridden over him, and she had played his interest in her against his interest in his work—for fun. She had done everything to him except to criticise him—this she had not done—it seemed to him only because it might have sullied the utter indifference she manifested and sincerely felt toward him.

When autumn had come and gone again it occurred to him that he could not have Judy Jones. He had to beat this into his mind but he convinced himself at last. He lay awake at night for a while and argued it over. He told himself the trouble and the pain she had caused him, he enumerated her glaring deficiencies as a wife. Then he said to himself that he loved her, and after a while he fell asleep. For a week, lest he imagined her husky voice over the telephone or her eyes opposite him at lunch, he worked hard and late, and at night he went to his office and plotted out his years.

At the end of a week he went to a dance and cut in on her once. For almost the first time since they had met he did not ask her to sit out with him or tell her that she was lovely. It hurt him that she did not miss these things—that was all. He was not jealous when he saw that there was a new man to-night. He had been hardened against jealousy long before.

He stayed late at the dance. He sat for an hour with Irene Scheerer and talked about books and about music. He knew very little about either. But he was beginning to be master of his own time now, and he had a rather priggish notion that he—the young and already fabulously successful Dexter Green—should know more about such things.

That was in October, when he was twenty-five. In January, Dexter and Irene became engaged. It was to be announced in June, and they were to be married three months later.

The Minnesota winter prolonged itself interminably, and it was almost May when the winds came soft and the snow ran down into Black Bear Lake at last. For the first time in over a year Dexter was enjoying a certain tranquillity of spirit. Judy Jones had been in Florida, and afterward in Hot Springs, and somewhere she had been engaged, and somewhere she had broken it off. At first, when Dexter had definitely given her up, it had made him sad that people still linked them together and asked for news of her, but when he began to be placed at dinner next to Irene Scheerer people didn't ask him about her any more—they told him about her. He ceased to be an authority on her.

May at last. Dexter walked the streets at night when the darkness was damp as rain, wondering that so soon, with so little done, so much of ecstasy had gone from him. May one year back had been marked by Judy's poignant, unforgivable, yet forgiven turbulence—it had been one of those rare times when he fancied she had grown to care for him. That old penny's worth of happiness he had spent for this bushel of content. He knew that Irene would be no more than a curtain spread behind him, a hand moving among gleaming teacups, a voice calling to children . . . fire and loveliness were gone, the magic of nights and the wonder of the varying hours and seasons . . . slender lips, down-turning, dropping to his lips and bearing him up into a heaven of eyes. . . . The thing was deep in him. He was too strong and alive for it to die lightly.

In the middle of May when the weather balanced for a few days on the thin bridge that led to deep summer he turned in one night at Irene's house. Their engagement was to be announced in a week now—no one would be surprised at it. And to-night they would sit together on the lounge at the University Club and look on for an hour at the dancers. It gave him a sense of solidity to go with her—she was so sturdily popular, so intensely "great."

He mounted the steps of the brownstone house and stepped inside.

"Irene," he called.

Mrs. Scheerer came out of the living-room to meet him.

"Dexter," she said, "Irene's gone up-stairs with a splitting headache. She wanted to go with you but I made her go to bed."

"Nothing serious, I——"

"Oh, no. She's going to play golf with you in the morning. You can spare her for just one night, can't you, Dexter?"

Her smile was kind. She and Dexter liked each other. In the living-room he talked for a moment before he said good-night.

Returning to the University Club, where he had rooms, he stood in the doorway for a moment and watched the dancers. He leaned against the door-post, nodded at a man or two—yawned.

"Hello, darling."

The familiar voice at his elbow startled him. Judy Jones had left a man and crossed the room to him—Judy Jones, a slender enamelled doll in cloth of gold; gold in a band at her head, gold in two slipper points at her dress's hem. The fragile glow of her face seemed to blossom as she smiled at him. A breeze of warmth and light blew through the room. His hands in the pockets of his dinner-jacket tightened spasmodically. He was filled with a sudden excitement.

"When did you get back?" he asked casually.

"Come here and I'll tell you about it."

She turned and he followed her. She had been away—he could have wept at the wonder of her return. She had passed through enchanted streets, doing things that were like provocative music. All mysterious happenings, all fresh and quickening hopes, had gone away with her, come back with her now.

She turned in the doorway.

"Have you a car here? If you haven't, I have."

"I have a coupé."

In then, with a rustle of golden cloth. He slammed the door. Into so many cars she had stepped—like that—her back against the leather, so—her elbow resting on the door—waiting. She would have been soiled long since had there been anything to soil her —except herself—but this was her own self outpouring.

With an effort he forced himself to start the car and back into the street. This was nothing, he must remember. She had done this before, and he had put her behind him, as he would have crossed a bad account from his books.

He drove slowly down-town and, affecting abstraction, traversed the deserted streets of the business section, peopled here and there where a movie was giving out its crowd or where consumptive or pugilistic youth lounged in front of pool halls. The clink of glasses and the slap of hands on the bars issued from saloons, cloisters of glazed glass and dirty yellow light.

She was watching him closely and the silence was embarrassing, yet in this crisis he could find no casual word with which to profane the hour. At a convenient turning he began to zigzag back toward the University Club.

"Have you missed me?" she asked suddenly.

"Everybody missed you."

He wondered if she knew of Irene Scheerer. She had been back only a day—her absence had been almost contemporaneous with his engagement.

"What a remark!" Judy laughed sadly—without sadness. She looked at him searchingly. He became absorbed in the dashboard.

"You're handsomer than you used to be," she said thoughtfully. "Dexter, you have the most rememberable eyes."

He could have laughed at this, but he did not laugh. It was the sort of thing that was said to sophomores. Yet it stabbed at him.

"I'm awfully tired of everything, darling." She called every one darling, endowing the endearment with careless, individual camaraderie. "I wish you'd marry me."

The directness of this confused him. He should have told her now that he was going to marry another girl, but he could not tell her. He could as easily have sworn that he had never loved her.

"I think we'd get along," she continued, on the same note, "unless probably you've forgotten me and fallen in love with another girl."

Her confidence was obviously enormous. She had said, in effect, that she found such a thing impossible to believe, that if it were true he had merely committed a childish indiscretion—and probably to show off. She would forgive him, because it was not a matter of any moment but rather something to be brushed aside lightly.

"Of course you could never love anybody but me," she continued, "I like the way you love me. Oh, Dexter, have you forgotten last year?"

"No, I haven't forgotten."

"Neither have I!"

Was she sincerely moved—or was she carried along by the wave of her own acting?

"I wish we could be like that again," she said, and he forced himself to answer:

"I don't think we can."

"I suppose not. . . . I hear you're giving Irene Scheerer a violent rush."

There was not the faintest emphasis on the name, yet Dexter was suddenly ashamed.

"Oh, take me home," cried Judy suddenly; "I don't want to go back to that idiotic dance—with those children."

Then, as he turned up the street that led to the residence district, Judy began to cry quietly to herself. He had never seen her cry before.

The dark street lightened, the dwellings of the rich loomed up around them, he stopped his coupé in front of the great white bulk of the Mortimer Joneses' house, somnolent, gorgeous, drenched with the splendor of the damp moonlight. Its solidity startled him. The strong walls, the steel of the girders, the breadth and beam and pomp of it were there only to bring out the contrast with the young beauty beside him. It was sturdy to accentuate her slightness—as if to show what a breeze could be generated by a butterfly's wing.

He sat perfectly quiet, his nerves in wild clamor, afraid that if he moved he would find her irresistibly in his arms. Two tears had rolled down her wet face and trembled on her upper lip.

"I'm more beautiful than anybody else," she said brokenly, "why can't I be happy?" Her moist eyes tore at his stability—her mouth turned slowly downward with an exquisite sadness: "I'd like to marry you if you'll have me, Dexter. I suppose you think I'm not worth having, but I'll be so beautiful for you, Dexter."

A million phrases of anger, pride, passion, hatred, tenderness fought on his lips. Then a perfect wave of emotion washed over him, carrying off with it a sediment of wisdom, of convention, of doubt, of honor. This was his girl who was speaking, his own, his beautiful, his pride.

"Won't you come in?" He heard her draw in her breath sharply.

Waiting.

"All right," his voice was trembling, "I'll come in."

v

It was strange that neither when it was over nor a long time afterward did he regret that night. Looking at it from the perspective of ten years, the fact that Judy's flare for him endured just one month seemed of little importance. Nor did it matter that by his yielding he subjected himself to a deeper agony in the end and gave serious hurt to Irene Scheerer and to Irene's parents, who had befriended him. There was nothing sufficiently pictorial about Irene's grief to stamp itself on his mind.

Dexter was at bottom hard-minded. The attitude of the city

on his action was of no importance to him, not because he was going to leave the city, but because any outside attitude on the situation seemed superficial. He was completely indifferent to popular opinion. Nor, when he had seen that it was no use, that he did not possess in himself the power to move fundamentally or to hold Judy Jones, did he bear any malice toward her. He loved her, and he would love her until the day he was too old for loving —but he could not have her. So he tasted the deep pain that is reserved only for the strong, just as he had tasted for a little while the deep happiness.

Even the ultimate falsity of the grounds upon which Judy terminated the engagement that she did not want to "take him away" from Irene—Judy, who had wanted nothing else—did not revolt him. He was beyond any revulsion or any amusement.

He went East in February with the intention of selling out his laundries and settling in New York—but the war came to America in March and changed his plans. He returned to the West, handed over the management of the business to his partner, and went into the first officers' training-camp in late April. He was one of those young thousands who greeted the war with a certain amount of relief, welcoming the liberation from webs of tangled emotion.

VI

This story is not his biography, remember, although things creep into it which have nothing to do with those dreams he had when he was young. We are almost done with them and with him now. There is only one more incident to be related here, and it happens seven years farther on.

It took place in New York, where he had done well—so well that there were no barriers too high for him. He was thirty-two years old, and, except for one flying trip immediately after the war, he had not been West in seven years. A man named Devlin from Detroit came into his office to see him in a business way, and then and there this incident occurred, and closed out, so to speak, this particular side of his life.

"So you're from the Middle West," said the man Devlin with careless curiosity. "That's funny—I thought men like you were probably born and raised on Wall Street. You know—wife of one of my best friends in Detroit came from your city. I was an usher at the wedding."

Dexter waited with no apprehension of what was coming.

"Judy Simms," said Devlin with no particular interest; "Judy Jones she was once."

"Yes, I knew her." A dull impatience spread over him. He had heard, of course, that she was married—perhaps deliberately he had heard no more.

"Awfully nice girl," brooded Devlin meaninglessly, "I'm sort of sorry for her."

"Why?" Something in Dexter was alert, receptive, at once.

"Oh, Lud Simms has gone to pieces in a way. I don't mean he ill-uses her, but he drinks and runs around——"

"Doesn't she run around?"

"No. Stays at home with her kids."

"Oh."

"She's a little too old for him," said Devlin.

"Too old!" cried Dexter. "Why, man, she's only twenty-seven." He was possessed with a wild notion of rushing out into the streets and taking a train to Detroit. He rose to his feet spasmodically.

"I guess you're busy," Devlin apologized quickly. "I didn't realize——"

"No, I'm not busy," said Dexter, steadying his voice. "I'm not busy at all. Not busy at all. Did you say she was—twenty-seven? No, I said she was twenty-seven."

"Yes, you did," agreed Devlin dryly.

"Go on, then. Go on."

"What do you mean?"

"About Judy Jones."

Devlin looked at him helplessly.

"Well, that's—I told you all there is to it. He treats her like the devil. Oh, they're not going to get divorced or anything. When he's particularly outrageous she forgives him. In fact, I'm inclined to think she loves him. She was a pretty girl when she first came to Detroit."

A pretty girl! The phrase struck Dexter as ludicrous.

"Isn't she—a pretty girl, any more?"

"Oh, she's all right."

"Look here," said Dexter, sitting down suddenly. "I don't understand. You say she was a 'pretty girl' and now you say she's 'all right.' I don't understand what you mean—Judy Jones wasn't a pretty girl, at all. She was a great beauty. Why, I knew her, I knew her. She was——"

Devlin laughed pleasantly.

"I'm not trying to start a row," he said. "I think Judy's a nice girl and I like her. I can't understand how a man like Lud Simms could fall madly in love with her, but he did." Then he added: "Most of the women like her."

Dexter looked closely at Devlin, thinking wildly that there must be a reason for this, some insensitivity in the man or some private malice.

"Lots of women fade just like *that*," Devlin snapped his fingers. "You must have seen it happen. Perhaps I've forgotten how pretty she was at her wedding. I've seen her so much since then, you see. She has nice eyes."

A sort of dullness settled down upon Dexter. For the first time in his life he felt like getting very drunk. He knew that he was laughing loudly at something Devlin had said, but he did not know what it was or why it was funny. When, in a few minutes, Devlin went he lay down on his lounge and looked out the window at the New York sky-line into which the sun was sinking in dull lovely shades of pink and gold.

He had thought that having nothing else to lose he was invulnerable at last—but he knew that he had just lost something more, as surely as if he had married Judy Jones and seen her fade away before his eyes.

The dream was gone. Something had been taken from him. In a sort of panic he pushed the palms of his hands into his eyes and tried to bring up a picture of the waters lapping on Sherry Island and the moonlit veranda, and gingham on the golf-links and the dry sun and the gold color of her neck's soft down. And her mouth damp to his kisses and her eyes plaintive with melancholy and her freshness like new fine linen in the morning. Why, these things were no longer in the world! They had existed and they existed no longer.

For the first time in years the tears were streaming down his face. But they were for himself now. He did not care about mouth and eyes and moving hands. He wanted to care, and he could not care. For he had gone away and he could never go back any more. The gates were closed, the sun was gone down, and there was no beauty but the gray beauty of steel that withstands all time. Even the grief he could have borne was left behind in the country of illusion, of youth, of the richness of life, where his winter dreams had flourished.

"Long ago," he said, "long ago, there was something in me, but now that thing is gone. Now that thing is gone, that thing is gone. I cannot cry. I cannot care. That thing will come back no more."

[1922]

THE GREAT GATSBY *and its world*

part 2

THE INSIGHTS Fitzgerald offers into the psychological conditions posed by wealth (by the possession of it, the desire for it, the expectation of it) are many and varied. For the most part, he is concerned to represent two kinds of moneyed circumstance: that of money recently inherited, in which there has been little time for the development of an aristocratic "code," as analyzed in the fiction of Henry James, William Dean Howells, and Edith Wharton; that of money acquired quickly and in a special milieu, such as that of Gatsby's and Meyer Wolfsheim's Prohibition underworld. The major analyses in Fitzgerald's work concern these matters: the question of privilege and mobility granted those who are born into money (as well as the desire for this privilege in those who do not have it but covet it); the phenomena of the underworld, and its function in releasing those who live in it from conventional standards and creating an entirely new set of manners and mores; the role of the young girl and her place in the economy of the "rich boy."

In one of his "Notebook" entries, under the title "Descriptions of Girls," Fitzgerald notes of one of his heroines, "She was lovely and expensive, and about nineteen." (The Crack-Up, p. 133) His stories from the beginning ring many changes upon that formula. Rosalind Connage of This Side of Paradise and Gloria Gilbert of The Beautiful and Damned are preliminary sketches, and within their limits, good ones. But Daisy Fay Buchanan is a full and mature study of the "flapper" heroine's place in Fitzgerald's spe-

115

cial world. It is interesting to compare notes on Daisy's dependence upon wealth for the security and "respectability" it grants, with Myrtle Wilson's lusty and even primitively arrogant assumptions of its momentary privileges, in the apartment Tom Buchanan provides for her on 158th Street.

"Let me tell you about the very rich," the narrator of "The Rich Boy" begins. "They are different from you and me. They possess and enjoy early, and it does something to them, makes them soft where we are hard, and cynical where we are trustful, in a way that, unless you were born rich, it is very difficult to understand. They think, deep in their hearts, that they are better than we are because we had to discover the compensations and refuges of life for ourselves. Even when they enter deep into our world, they still think they are better than we are. . . ."[1] This is by way of introducing Anson Hunter, one of six children who are due to inherit fifteen millions. Fitzgerald is especially interested in short-term inheritances. These people usually have no genuine or clear moral conventions to assist in the control of the wealth or of the social privileges it conveys. Tom Buchanan is the true master symbol of this type, its culmination in Fitzgerald's fiction, as Daisy is the culmination of the "lovely, expensive, nineteen" type of heroine.

Fitzgerald is master of the literary study of wealth in terms of the pace of its inheritance or acquisition. The Charlie Wales of "Babylon Revisited" (written in 1931; published in Taps at Reveille) shows the disastrous moral consequences of money quickly achieved and quickly spent. Buchanan belongs to a group of "careless people" who "smashed up things and then retreated back into their money or their vast carelessness, or whatever it was that kept them together, and let other people clean up the mess they had made . . ." (Gatsby, pp. 180-81). Wales speaks of the men of the 1920s who spent their money lavishly and foolishly, in the illusion that money might translate them beyond ordinary

[1] Babylon Revisited and Other Stories, The Scribner Library Edition, (New York: Charles Scribner's Sons, 1960), p. 152.

moral responsibilities: "—The men who locked their wives out in the snow, because the snow of twenty-nine wasn't real snow. If you didn't want it to be snow, you paid some money."[2] There is a sufficient difference between these two to suggest that in Fitzgerald the rate and power of release from ordinary moral convention increase in terms of the speed and ease with which money is acquired.

At a certain point in Fitzgerald's judgment of wealth, the representation becomes fantasy. The economy of balances between money and convention is all but lost, and the result is a kind of lyrical creation, comical at times but with overtones of horror. Only Henry James's Christopher Newman (The American, 1877) occasionally resembles Fitzgerald's creatures in this respect: he has much money; the evidences of his wealth are obvious and on display; he has no real power of evaluation or taste. But of course the comparison cannot be carried very far, and in any case Newman is a moral sophisticate compared with Jay Gatsby. There is something, however, in the horror and the glory of wealth which transcends reality. Gatsby's relationship to money is pure and disinterested, unselfish; he wants it only to use it as a means of transcending time, reinstating the past, but most of all redirecting the "Platonic conception of himself" of which Nick Carraway speaks.

The world of The Great Gatsby is therefore sufficiently a mixture of fantasy and prosaic reality to give its ideas a vital, dramatic exposition. In his relations to Meyer Wolfsheim and to Carraway, Gatsby comprehends an entire range of fantasy and reality with respect to the phenomena of wealth. The novel touches upon and suggests every conceivable literary reflection of wealth in Fitzgerald's world.

[2] Ibid., p. 229.

THE DELEGATE FROM GREAT NECK*

Edmund Wilson

Wilson originally wrote a series of "imaginary dialogues" for the New Republic. *This one, between Fitzgerald and Van Wyck Brooks, was published in the issue of April 30, 1924, and was subsequently printed with its fellows in a collection called Discordant Encounters (New York: Boni, 1926). Note especially the reference to the millionaires of the generation before Fitzgerald's, especially to James J. Hill (whose mansion in Saint Paul Fitzgerald could see daily in his youth, at the "other end" of Summit Avenue).*

Mr. F. Scott Fitzgerald and Mr. Van Wyck Brooks

MR. FITZGERALD. How do you do, Mr. Brooks. I'm afraid it's an awful nuisance for you to see me.

MR. BROOKS. Not at all. I'm very glad to. I'm only sorry to have had to put it off. But I've been so frightfully busy with my book that I haven't been able to do anything else.

MR. FITZGERALD. What's that—the James? I suppose you're hurrying to have it out in time to get the benefit of the publicity of the *Dial* award.

* Edmund Wilson, "The Delegate from Great Neck," Shores of Light (New York: Farrar, Straus and Young, 1952), pp. 141-55. Reprinted with the permission of the author.

MR. BROOKS. Oh, no: it may take me a long time yet. But it's really rather a complicated job, and I don't like to drop a chapter in the middle or I lose all the threads. I've just come to a breathing-space.

MR. FITZGERALD. I should think you'd want to rush it right through and get it out now: it might double your sales.

MR. BROOKS. Oh, I couldn't possibly: I still have a good deal of work to do on it.

MR. FITZGERALD. I suppose you must read hundreds of books, don't you? How many books do you suppose you've read for the James? Two hundred? Five hundred?

MR. BROOKS. Oh, I don't know, I'm sure—everything I could get hold of that threw any light on him.

MR. FITZGERALD. I suppose you must quote on an average of four or five books on every page of your biographies, don't you? —and you probably refer to four or five others—and you've probably read half a dozen others that you didn't get anything out of. That makes fifteen or sixteen books to a page. Think of it! Reading fifteen or sixteen books just to write a single page! For a book of two hundred and fifty pages that would be—

MR. BROOKS. They're not all different books, you know. One uses the same books again and again.

MR. FITZGERALD. I know: but even so—it's perfectly amazing! I suppose you must know more about American literature than anybody else in the world, don't you?

MR. BROOKS. Oh, no! not by any means.

MR. FITZGERALD. Well, you're the greatest writer on the subject, anyway. That's the reason we've sent you this letter. As I told you, I've been delegated by the Younger Generation of American writers to congratulate you on getting the prize. They chose me as really the original member of the Younger Generation. Of course there were a lot of people writing before *This Side of Paradise*—but the Younger Generation never really became self-conscious till then nor did the public at large become conscious of it. My slogan is that I am the man who made America Younger-Generation-conscious.

MR. BROOKS. I am certainly very much flattered—

MR. FITZGERALD. Besides, I'm about the only one who still looks really young. Most of the others are getting old and bald and discouraged. So they picked me out to represent them. They thought they ought to send somebody under thirty. —Well, could you stand to have me read you the letter they've written you or would you rather read it yourself?

MR. BROOKS. No: Certainly—read it. Do!

MR. FITZGERALD. (*reading*). "Dear Van Wyck Brooks: We, the undersigned American writers, desire to offer you our heartiest congratulations on the occasion of your receiving the *Dial* award. If it is a question of critical service to American letters, we believe that there is no one living to whom it might more fitly be given. We soon found, when we first began writing, that your books were among the few that could help us to orient ourselves." —This first part's pretty heavy—but it gets a little more interesting later on. —I didn't draft the letter myself.

"You yourself had called a caustic roll of the critics whom we found in authority: Professor Irving Babbitt, who, refusing to see in romanticism one of the great creative movements of our time, could do nothing but scold at young writers who derived inspiration from it; Mr. Paul Elmer More, who, for all his sound standards of learning and literary competence—an anti-romantic like Professor Babbitt—had denounced as a form of debauchery what is actually a necessary condition of any artistic activity: the response to irrational impulse, and who thus, if he could have enforced his injunction, would have shut off the arts at their source; and Professor Stuart P. Sherman, who, borrowing the severity of Mr. More's manner without sharing his moral convictions, soon gave out such discordant sounds that he has now been forced to change his tune in the interests of a liberal sweetness. These critics had been preaching restraint to a people bound hand and foot.

The country at large may have been suffering, as they thought, from a phase of anarchic expansion; but the failing of our literature was the timidity of the 'genteel tradition.' You were among the first to stand up for the romantic doctrine of 'experience for its own sake' and to insist on the importance of literature as a political and social influence. These ideas are perhaps open to criticism as a definitive aesthetic program; but they have served at least to awaken us to a sense of the drama in which we were playing. Our fathers had been further than our grandfathers from the civilization of Europe, and you goaded us back to our place in the world. You roused us with the cry that the hour had come 'to put away childish things and to walk the stage as poets do.'

"For all this we are forever in your debt, and we have wished to express our gratitude. Do not think us ungracious, we beg, if we accompany it with a plea. You were almost alone, when you first began to write, in taking American literature seriously—in appraising it as rigorously as possible, in comparison with other literatures, and in exhorting us to better our achievements. Yet, in your zeal to confess our deficiencies, you seem sometimes to create the impression that we have so far accomplished nothing. The older generation of critics had fallen down, primarily, as humanists— that is, they had been weak, not in intellect, but in aesthetic sensibility. They had not been able to feel the value of the widely varying forms of beauty which the men of other races and ages had distilled from their varied experience. Can it be that, with more generous intentions than theirs, you, too, with different preconceptions, are tending to fail in appreciation? After all, a good many of the Americans whose inadequacies you have analyzed so damagingly have had each his peculiar sense of life, his particular aspect of America, that he succeeded in getting on paper in some more or less vivid form. Emerson pursuing happy guides through the winey yet fumeless air in his commerce, so blithe and so homely, with the high places of light; Thoreau with his compact prose and his strong and dense colors, like the white of opaque clouds against blue Massachusetts sky, like the clustered green masses of trees around foursquare New England houses—both these men have conveyed to us the beauty of a particular kind of life. We feel in them a freshness and a freedom as of lawns that slope away to fenceless meadows, and we taste a frosty sea-captain sarcasm that seasons ideal and discipline. So Mark Twain has most poignant pages which give us something that we scarcely find in your *Ordeal of Mark Twain*; it is not only the sadness of the Mississippi in the days when life there was poor, but the romance and the humor of the pioneers straying wide across the empty continent; and we recognize in that sadness, that rough romance and that humor, at once genial and cruel, something more than the outlandish product of a particular time and place: we are moved by the troubling compound of life at all times in all places."—

MR. BROOKS. Will you forgive me if I interrupt you a moment? I don't want to find fault so much with your description of the New England writers—though I'm not sure that even there you haven't allowed distance to gild with an imaginary glamor a society that turns out, when we examine it, rather disappointingly barren—but in regard to the West, one is driven, when one comes to look into the subject, to the conclusion that its reputed romance and humor are almost entirely fictitious. The life along the Mississippi that Mark Twain knew in his boyhood was depressing in the extreme—a mere matter of lonely villages scattered along a muddy shore; and such excitement as he afterwards found in Nevada and California was mainly limited to drinking and gambling, with outbursts of violent profanity and occasional outbreaks of murder. The lies and the practical jokes that constituted frontier humor were merely, like those other manifestations, in the nature of hysterical relief from intolerable privations and repressions.

MR. FITZGERALD. Well, I come from the West—the *Middle West*—myself, and of course it's pretty bad in some ways. But

don't you think there must have been still a certain romance
about it at the time that Mark Twain went there? Don't you
imagine even a pilot on the Mississippi, like Mark Twain was in
his youth, must have felt a real thrill at knowing that he was personally playing a part in dominating the American continent?
And there must have been a marvellous kind of comradeship in
the ranches and the mining-camps—when they called each other
Captain and Colonel. I always have a feeling of something heroic
in the old songs and stories of the West. Think of the men from
New York and New England who first dared to build their settle-
ments in the gigantic amphitheaters of Utah, where the great
black rock-ranges wall you round like the ramparts of the world!
And the red sandstone hills of Nevada! Can you imagine what it
must have been like to try to live the white man's life among
those fantastic shapes, in the presence of those faceless prehistoric
gods? And the first men who went to California, the prospectors
of Mark Twain's sixties—they must have been drunk with the sunshine even more than the San Franciscans today—as well as with
liquor, of course. I imagine them shaking off their hardships in a
tremendous exhilaration when they first found themselves on
that golden coast, where no worry from the old world ever comes,
where Time itself seems to have been left behind like some tyran-
nous medieval institution, where man's life seems restored at least
to the primeval leisure of Eden, where it is always summertime
and always afternoon! Have you ever seen the mountains turning
purple at sunset and the purple-fringed sea? Think of the men
from the shacks and the diggings looking out on that new horizon,
that new ocean that opened to the Orient, and hearing the drums
of the surf that beat out the somnolent rhythms of the reefs and
white sands of the South Seas! No older generation and no
taboos! Big fortunes easy to make! Don't you think that, if ever
Americans have really felt free in America, those early Californians
must have?

    MR. BROOKS. The condition of survival for the pioneer, even in

California, was the suppression of all those instincts which might tend to conflict with his adjustment to his rude environment. You assume that a man of Mark Twain's generation would have been capable of the enjoyment of landscape. But we find no evidence that this was the case. The enjoyment of landscape results in an enrichment of the spiritual soil which bears its fruits in artistic creation, and the generation of Mark Twain—who can doubt it?—throttled its impulse to delight in natural beauty as an interference with its concentration upon its immediate material task. The psychology of the Puritan and the pioneer has always, it seems to me, made Americans rather blind to natural beauty. It may, in fact, be seriously questioned whether America has ever had a writer who can be said to have appreciated it properly. Think of the vital relation to natural objects that one finds in a Ruskin or a Jeffries, and then summon the most distinguished examples that our literature is able to show. How meager, how relatively pale, how lacking in genuine significance, the latter must inevitably appear!

MR. FITZGERALD. Well, I really oughtn't to try to talk about it because I don't know the subject the way you do.—I dare say that that part of the letter does lay it on pretty thick, but they wanted a purple passage to show you what they meant about enthusiasm. —Shall I go on reading?

MR. BROOKS. Do.

MR. FITZGERALD. "In the case of Henry James, again, we have been a little disappointed as we have read the published chapters of your forthcoming book about him. What we had hoped for was a definitive study of a novelist of genius who, fortunately for us, happened to be an American; but what we seem to be getting is the tragedy of an American who was rash enough to try to become a novelist. Yet, for all James's partial failures at filling in the outlines of his canvases, he was surely a first-rate artist, one of the few real masters of literature that the United States has produced; and his position as an American expatriate must have

given him a peculiar advantage as an international critic of society
that made up for whatever he had missed in intimate experience
of American life. Must we believe that his social maladjustment as
an American of his period had really for his work the disastrous
results on which you insist in these chapters? Your first instalment
is based on James's own autobiographical volumes; yet what interests us when we read these books is less the record of the
provincial background and the writer's relation to it than the
wonder and excitement of the artist enchanted by the spectacle
of life—life even in the nineteenth century, even in the United
States. Do not, we beg you—it is the burden of our plea—lose too
much the sense of that wonder!"—

MR. BROOKS. I beg your pardon: but I really do think you overestimate those autobiographical volumes! To me, there has
always seemed to be something rather flaccid and empty about
them. Think how much more colorful and spirited is Cellini's
autobiography! How much more candid Rousseau's! How infinitely
much more alive to the intellectual currents of their time the auto-
biographies of Renan and Mill! How much richer in psychological
interest the memoirs of Marie Bashkirtseff! James wrote in his
later years, you know, of "the starved romance of my life." And
what I feel in his autobiography is the starvation rather than the
romance. What American can fail to recognize the inexorable
spiritual blight of which James himself spoke so often? Have we
not all run up against it—an impotence and a blindness of the
soul—like one of those great blank implacable walls that balk the
view in American cities?

MR. FITZGERALD. The Puritan thing, you mean. I suppose you're
probably right. I don't know anything about James myself. I've
never read a word of him. —Just let me finish this letter; there's
not very much more.

"We thus deprecate your gloomy verdicts on the value of the
American classics; yet, feeling as we do the force of your criticism
of our general culture, we should never have thought of complain-

ing, if we had not lately come to fear that, intent upon the diagnosis of the diseases from which we have suffered, you have ended by becoming inhibited by an a priori theory which prevents you from hoping for improvement. You have discovered so many reasons why artistic achievement should be difficult that you seem to have become convinced that it must always remain impossible. When you write of contemporary literature, it is politely but without conviction: the modern writers who have been most successful in realizing the ideal you proposed have not received your accolade. And the effect, in the long run, has been more than a little discouraging. The other day, one of the youngest of our number, reading your essay *The Literary Life*, broke down into a wild fit of weeping and cursed God for having made him an American."—

MR. BROOKS. Dear me! How distressing! Really—

MR. FITZGERALD. Oh, that's just a silly joke! It didn't really happen, of course. I made it up myself and had them put it in. It's the only part I wrote. —I'm sorry: I suppose it was bad taste!

MR. BROOKS. No—no: not at all! I see! I beg your pardon. Go ahead.

MR. FITZGERALD. "It is true that our newer critics tend to err through too easy enthusiasm: it is usually enough for a book to make pretensions to artistic seriousness for them to hail it as a masterpiece. But their indiscriminate excitement hardly compensates us for your indifference. It is certainly a mistake to behave as if all our contemporary writers were equally successful as artists, but we have the uncomfortable feeling that you may think them all equally deplorable—merely the most recent examples of the various depressing ways in which writers may fail in America—not the beginnings of a literary renascence but fresh waxworks for a Chamber of Horrors; and we wonder whether your disinclination to write anything about your contemporaries may not be due merely to a delicacy that prevents you from cutting up people before they are quite dead.

"Yet the younger generation of writers have been trying to put your precepts into practice. They have not blenched before the boldness of the European masters, as you accuse their fathers of doing: they have tried to follow great examples. They are interested, as you urged them to be, in the life of their own country; and they have opened their souls to experience. For all their pessimistic pronouncements, they are confident, hopeful and gay. But when they have looked for your snow-white banner flying beside their more motley ones, they have found you still brooding the wrongs of an earlier generation, the defeats of an older army. They find you shivering among the archives, and they shiver at the sight of your chill. Meantime, there is life in America—artistic life even—to warm us all. If we reproach you for failing to enjoy it, we are only giving back to you a gospel we have learned from your own books."

And then the names—I won't read the list—but practically everybody, you see.

MR. BROOKS. It was really awfully kind of you to take the trouble to write me like this. I'm very much interested in what you say. —But I can't reconcile the picture that you draw of yourselves at the end of your letter with the account that you gave me yourself when you were talking about your friends just now. You said, I think, that the younger generation was "getting old and bald and discouraged," and that is not a very cheerful picture. I appreciate your gallant effort to make the best of your situation; but I am afraid that your admirable spirit has already been partly broken by the indifference of a commercial society, that your gestures are lost in the void.

MR. FITZGERALD. Oh, I was just kidding about that. They're not really old and discouraged. I'm the only one that's discouraged, because I find that I can't live at Great Neck on anything under thirty-six thousand a year, and I have to write a lot of rotten stuff that bores me and makes me depressed.

MR. BROOKS. Couldn't you live more cheaply somewhere else?

MR. FITZGERALD. Nowhere that's any fun.

MR. BROOKS. I can't help thinking it a pity that a writer as gifted as you should be let in for such heavy expenses. As you say, it lays you open to exploitation by the popular magazines; and, though you charge me with indifference, I can tell you that that is something I regret very much. I should hate to see your whole generation fall a victim to that sort of thing. You are "the man," you told me, you know, at the beginning of our conversation, "who has made America Younger-Generation-conscious." Did you realize, when you used that expression, that you had dropped into the language of advertising? In describing your literary activities, you could not avoid the jargon of business; and it strikes me that the production of books by the younger generation has now become an industry much like another. The first crop of younger writers had scarcely scored their first successes when a new race of editors and publishers met them with open arms, eager to commercialize them—not by turning them into hacks of the old sort who would have had to do work of a kind altogether against their conscience but by stimulating them to write much and often rather than responsibly and well, by putting a premium on their secondbest; so that, instead of improving on their first attempts, they have often, it seems to me, sunk below them. A half-educated public has created a demand for half-baked work. And I'm not at all sure that you younger writers are very much better off than your predecessors were: in the eighties and nineties, at least, there was a small cultivated public and not much question of pleasing the rest. I will say of the distinguished writers of the day before yesterday, whom you accuse me of undervaluing, that they usually followed their art with a very high sense of its dignity, so that even their journalism sounds like the work of serious men of letters—and this is true of Stephen Crane as much as of Henry James; whereas, in the case of you younger men, one sometimes cannot help feeling that your most ambitious productions are a species of journalism. Is it possible to resist the conclusion that you are succumbing to our capitalist civilization in a way you could never have foreseen?

MR. FITZGERALD. I knew that what I said about making America Younger-Generation-conscious sounded like advertising. I was just making fun of the way that the advertising people talk.

MR. BROOKS. Let me remind you that Freud has shown us that the things we say in jest are as significant as the things we say in earnest—they may, in fact, be more significant, because they reveal the thoughts that are really at the back of our minds and that we do not care to avow to the world. I was struck, also, by that other joke, which you contributed to the letter—I mean about the man who cursed God for having made him an American. Who can fail to detect in this desperate image an involuntary tragic cry which contradicts everything else you have been straining so hard to affirm?—Another detail that betrays: I notice that when you mention the signatories, who explicitly include yourself, you always speak of them as "they" instead of "we." In doing so, I can't help feeling, you furnish irresistible evidence that the unity you assume in collaborating is more or less artificial, that you are actually, in spirit and point of view, as isolated from one another as it has always seemed that literary men are bound to be in America. In allowing your art to become a business, you have rendered true unity impossible and have given yourselves up to the competitive anarchy of American commercial enterprise. You can at best, I fear, gain nothing but money and big hollow reputations—each man out for himself—and these things for fifty years in America have brought nothing but disillusion.

MR. FITZGERALD. Don't you suppose, though, that the American millionaires must have had a certain amount of fun making and spending their money? Can't you imagine a man like Harriman or Hill feeling a certain creative ecstasy as he piled up all that power? Just think of being able to buy absolutely anything you wanted— houses, railroads, enormous industries!—dinners, automobiles, stunning clothes for your wife, clothes like nobody else in the world could wear!—all the finest paintings in Europe, all the books that had ever been written! Think of what it would be like to give parties that went on for days and days, with everything that anybody could want to drink and a medical staff in attendance and the biggest jazz orchestras in the city alternating night and day! I confess that I get a big kick out of all the glittering expensive things. Why, once, when I'd just arrived in New York with lot of money to spend, after being away in the West, and I came back to the Plaza the first night and looked up and saw that great creamy palace all blazing with green and gold lights, and the taxis and the limousines streaming up and down the Avenue—why, I jumped into the Pulitzer fountain just out of sheer joy! And I wasn't boiled either.

MR. BROOKS. Are you sure you weren't a little hysterical?

MR. FITZGERALD. No: I've been hysterical, too. This was exhilaration. —Look: I don't suppose you could possibly be persuaded to come down to Great Neck this weekend. We're having a little party ourselves. Maybe it would bore you to death—but we're asking some people down who ought to be pretty amusing. Gloria Swanson's coming. And Dos Passos and Sherwood Anderson. And Marc Connelly and Dorothy Parker. And Rube Goldberg. And Ring Lardner will be there. You probably think some of those people are lowbrow, but Ring Lardner, for instance, is really a very interesting fellow—he's really not just a popular writer: he's pretty morose about things. I'd like to have you meet him. There'll be some dumb-bell friends of mine from the West, but I don't believe you'd mind them. And then there's going to be a man who sings a song called, *Who'll Bite Your Neck When My Teeth Are Gone?* Neither my wife nor I knows his name—but this song is one of the funniest things we've ever heard!

MR. BROOKS. Why, thank you ever so much. I'd like ever so much to go—and I'd like to meet all those people. But I'm really afraid that I can't. I'm not nearly done with the James, and I have to devote all my free time to it. And, since you feel that I'm being unfair to him, I must go over my material again and think about it from that point of view. —You know, I appreciate very much your taking the trouble to write me. I'm sorry you find me discouraging: of course, I don't mean to be. On the contrary, I think that your generation is showing a great deal of promise.

MR. FITZGERALD. Well, I'm sorry if I've been a nuisance. It was good of you to listen to the letter.

MR. BROOKS. It was very good of you to write it.

MR. FITZGERALD. Well, I won't bother you any longer. —I'm sorry you can't come down Saturday.

MR. BROOKS. Thank you ever so much. I wish I could!

April 30, 1924

HOW TO LIVE ON $36,000 A YEAR*

F. Scott Fitzgerald

This piece, written for the Saturday Evening Post of April 5, 1924, is a humorous record of Fitzgerald's financial troubles following upon his elevation to the status of best-selling author. It will suggest something of the bright confusion and the erratic failure to account for daily, conventional responsibilities, as well as the world of suburban New York which is the setting of The Great Gatsby.

"You ought to start saving money," The Young Man With a Future assured me just the other day. "You think it's smart to live up to your income. Some day you'll land in the poorhouse."

I was bored, but I knew he was going to tell me anyhow, so I asked him what I'd better do.

"It's very simple," he answered impatiently; "only you establish a trust fund where you can't get your money if you try."

I had heard this before. It is System Number 999. I tried System Number 1 at the very beginning of my literary career four years ago. A month before I was married I went to a broker and asked his advice about investing some money.

*F. Scott Fitzgerald, "How to Live on $36,000 a Year," Afternoon of an Author, ed. Arthur Mizener (New York: Charles Scribner's Sons, 1957), pp. 87-99. Copyright 1924 The Curtis Publishing Company; renewal copyright 1952 Frances Scott Fitzgerald Lanahan. Reprinted by permission of Charles Scribner's Sons.

"It's only a thousand," I admitted, "but I feel I ought to begin to save right now."

He considered.

"You don't want Liberty Bonds," he said. "They're too easy to turn into cash. You want a good, sound, conservative investment, but also you want it where you can't get at it every five minutes."

He finally selected a bond for me that paid 7 per cent and wasn't listed on the market. I turned over my thousand dollars, and my career of amassing capital began that day.

On that day, also, it ended.

The heirloom no one would buy

My wife and I were married in New York in the spring of 1920, when prices were higher than they had been within the memory of man. In the light of after events it seems fitting that our career should have started at that precise point in time. I had just received a large check from the movies and I felt a little patronizing toward the millionaires riding down Fifth Avenue in their limousines—because my income had a way of doubling every month. This was actually the case. It had done so for several months— I had made only thirty-five dollars the previous August, while here in April I was making three thousand—and it seemed as if it was going to do so forever. At the end of the year it must reach half a million. Of course with such a state of affairs, economy seemed a waste of time. So we went to live at the most expensive hotel in New York, intending to wait there until enough money accumulated for a trip abroad.

To make a long story short, after we had been married for three months I found one day to my horror that I didn't have a dollar in the world, and the weekly hotel bill for two hundred dollars would be due next day.

I remember the mixed feelings with which I issued from the bank on hearing the news.

"What's the matter?" demanded my wife anxiously, as I joined her on the sidewalk. "You look depressed."

"I'm not depressed," I answered cheerfully; "I'm just surprised. We haven't got any money."

"Haven't got any money," she repeated calmly, and we began to walk up the Avenue in a sort of trance. "Well, let's go to the movies," she suggested jovially.

It all seemed so tranquil that I was not a bit cast down. The cashier had not even scowled at me. I had walked in and said to him, "How much money have I got?" And he had looked in a big book and answered, "None."

That was all. There were no harsh words, no blows. And I knew that there was nothing to worry about. I was now a successful author, and when successful authors ran out of money all they had to do was to sign checks. I wasn't poor—they couldn't fool me. Poverty meant being depressed and living in a small remote room and eating at a *rôtisserie* on the corner, while I—why, it was impossible that I should be poor! I was living at the best hotel in New York!

My first step was to try to sell my only possession—my $1000 bond. It was the first of many times I made the attempt; in all financial crises I dig it out and with it go hopefully to the bank, supposing that, as it never fails to pay the proper interest, it has at last assumed a tangible value. But as I have never been able to sell it, it has gradually acquired the sacredness of a family heir-loom. It is always referred to by my wife as "your bond," and it was once turned in at the Subway offices after I left it by accident on a car seat!

This particular crisis passed next morning when the discovery that publishers sometimes advance royalties sent me hurriedly to mine. So the only lesson I learned from it was that my money usually turns up somewhere in time of need, and that at the worst you can always borrow—a lesson that would make Benjamin Franklin turn over in his grave.

For the first three years of our marriage our income averaged a little more than $20,000 a year. We indulged in such luxuries as a baby and a trip to Europe, and always money seemed to come easier and easier with less and less effort, until we felt that with just a little more margin to come and go on, we could begin to save.

Plans

We left the Middle West and moved East to a town about fifteen miles from New York, where we rented a house for $300 a month. We hired a nurse for $90 a month; a man and his wife—they acted as butler, chauffeur, yard man, cook, parlor maid and chambermaid—for $160 a month; and a laundress, who came twice a week, for $36 a month. This year of 1923, we told each other, was to be our saving year. We were going to earn $24,000, and live on $18,000, thus giving us a surplus of $6,000 with which to buy safety and security for our old age. We were going to do better at last.

Now as everyone knows, when you want to do better you first buy a book and print your name in the front of it in capital letters. So my wife bought a book, and every bill that came to the house was carefully entered in it, so that we could watch living expenses and cut them away to almost nothing—or at least to $1,500 a month.

We had, however, reckoned without our town. It is one of those little towns springing up on all sides of New York which are built especially for those who have made money suddenly but have never had money before.

My wife and I are, of course, members of this newly rich class. That is to say, five years ago we had no money at all, and what we now do away with would have seemed like inestimable riches to us then. I have at times suspected that we are the only newly rich people in America, that in fact we are the very couple at whom all the articles about the newly rich were aimed.

Now when you say "newly rich" you picture a middle-aged and

corpulent man who has a tendency to remove his collar at formal dinners and is in perpetual hot water with his ambitious wife and her titled friends. As a member of the newly rich class, I assure you that this picture is entirely libelous. I myself, for example, am a mild, slightly used young man of twenty-seven, and what corpulence I may have developed is for the present a strictly confidential matter between my tailor and me. We once dined with a bona fide nobleman, but we were both far too frightened to take off our collars or even to demand corned beef and cabbage. Nevertheless we live in a town prepared for keeping money in circulation.

When we came here, a year ago, there were, all together, seven merchants engaged in the purveyance of food—three grocers, three butchers and a fisherman. But when the word went around in food-purveying circles that the town was filling up with the recently enriched as fast as houses could be built for them, the rush of butchers, grocers, fishmen and delicatessen men became enormous. Trainloads of them arrived daily with signs and scales in hand to stake out a claim and sprinkle sawdust upon it. It was like the gold rush of '49, or a big bonanza of the 70's. Older and larger cities were denuded of their stores. Inside of a year eighteen food dealers had set up shop in our main street and might be seen any day waiting in their doorways with alluring and deceitful smiles.

Having long been somewhat overcharged by the seven previous food purveyors we all naturally rushed to the new men, who made it known by large numerical signs in their windows that they intended practically to give food away. But once we were snared, the prices began to rise alarmingly, until all of us scurried like frightened mice from one new man to another, seeking only justice, and seeking it in vain.

Great expectations

What had happened, of course, was that there were too many food purveyors for the population. It was absolutely impossible for eighteen of them to subsist on the town and at the same time charge moderate prices. So each was waiting for some of the others to give up and move away; meanwhile the only way the rest of them could carry their loans from the bank was by selling things at two or three times the prices in the city fifteen miles away. And that is how our town became the most expensive one in the world.

Now in magazine articles people always get together and found community stores, but none of us would consider such a step. It would absolutely ruin us with our neighbors, who would suspect that we actually cared about our money. When I suggested one day to a local lady of wealth—whose husband, by the way, is reputed to have made his money by vending illicit liquids—that I start a community store known as "F. Scott Fitzgerald—Fresh Meats," she was horrified. So the idea was abandoned.

But in spite of the groceries, we began the year in high hopes. My first play was to be presented in the autumn, and even if living in the East forced our expenses a little over $1,500 a month, the play would easily make up for the difference. We knew what colossal sums were earned on play royalties, and just to be sure, we asked several playwrights what was the maximum that could be earned on a year's run. I never allowed myself to be rash. I took a sum halfway between the maximum and the minimum, and put that down as what we could fairly count on its earning. I think my figures came to about $100,000.

It was a pleasant year; we always had this delightful event of the play to look forward to. When the play succeeded we could buy a house, and saving money would be so easy that we could do it blindfolded with both hands tied behind our backs.

As if in happy anticipation we had a small windfall in March from an unexpected source—a moving picture—and for almost the first time in our lives we had enough surplus to buy some bonds. Of course we had "my" bond, and every six months I clipped the little coupon and cashed it, but we were so used to it that we never counted it as money. It was simply a warning never to tie up cash where we couldn't get at it in time of need.

No, the thing to buy was Liberty Bonds, and we bought four of them. It was a very exciting business. I descended to a shining and impressive room downstairs, and under the chaperonage of a guard deposited my $4,000 in Liberty Bonds, together with "my" bond, in a little tin box to which I alone had the key.

Less cash than company

I left the bank, feeling decidedly solid. I had at last accumulated a capital. I hadn't exactly accumulated it, but there it was anyhow, and if I had died next day it would have yielded my wife $212 a year for life—or for just as long as she cared to live on that amount.

"That," I said to myself with some satisfaction, "is what is called providing for the wife and children. Now all I have to do is to deposit the $100,000 from my play and then we're through with worry forever."

I found that from this time on I had less tendency to worry about current expenses. What if we did spend a few hundred too much now and then? What if our grocery bills did vary mysteriously from $85 to $165 a month, according as to how closely we watched the kitchen? Didn't I have bonds in the bank? Trying to keep under $1,500 a month the way things were going was merely niggardly. We were going to save on a scale that would make such petty economies seem like counting pennies.

The coupons on "my" bond are always sent to an office on lower Broadway. Where Liberty Bond coupons are sent I never had a chance to find out, as I didn't have the pleasure of clipping any. Two of them I was unfortunately compelled to dispose of just one month after I first locked them up. I had begun a new novel, you see, and it occurred to me it would be much better business in the end to keep at the novel and live on the Liberty Bonds while I was writing it. Unfortunately the novel progressed slowly, while the Liberty Bonds went at an alarming rate of speed. The novel was interrupted whenever there was any sound above a whisper in the house, while the Liberty Bonds were never interrupted at all.

And the summer drifted too. It was an exquisite summer and it became a habit with many world-weary New Yorkers to pass their week-ends at the Fitzgerald house in the country. Along near the end of a balmy and insidious August I realized with a shock that only three chapters of my novel were done—and in the little tin safety-deposit vault, only "my" bond remained. There it lay—paying storage on itself and a few dollars more. But never mind; in a little while the box would be bursting with savings. I'd have to hire a twin box next door.

But the play was going into rehearsal in two months. To tide over the interval there were two courses open to me—I could sit down and write some short stories or I could continue to work on the novel and borrow the money to live on. Lulled into a sense of security by our sanguine anticipations I decided on the latter course, and my publishers lent me enough to pay our bills until the opening night.

So I went back to my novel, and the months and money melted away; but one morning in October I sat in the cold interior of a New York theater and heard the cast read through the first act of my play. It was magnificent; my estimate had been too low. I could almost hear the people scrambling for seats, hear the ghostly voices of the movie magnates as they bid against one another for the picture rights. The novel was now laid aside; my days were spent at the theater and my nights in revising and improving the two or three little weak spots in what was to be the success of the year.

The time approached and life became a breathless affair. The November bills came in, were glanced at, and punched onto a bill file on the bookcase. More important questions were in the air. A disgusted letter arrived from an editor telling me I had written only two short stories during the entire year. But what did that matter? The main thing was that our second comedian got the wrong intonation in his first-act exit line.

The play opened in Atlantic City in November. It was a colossal frost. People left their seats and walked out, people rustled their programs and talked audibly in bored impatient whispers. After the second act I wanted to stop the show and say it was all a mistake but the actors struggled heroically on.

There was a fruitless week of patching and revising, and then we gave up and came home. To my profound astonishment the year, the great year, was almost over. I was $5,000 in debt, and my one idea was to get in touch with a reliable poorhouse where we could hire a room and bath for nothing a week. But one satisfaction nobody could take from us. We had spent $36,000, and purchased for one year the right to be members of the newly rich class. What more can money buy?

Taking account of stock

The first move, of course, was to get out "my" bond, take it to the bank and offer it for sale. A very nice old man at a shining table was firm as to its value as security, but he promised that if I became overdrawn he would call me up on the phone and give me a chance to make good. No, he never went to lunch with depositors. He considered writers a shiftless class, he said, and assured me that the whole bank was absolutely burglarproof from cellar to roof.

Too discouraged even to put the bond back in the now yawning deposit box, I tucked it gloomily into my pocket and went home. There was no help for it—I must go to work. I had exhausted my resources and there was nothing else to do. In the train I listed all our possessions on which, if it came to that, we could possibly raise money. Here is the list:

1 Oil stove, damaged.
9 Electric lamps, all varieties.
2 Bookcases with books to match.
1 Cigarette humidor, made by a convict.

2 Framed crayon portraits of my wife and me.
1 Medium-priced automobile, 1921 model.
1 Bond, par value $1,000; actual value unknown.

"Let's cut down expenses right away," began my wife when I reached home. "There's a new grocery in town where you pay cash and everything costs only half what it does anywhere else. I can take the car every morning and—"

"Cash!" I began to laugh at this. "Cash!"

The one thing it was impossible for us to do now was to pay cash. It was too late to pay cash. We had no cash to pay. We should rather have gone down on our knees and thanked the butcher and grocer for letting us charge. An enormous economic fact became clear to me at that moment—the rarity of cash, the latitude of choice that cash allows.

"Well," she remarked thoughtfully, "that's too bad. But at least we don't need three servants. We'll get a Japanese to do general housework, and I'll be nurse for a while until you get us out of danger."

"Let them go?" I demanded incredulously. "But we can't let them go! We'd have to pay them an extra two weeks each. Why, to get them out of the house would cost us $125—in cash! Besides, it's nice to have the butler; if we have an awful smash we can send him up to New York to hold us a place in the bread line."

"Well, then, how can we economize?"

"We can't. We're too poor to economize. Economy is a luxury. We could have economized last summer—but now our only salvation is in extravagance."

"How about a smaller house?"

"Impossible! Moving is the most expensive thing in the world; and besides, I couldn't work during the confusion. No," I went on, "I'll just have to get out of this mess the only way I know how, by making more money. Then when we've got something in the bank we can decide what we'd better do."

Over our garage is a large bare room whither I now retired with pencil, paper and the oil stove, emerging the next afternoon at five o'clock with a 7,000-word story. That was something; it would pay the rent and last month's overdue bills. It took twelve hours a day for five weeks to rise from abject poverty back into the middle class, but within that time we had paid our debts, and the cause for immediate worry was over.

But I was far from satisfied with the whole affair. A young man can work at excessive speed with no ill effects, but youth is unfortunately not a permanent condition of life.

I wanted to find out where the $36,000 had gone. Thirty-six thousand is not very wealthy—not yacht-and-Palm-Beach wealthy—but it sounds to me as though it should buy a roomy house full of furniture, a trip to Europe once a year, and a bond or two besides. But our $36,000 had bought nothing at all.

So I dug up my miscellaneous account books, and my wife dug up her complete household record for the year 1923, and we made out the monthly average. Here it is:

Household Expenses	Apportioned per Month
Income tax	$ 198.00
Food	202.00
Rent	300.00
Coal, wood, ice, gas, light, phone and water	114.50
Servants	295.00
Golf clubs	105.50
Clothes—three people	158.00
Doctor and dentist	42.50
Drugs and cigarettes	32.50
Automobile	25.00
Books	14.50
All other household expenses	112.50
Total	$1,600.00

"Well, that's not bad," we thought when we had got thus far. "Some of the items are pretty high, especially food and servants. But there's about everything accounted for, and it's only a little more than half our income."

Then we worked out the average monthly expenditures that could be included under pleasure.

Hotel bills—this meant spending the night or charging meals in New York	$ 51.00
Trips—only two, but apportioned per month	43.00
Theater tickets	55.00
Barber and hairdresser	25.00
Charity and loans	15.00
Taxis	15.00
Gambling—this dark heading covers bridge, craps and football bets	33.00
Restaurant parties	70.00
Entertaining	70.00
Miscellaneous	23.00
Total	$400.00

Some of these items were pretty high. They will seem higher to a Westerner than to a New Yorker. Fifty-five dollars for theater tickets means between three and five shows a month, depending on the type of show and how long it's been running. Football games are also included in this, as well as ringside seats to the Dempsey-Firpo fight. As for the amount marked "restaurant parties"—$70 would perhaps take three couples to a popular after-theater cabaret—but it would be a close shave.

We added the items marked "pleasure" to the items marked "household expenses," and obtained a monthly total.

"Fine," I said. "Just $3,000. Now at least we'll know where to cut down, because we know where it goes."

She frowned; then a puzzled, awed expression passed over her face.

"What's the matter?" I demanded. "Isn't it all right? Are some of the items wrong?"

"It isn't the items," she said staggeringly; "it's the total. This only adds up to $2,000 a month."

I was incredulous, but she nodded.

"But listen," I protested; "my bank statements show that we've spent $3,000 a month. You don't mean to say that every month we lose $1,000 dollars?"

"This only adds up to $2,000," she protested, "so we must have."

"Give me the pencil."

For an hour I worked over the accounts in silence, but to no avail.

"Why, this is impossible!" I insisted. "People don't lose $12,000 in a year. It's just—it's just missing."

There was a ring at the doorbell and I walked over to answer it, still dazed by these figures. It was the Banklands, our neighbors from over the way.

"Good heavens!" I announced. "We've just lost $12,000!"

Bankland stepped back alertly.

"Burglars?" he inquired.

"Ghosts," answered my wife.

Mrs. Bankland looked nervously around.

"Really?"

We explained the situation, the mysterious third of our income that had vanished into thin air.

"Well, what we do," said Mrs. Bankland, "is, we have a budget."

"We have a budget," agreed Bankland, "and we stick absolutely to it. If the skies fall we don't go over any item of that budget. That's the only way to live sensibly and save money."

"That's what we ought to do," I agreed.

Mrs. Bankland nodded enthusiastically.

"It's a wonderful scheme," she went on. "We make a certain deposit every month, and all I save on it I can have for myself to do anything I want with."

I could see that my own wife was visibly excited.

"That's what I want to do," she broke out suddenly. "Have a budget. Everybody does it that has any sense."

"I pity anyone that doesn't use that system," said Bankland solemnly. "Think of the inducement to economy—the extra money my wife'll have for clothes."

"How much have you saved so far?" my wife inquired eagerly of Mrs. Bankland.

"So far?" repeated Mrs. Bankland. "Oh, I haven't had a chance so far. You see we only began the system yesterday."

"Yesterday!" we cried.

"Just yesterday," agreed Bankland darkly. "But I wish to heaven I'd started it a year ago. I've been working over our accounts all week, and do you know, Fitzgerald, every month there's $2,000 I can't account for to save my soul."

Headed toward easy street

Our financial troubles are now over. We have permanently left the newly rich class and installed the budget system. It is simple and sensible, and I can explain it to you in a few words. You consider your income as an enormous pie all cut up into slices, each slice representing one class of expenses. Somebody has worked it all out; so you know just what proportion of your income you can spend on each slice. There is even a slice for founding universities, if you go in for that.

For instance, the amount you spend on the theater should be half your drug-store bill. This will enable us to see one play every five and a half months, or two and a half plays a year. We have already picked out the first one, but if it isn't running five and a half months from now we shall be that much ahead. Our allowance for newspapers should be only a quarter of what we spend on self-improvement, so we are considering whether to get the Sunday paper once a month or to subscribe for an almanac.

According to the budget we will be allowed only three-quarters of a servant, so we are on the lookout for a one-legged cook who can come six days a week. And apparently the author of the budget book lives in a town where you can still go to the movies for a nickel and get a shave for a dime. But we are going to give up the expenditure called "Foreign missions, etc.," and apply it to the life of crime instead. Altogether, outside of the fact that there is no slice allowed for "missing" it seems to be a very complete book, and according to the testimonials in the back, if we make $36,000 again this year, the chances are that we'll save at least $35,000.

"But we can't get any of that first $36,000 back," I complained around the house. "If we just had something to show for it I wouldn't feel so absurd."

My wife thought a long while.

"The only thing you can do," she said finally, "is to write a magazine article and call it How to Live on $36,000 a Year."

"What a silly suggestion!" I replied coldly.

THE MAN WHO FIXED THE SERIES*

Leo Katcher

Arnold Rothstein is said to have been the model of Meyer Wolfsheim of The Great Gatsby. Fitzgerald knew little enough about
Rothstein, and that largely from contemporary gossip. But Rothstein was a notorious and "epochal" figure, who, according to
Katcher, modernized the underworld to adapt it to the changing
milieu of the Prohibition decade. He was primarily a gambler,
though he put his resources of hoodlumism at the disposal of
bootleggers, was at one time in the business himself, was in some
mysterious way involved in the Liberty Bond thefts, and (at the
time he was murdered in 1928) was the master-mind of a world-
wide opium and heroin enterprise. He did not "fix the World
Series in 1919," nor can it be said strictly that the Series was
actually fixed. But he was involved, in the background, and there
are other points of association with the mysterious world of Gatsby's telephone calls and his business "gonnegtions."

> "Who is he, anyhow, an actor?"
> "No."
> "A dentist?"

* Leo Katcher, "The Man Who Fixed the Series," The Big Bankroll (New
York: Harper and Brothers, 1959), pp. 138-48. Copyright © 1958, 1959 by
Leo Katcher. Reprinted by permission of Harper & Brothers.
148

"Meyer Wolfsheim? No, he's a gambler." Gatsby hesitated, then added coolly: "He's the man who fixed the World's Series back in 1919."

"Fixed the World's Series?" I repeated.

The idea staggered me. I remembered, of course, that the World's Series had been fixed in 1919, but if I had thought of it at all I would have thought of it as a thing that merely happened, the end of some inevitable chain. It never occurred to me that one man could start to play with the faith of fifty million people—with the singlemindedness of a burglar blowing a safe.

"How did he happen to do that?" I asked after a minute.

"He just saw the opportunity."

"Why isn't he in jail?"

"They can't get him, old sport. He's a smart man."

—F. SCOTT FITZGERALD, *The Great Gatsby*

Fitzgerald, in Nick Carraway's interior monologue, came closer to the truth of the 1919 World Series than most. The fix did happen as the end of an inevitable chain of events.

The world in which Arnold Rothstein lived is now long gone. Far more deserving men than he have been forgotten. But not Rothstein. His memory is disinterred each autumn when the World Series time rolls around. He is the legendary figure, the "man who fixed the Series."

He did not fix the Series.

The Series, however, could not have been fixed had there been no Arnold Rothstein.

These statements are not contradictory, but complementary. Rothstein's name, his reputation, and his reputed wealth were all used to influence the crooked baseball players. But Rothstein, knowing this, kept apart from the actual fix. He just let it happen.

The story of the fix is the story of a flock of lambs who appealed to a wolf to protect them. What happened thereafter was inevitable.

Looking back almost four decades, it is hard to find one adjective which would describe the actions of the ballplayers. They were inept. They were naïve. They were stupid. They did everything wrong and, in the end, were cheated of their promised reward.

The gamblers who were let in on a sure thing, whether amateurs, like Bill Burns and Billy Maharg, or professionals, like Rothstein and Sport Sullivan, never realized on the potential that lay before them.

From beginning to end—and even beyond the end—there was no logic to what happened. There were confessions and these were recanted. There were affidavits and these disappeared from the locked files of the authorities. There were indictments and most of these were dismissed. There was a trial and it never went to the jury.

The records of the Series show that some of the fixers played better than had been expected. Some players, beyond suspicion, made the damaging errors on the field, failed to hit at the plate. It was a Greek tragedy that was played as a farce.

The Chicago White Sox team of 1919 was one of the great baseball teams of all time. It had the potential to rank with Connie Mack's Philadelphia Athletics with its "Million-Dollar Infield." It was a team on the way up.

Charles Comiskey, the "Old Roman," owned the team. (His heirs still control it.)[1] Comiskey, a great baseball man, was one of the founders of the American League. He was the type of employer who believed that labor should be bought as cheaply as possible. His reasoning was blunt and simple. "If they don't play for me, they can't play for anyone."

He was, of course, correct. Baseball's reserve clause, which bound a player to one team so long as that team desired his services, was in effect then as it is now. A ballplayer had no freedom of choice, could play only for the team with which he had originally signed.

Comiskey, more than any other team owner, used this power to keep wages low. Some of his better players were paid less than

[1] As of 1959. The ownership has changed twice since then.

$4,500, others were paid the big league minimum of $2,500. True, this was before the era of Babe Ruth and his $80,000 salary, but Comiskey paid bottom wages even by 1919 standards.

In the middle of the 1919 season the players staged a mild revolt. Their first step was orderly.

A group of them asked William ("Kid") Gleason, their manager, to intercede with Comiskey to get them raises. Gleason, whose sympathies were with the players, did go to Comiskey with the request. He returned with Comiskey's answer, a blunt "No."

The players sulked, but won ball games. They clinched the pennant early on their last Eastern swing. And during that swing, they—not all, but a sizable group—conceived the idea of throwing the World Series.

The ring leader, as he later admitted, was Eddie Cicotte, the team's leading pitcher. Chick Gandil, the first baseman, has written that he connived with Cicotte from the start.

The World Series was always one of the big gambling events of the year. Adult males took their baseball partisanship as seriously as their political partisanship, and were more likely to back up the baseball loyalty with cash. It looked, to the scheming ballplayers, as though they could not miss making large fortunes. All they needed to assure this was a gambler to work with them.

Their choice was Joseph ("Sport") Sullivan, of Boston. Sullivan was the biggest gambler in New England. Cicotte laid the proposition on the line for Sullivan.

The White Sox would deliberately lose to Cincinnati, the National League pennant winner, if Sullivan would pay $10,000 to each of the players who would be involved in the plot. Cicotte thought it would require ten men to assure certainty. His price for throwing the Series was set, in round figures, at $100,000, payable in advance.

Sullivan agreed the deal had merit. However, he explained, there was one drawback. He didn't have $100,000. But there was one gambler to whom that kind of money was ordinary—Arnold

Rothstein. "I'll talk to 'A.R.,' " Sullivan told Cicotte and Gandil, who were the two players present at this meeting. He expressed certainty that Rothstein would provide the bribe money.

Gandil and Cicotte regarded the deal as good as arranged. Their next step was to enlist other players in their cabal. It was later charged there were eight players involved. These were Cicotte and Gandil, the ringleaders; Claude Williams, second-best pitcher on the team; Swede Risberg, shortstop; Buck Weaver, third baseman; Joe Jackson (next to Ty Cobb the best hitter in the league) and Happy Felsch, outfielders; and Fred McMullin, utility infielder.

The group included five of the eight regular starters, the team's two best pitchers, and, in McMullin, the player who would "scout" the Cincinnati team.

Of this group, Cicotte, Jackson and Williams confessed their part in the plot to a Cook County (Chicago) Grand Jury. Felsch and Gandil gave signed confessions to newspapers. Weaver denied complicity in the plot and neither McMullin nor Risberg ever made any statement. All eight, however, were indicted for throwing the Series.

The plot was all arranged, but no word had come from Sullivan. When Cicotte, growing anxious, sought to telephone him, Sullivan could not be reached.

Cicotte sought another gambler to implement the scheme. He chose Bill Burns, a former baseball player who had grown wealthy in the oil business but who gambled heavily on the side.

Burns, like Sullivan, agreed this was a foolproof way to make a fortune. However, like Sullivan, he pleaded inability to raise $100,000 in cash and, to continue the parallel, he suggested Rothstein as the best source for that much money. He said he did not know Rothstein, but he did have "connections" through whom he could reach him.

Cicotte told Burns to try.

The middleman whom Burns chose was a former boxer and petty gambler, William Maharg, of Philadelphia.

What then ensued was told in the testimony which Maharg gave at the trial of the ballplayers late in 1920. Here is a portion of his testimony:

"In the autumn of last year," Maharg told the jury, "I received a call from Burns from New York. I hopped a train and met Bill at the Ansonia. . . .

"He said a group of the most prominent players of the White Sox would be willing to throw the coming World Series if a syndicate of gamblers would give them $100,000 the morning of the first game. Burns said, 'Do you know any gamblers who would be interested in the proposition?'

"I said I would go back to Philadelphia and see what I could do. Burns said he would have to go to Montreal to close an oil deal and that he would wire me about the progress of the [baseball] deal. That explains a telegram sent to me from Montreal, when he wired:—'What have you done about the ball games?'

"I saw some gamblers in Philadelphia. They told me it was too big a proposition for them to handle, and they recommended me to Arnold Rothstein, a well-known and wealthy New York gambler.

"When Burns returned from Montreal, I went over to New York and joined him. Through my Philadelphia connections, I made an appointment with Rothstein. We met Rothstein by appointment in the Astor and put the proposition to him. He declined to get into it. He said he did not think such a frame-up would be possible.

"We left Rothstein and I hung around a while in New York. Then I returned to Philadelphia, thinking everything was off until I received the following wire from Bill Burns:—'Arnold R. has gone through with everything. Got eight [players] in. Leaving for Cincinnati at 4:30. Bill Burns.' This was only a few days before the Series.

"I went to Cincinnati the next day and joined Burns. He said that after I had left New York he ran into Abe Attell, the fighter, who had gone to Rothstein and fixed things. Burns added that

Rothstein had 'laid off' us because he didn't know us, but was very willing to talk turkey with Attell whom he knew.

"Attell was in Cincinnati, quartered in a large suite in the Sinton Hotel. He had a gang of about twenty-five gamblers with him. He said they were all working for Rothstein.

"Their work was very raw. They stood in the lobby of the Sinton and buttonholed everybody who came in. They accepted bets right and left and it was nothing to see $1,000 bills wagered.

"I had my first suspicion on the morning of the first game when Burns and I visited Attell. We asked for the $100,000 to turn over to the White Sox players for this part of the deal. [This was the sum Burns had promised Cicotte, rather than the original $10,000 per man.] Attell refused to turn over the $100,000, saying that they needed the money to make bets.

"He made a counter proposition that $20,000 would be handed the players at the end of each losing game. [In 1919 the Series was played until one team won five games.] Burns went to the Sox players and told them and they seemed satisfied with the new arrangements.

"We all bet on Cincinnati the first day and won. The next day, Burns and I went around again to Attell at his headquarters. I never saw so much money in my life. Stacks of bills were being counted on dressers and tables. I asked for the money for the players and Attell said that he would pay them at the end of the Series. I said they wanted their money now.

"When Attell refused to pay the money that he had promised the players, Burns said I should go to New York and talk to Rothstein. I went to New York and called on Rothstein."

Here Maharg's testimony concluded. The defense objected that details of the meeting—if there had been a meeting—were not relevant. The judge upheld the objection.

This was the last time that Rothstein's name appeared in any official proceeding resulting from the fixed Series. The coupling of his name and the 1919 Series, a coupling that began with the plotting, has continued to today.

The first person to accuse Rothstein directly of fixing the Series was Ban Johnson, president of the American League. Johnson, on the basis of widespread rumors that the Series had been crooked, hired private detectives to make an investigation before the last game of the Series was over. In September, 1920, Johnson announced the results of that investigation. He stated categorically that the Series had been deliberately lost by the White Sox and added:

"The man behind the fixing of the Series was Arnold Rothstein."

Rothstein issued an immediate denial, the first of many. He said, "There is not a word of truth in the report that I had anything to do with the World Series of last fall. I do not know if it was fixed. . . . My only connection was to refuse to do business with some men who said they could fix it. . . . I intend to sue Ban Johnson for libel. . . ."

Rothstein, of course, did not sue. Perhaps he had in mind Tim Sullivan's old warning: "Never sue. They might prove it."

Johnson's charges set off an official investigation in Chicago. State's Attorney Maclay Hoyne began presenting evidence to a Grand Jury. The three players made their confessions. And, in every report of what was happening, Rothstein's name led all the rest.

Rothstein, asked for a statement, announced that he was "sick and tired" of rumors and allegations. To put an end to them, he was going to make a voluntary appearance before the Grand Jury.

Rothstein had a prepared statement ready. He read part of it to newspapermen before he went in to testify.

"Attell did the fixing.

"I've come here to vindicate myself. If I wasn't sure I was going to be vindicated, I would have stayed home. As far as my story is concerned, I've already told most of it, but I guess you [the Grand Jury] want it on the official record.

"The whole thing started when Attell and some other cheap gamblers decided to frame the Series and make a killing. The world knows I was asked in on the deal and my friends know how

I turned it down flat. I don't doubt that Attell used my name to put it over. That's been done by smarter men than Abe. But I wasn't in on it, wouldn't have gone into it under any circumstances and didn't bet a cent on the Series after I found out what was under way. My idea was that whatever way things turned out, it would be a crooked Series anyhow and that only a sucker would bet on it.

"I'm not going to hold anything back from you [the jury]. I'm here to clear myself and I expect to get out of here with a clean bill of health."

After Rothstein testified, State's Attorney Hoyne told reporters that Rothstein's statement had been read to the Grand Jury exactly as Rothstein had read it to the reporters. "It's part of the record," he said.

The reporters asked Hoyne for his reaction to Rothstein's appearance and testimony.

"I don't think Rothstein was involved in it [the fix]."

Alfred Austrian, attorney for Comiskey and the White Sox, said to the same reporters, "Rothstein, in his testimony today, proved himself guiltless."

Obviously the Grand Jury also believed Rothstein. At the end of its deliberations it returned indictments against the eight players, Attell, Sullivan and Rachel Brown. Mrs. Brown was Rothstein's chief bookkeeper. She had been in Cincinnati and Chicago with Attell and had kept the records of all the bets.

Sometime between the Grand Jury hearings and the following September a peculiar happening occurred. All the records and minutes of the Grand Jury hearings disappeared. So, too, did the signed confessions of Cicotte, Williams and Jackson.

When the case went to trial, Attell was not present; he had gone to Canada, where he successfully resisted extradition.

The state, virtually all of its evidence gone, sought to get the players to repeat their confessions on the stand. This they refused to do, citing the Fifth Amendment. To talk would "tend to incriminate or degrade them." This was a new tactic in the Chicago court, but not new in New York. It was a favorite device of William J. Fallon's.

The state was left with only Maharg's testimony. Since he was one of the conspirators, his testimony required corroboration before it could be used as evidence. When no corroboration was forthcoming, the judge had to dismiss the case.

Thus, on the official record and on the basis of Hoyne's statement, Rothstein was never involved in the fixing of the Series. Also, on the official record, it was never proved that the Series had been fixed.

Nick Carraway was right. It just happened.

Nevertheless, trial or no trial, Grand Jury or no Grand Jury, Rothstein was fixed in the public mind, in history, as the man who fixed the Series. That judgment is fair enough. By reason of his being what he was, he was responsible for the crooked Series.

Here is the record of his involvement:

Immediately after Sullivan talked with Cicotte he went to New York, where he offered the deal to Rothstein.

"I don't want any part of it," Rothstein said. "It's too raw. Besides, you can't get away with it."

Sullivan pressed Rothstein, suggesting he at least look into it. "Not for my $100,000," Rothstein said. "You might be able to fix a game, but not the Series. You'd get lynched if it ever came out."

To Rothstein, as to millions of others, baseball ranked with love of mother and respect for the flag as untouchable. It was the "Great American Game." Its stars were among the folk heroes of the age. A man who would trifle with the honor of the game was a Benedict Arnold.

But, much as he respected baseball, Rothstein loved money more. It was hard to pass up the chance for so big a winning. He might have decided to play along with Sullivan had not Burns and Maharg appeared on the scene. They impressed him as amateurs and bunglers.

What bothered Rothstein most was that the deal was being peddled. His eleven times eleven progression had reached an astronomical total. To succeed, a fix should be a secret, not public property.

But one thought gnawed at him. Maybe it could be done. Maybe, despite all the stupidity involved, the fix could be brought off.

If there really was a sure thing going, he could make hundreds of thousands of dollars. He had to find out. For this purpose, he used Attell. He told him to maintain contact with Burns and Maharg. "I think they're puffing a pipe," he said, "but keep an eye on them."

Burns knew that Attell worked for Rothstein. He had no hesitancy about repeating his story. He added that he felt the deal could be made firm by a down payment of $10,000. Attell reported this back to Rothstein.

Now Rothstein discussed the Series with Nat Evans. He trusted Evans' judgment as he did that of few others. Evans, like Rothstein, was not too impressed. However, also like Rothstein, he felt there was too much risk in not knowing what was happening.

The $10,000 was a small sum to pay for "insurance." The money was given to Burns, its source not specified.

A few days before the Series opened, Evans went to Cincinnati, taking Attell and Rachel Brown with him. There, Evans again met with Burns and, after the meeting, he telephoned Rothstein and said, "I talked with Burns and some of the players. They're in so deep, they've got to throw the Series even if it don't mean a dime to them."

Rothstein still hesitated, but he knew time was growing short. He was taking bets on both teams, shaving the odds, of course, in his own favor. He could keep his books in balance and assure himself of a profit no matter which team won. Or he could start betting on Cincinnati.

His decision, reached twenty-four hours before the first game, was to accept Evans' judgment. But he coppered even that bet. "We'll play the Reds from game to game," he told Evans. "There's always the chance of a double-cross."

The situation was ironic. Rothstein could no longer doubt that the Series was fixed, yet he was unwilling to accept that as reality. He was certain the players were going to throw the Series, but he refused to bet on his own certainty. Bet, that is, to the limit.

And, though he had not fixed the Series, he was aware that already a gambler as well known as Honest John Kelly was announcing to would-be bettors that he would not take any bets on the Series because, "Everybody knows Arnold Rothstein has fixed it."

Rothstein took some steps to protect himself. He made a number of public wagers on the White Sox. He let it drop that he had heard the rumors but that they were untrue. And he stated, emphatically, that he would never have a part in anything as dirty as fixing a Series.

He was certain that the story would someday break. He wanted to have as good an alibi as possible when that day came.

The end result was that, while Rothstein won the Series, he won a small sum. He always maintained it was less than $100,000. It actually was about $350,000. It could have been much—very much—more. It wasn't because Rothstein chickened out. A World Series fix was too good to be true—even if it was true.

EXCERPTS FROM "DESCRIPTIONS OF GIRLS"*

F. Scott Fitzgerald

These are illustrative examples of Fitzgerald's interest in observing the American flapper. As they, as well as his early fiction, testify, he was anxious both to describe her and to give a suggestion of her role in the society of the "very young." Perhaps the most revealing expression is in the second of these quotations: "She was lovely and expensive, and about nineteen." Fitzgerald's portrayal of the young American girl steadily improved. In the beginning he was dazzled by her superficial beauty. Gradually, he came to realize that her being "expensive" was a major clue to the social scene of the 1920's, and to its moral implications. Contrast, for example, the observations of the first and last of these "Notes" with the characterization of Daisy in The Great Gatsby.

Becky was nineteen, a startling little beauty, with her head set upon her figure as though it had been made separately and then placed there with the utmost precision. Her body was sturdy, athletic; her head was a bright, happy composition of curves and shadows and vivid color, with that final kinetic jolt, the element that is eventually sexual in effect, which made strangers stare at

* F. Scott Fitzgerald, from "Descriptions of Girls," The Note-Books from The Crack-Up, ed. Edmund Wilson (New York: New Directions, 1945), pp. 132, 133, 135, 142 and 144. Copyright 1945 by New Directions. Reprinted by permission of New Directions, Publishers.

160

her. (Who has not had the excitement of seeing an apparent beauty from afar; then, after a moment, seeing that same face grow mobile and watching the beauty disappear moment by moment, as if a lovely statue had begun to walk with the meager joints of a paper doll?) Becky's beauty was the opposite of that. The facial muscles pulled her expressions into lovely smiles and frowns, disdains, gratifications and encouragements; her beauty was articulated, and expressed vividly whatever it wanted to express. [132]

She was a stalk of ripe corn, but bound not as cereals are but as a rare first edition, with all the binder's art. She was lovely and expensive, and about nineteen. [133]

Her face, flushed with cold and then warmed again with the dance, was a riot of lovely, delicate pinks, like many carnations, rising in many shades from the white of her nose to the high spot of her cheeks. Her breathing was very young as she came close to him—young and eager and exciting. [133]

Half an hour later, sitting a few feet from the judgment dais, he saw a girl detach herself from a group who were approaching it in threes—it was a girl in a white evening dress with red gold hair and under it a face so brave and tragic that it seemed that every eye in the packed hall must be fixed and concentrated on its merest adventures, the faintest impression upon her heart. [135]

. . . . is still a flapper. Fashions, names, manners, customs and morals change, but for . . . . it is still 1920. This concerns me, for there is no doubt that she originally patterned herself upon certain immature and unfortunate writings of mine, so I have a special indulgence for . . . . as for one who has lost an arm or leg in one's service.

She was a ripe grape, ready to fall for the mere shaking of a vine. [142]

Her face was a contrast between herself looking over a frontier—and a silhouette, an outline seen from a point of view, something finished—white, polite, unpolished—it was a destiny, scarred a little with young wars, worried with old white faiths . . . And out of it looked eyes so green that they were like phosphorescent marbles, so green that the scarcely dry clay of the face seemed dead beside it. [144]

part **3**

IT IS CLEAR from Fitzgerald's statements after its publication that he considered Gatsby to be his masterpiece. His introduction to the 1934 Modern Library edition testifies to his continuing belief in it, and only a few months before his death in December of 1940 he was writing his daughter that Gatsby had been his one clear triumph.

He did nevertheless have some doubts at the beginning, as his letters, given below, will testify. They are largely unfounded, but a discussion of the questions raised by him and by persons who wrote him about Gatsby should prove helpful.

The second half of Part Three consists of brief quotations from the novel itself, with the object of stressing certain specific critical issues. They are by no means intended to serve as a substitute for the novel, but simply to direct attention to key passages in it. The quotations are from The Scribner Library Edition (1960), which, because it is the only paper-back edition in print, should be the one most easily accessible.

CRITICAL PROBLEMS

AN INTRODUCTION TO *THE GREAT GATSBY**

F. Scott Fitzgerald

This brief statement is most illuminating in what it says of Fitzgerald's perspective as of nine years after publication.

To one who has spent his professional life in the world of fiction the request to "write an introduction" offers many facets of temptation. The present writer succumbs to one of them; with as much equanimity as he can muster, he will discuss the critics among us, trying to revolve as centripetally as possible about the novel which comes hereafter in this volume.

To begin with, I must say that I have no cause to grumble about the "press" of any book of mine. If Jack (who liked my last book) didn't like this one—well then John (who despised my last book) *did* like it; so it all mounts up to the same total. But I think the writers of my time were spoiled in that regard, living in generous days when there was plenty of space on the page for endless ratiocination about fiction—a space largely created by Mencken because of his disgust for what passed as criticism before he arrived and made his public. They were encouraged by his bravery and his tremendous and profound love of letters. In his

* F. Scott Fitzgerald, Introduction to The Modern Library Edition of The Great Gatsby (New York: Random House Inc., 1934). Copyright 1934 by The Modern Library, Inc. Reprinted by permission of Random House, Inc.

case, the jackals are already tearing at what they imprudently regard as a moribund lion, but I don't think many men of my age can regard him without reverence, nor fail to regret that he got off the train. To any new effort by a new man he brought an attitude; he made many mistakes—such as his early undervaluation of Hemingway—but he came equipped; he never had to go back for his tools.

And now that he has abandoned American fiction to its own devices, there is no one to take his place. If the present writer had seriously to attend some of the efforts of political diehards to tell him the values of a métier he has practised since boyhood—well, then, babies, you can take this number out and shoot him at dawn.

But all that is less discouraging, in the past few years, than the growing cowardice of the reviewers. Underpaid and overworked, they seem not to care for books, and it has been saddening recently to see young talents in fiction expire from sheer lack of a stage to act on: West, McHugh and many others.

I'm circling closer to my theme song, which is: that I'd like to communicate to such of them who read this novel a healthy cynicism toward contemporary reviews. Without undue vanity one can permit oneself a suit of chain mail in any profession. Your pride is all you have, and if you let it be tampered with by a man who has a dozen prides to tamper with before lunch, you are promising yourself a lot of disappointments that a hard-boiled professional has learned to spare himself.

This novel is a case in point. Because the pages weren't loaded with big names of big things and the subject not concerned with farmers (who were the heroes of the moment), there was easy judgment exercised that had nothing to do with criticism but was simply an attempt on the part of men who had few chances of self-expression to express themselves. How anyone could take up the responsibility of being a novelist without a sharp and concise attitude about life is a puzzle to me. How a critic could assume a point of view which included twelve variant aspects of the social scene in a few hours seems something too dinosaurean to loom over the awful loneliness of a young author.

To circle nearer to this book, one woman, who could hardly have written a coherent letter in English, described it as a book that one read only as one goes to the movies around the corner. That type of criticism is what a lot of young writers are being greeted with, instead of any appreciation of the world of imagination in which they (the writers) have been trying, with greater or lesser success, to live—the world that Mencken made stable in the days when he was watching over us.

Now that this book is being reissued, the author would like to say that never before did one try to keep his artistic conscience as pure as during the ten months put into doing it. Reading it over one can see how it could have been improved—yet without feeling guilty of any discrepancy from the truth, as far as I saw it; truth or rather the *equivalent* of the truth, the attempt at honesty of imagination. I had just re-read Conrad's preface to *The Nigger*, and I had recently been kidded half haywire by critics who felt that my material was such as to preclude all dealing with mature persons in a mature world. But, my God! it was my material, and it was all I had to deal with.

What I cut out of it both physically and emotionally would make another novel!

I think it is an honest book, that is to say, that one used none of one's virtuosity to get an effect, and, to boast again, one soft-pedalled the emotional side to avoid the tears leaking from the socket of the left eye, or the large false face peering around the corner of a character's head.

If there is a clear conscience, a book can survive—at least in one's feelings about it. On the contrary, if one has a guilty conscience, one reads what one wants to hear out of reviews. In addition, if one is young and willing to learn, almost all reviews have a value, even the ones that seem unfair.

The present writer has always been a "natural" for his profession, in so much that he can think of nothing he would have done as efficiently as to have lived deeply in the world of imagination. There are plenty other people constituted as he is, for giving expression to intimate explorations, the:

—Look—this is here!

—I saw this under my eyes.

—*This* is the way it was!

—No, it was like this.

"Look! Here is that drop of blood I told you about."

—"Stop everything! Here is the flash of that girl's eyes, here is the reflection that will always come back to me from the memory of her eyes.

—"If one chooses to find that face again in the non-refracting surface of a washbowl, if one chooses to make the image more obscure with a little sweat, it should be the business of the critic to recognize the intention.

—"No one felt like this before—says the young writer—but *I* felt like this; I have a pride akin to a soldier going into battle; without knowing whether there will be anybody there, to distribute medals or even to record it."

But remember, also, young man: you are not the first person who has ever been alone and alone.

LETTERS ABOUT *THE GREAT GATSBY*
FROM F. SCOTT FITZGERALD

To EDMUND WILSON, classmate and contemporary, and "literary conscience."*

[1925]
14 Rue de Tillsit
Paris, France

Dear Bunny:

Thanks for your letter about the book.[1] I was awfully happy that you liked it and that you approved of the design. The worst fault in it, I think is a BIG FAULT: I gave no account (and had no feeling about or knowledge of) the emotional relations between Gatsby and Daisy from the time of their reunion to the catastrophe. However the lack is so astutely concealed by the retrospect of Gatsby's past and by blankets of excellent prose that no one has noticed it—though everyone has felt the lack and called it by another name. Mencken said (in a most enthusiastic letter received today) that the only fault was that the central story was trivial and a sort of anecdote (that is because he has forgotten his admiration for Conrad and adjusted himself to the sprawling novel) and I felt that what he really missed was the lack of any emotional backbone at the very height of it.

[1] *The Great Gatsby.*
* This letter and the following two letters to John Peale Bishop and Frances Scott Fitzgerald are from The Crack-Up, ed. Edmund Wilson (New York: New Directions, 1945), pp. 270, 271, 272 and 294. Reprinted by permission of New Directions, publishers.

169

Without making any invidious comparisons between Class A and Class C, if my novel is an anecdote so is *The Brothers Karamazoff*. From one angle the latter could be reduced into a detective story. However the letters from you and Mencken have compensated me for the fact that of all the reviews, even the most enthusiastic, not one had the slightest idea what the book was about and for the even more depressing fact that it was in comparison with the others a financial failure (after I'd turned down fifteen thousand for the serial rights!) I wonder what Rosenfeld thought of it.

I looked up Hemminway. He is taking me to see Gertrude Stein tomorrow. This city is full of Americans—most of them former friends—whom we spend most of our time dodging, not because we don't want to see them but because Zelda's only just well and I've got to work; and they seem to be incapable of any sort of conversation not composed of semi-malicious gossip about New York courtesy celebrities. I've gotten to like France. We've taken a swell apartment until January. I'm filled with disgust for Americans in general after two weeks sight of the ones in Paris—these preposterous, pushing women and girls who assume that you have any personal interest in them, who have all (so they say) read James Joyce and who simply adore Mencken. I suppose we're no worse than anyone, only contact with other races brings out all our worse qualities. If I had anything to do with creating the manners of the contemporary American girl I certainly made a botch of the job.

I'd love to see you. God. I could give you some laughs. There's no news except that Zelda and I think we're pretty good, as usual, only more so.

Scott

Thanks again for your cheering letter.

To JOHN PEALE BISHOP, *classmate at Princeton, fellow novelist, poet and critic.*

[Postmarked, August 9, 1925]
Rue de Tilsitt
Paris, France

Dear John:

Thank you for your most pleasant, full, discerning and helpful letter about *The Great Gatsby*. It is about the only criticism that the book has had which has been intelligable, save a letter from Mrs. Wharton. I shall only ponder, or rather I have pondered, what you say about accuracy—I'm afraid I haven't quite reached the ruthless artistry which would let me cut out an exquisite bit that had no place in the context. I can cut out the almost exquisite, the adequate, even the brilliant—but a true accuracy is, as you say, still in the offing. Also you are right about Gatsby being blurred and patchy. I never at any one time saw him clear myself—for he started out as one man I knew and then changed into myself—the amalgam was never complete in my mind.

Your novel sounds fascinating and I'm crazy to see it. I'm beginning a new novel next month on the Riviera. I understand that MacLeish is there, among other people (at Antibes where we are going). Paris has been a mad-house this spring and, as you can imagine, we were in the thick of it. I don't know when we're coming back—maybe never. We'll be here till Jan. (except for a month in Antibes), and then we go Nice for the Spring, with Oxford for next summer. Love to Margaret and many thanks for the kind letter.

Scott

172 F. Scott Fitzgerald

To FRANCES SCOTT FITZGERALD, *his daughter.*

June 12, 1940

I could agree with you as opposed to Dean Thompson if you were getting "B's." Then I would say: As you're not going to be a teacher or a professional scholar, don't try for "A's"—don't take the things in which you can get "A," for you can learn them yourself. Try something hard and new, and try it hard, and take what marks you can get. But you have no such margin of respectability, and this borderline business is a fret to you. Doubt and worry— you are as crippled by them as I am by my inability to handle money or my self-indulgences of the past. It is your Achilles' heel —and no Achilles' heel ever toughened by itself. It just gets more and more vulnerable. What little I've accomplished has been by the most laborious and uphill work, and I wish now I'd *never* relaxed or looked back—but said at the end of *The Great Gatsby*: "I've found my line—from now on this comes first. This is my immediate duty—without this I am nothing."

LETTERS TO FITZGERALD ABOUT
THE GREAT GATSBY AND RELATED MATTERS

From MAXWELL PERKINS, his editor at Scribner's, November 20, 1924.*

Dear Scott:

I think you have every kind of right to be proud of this book.[1] It is an extraordinary book, suggestive of all sorts of thoughts and moods. You adopted exactly the right method of telling it, that of employing a narrator who is more of a spectator than an actor: this puts the reader upon a point of observation on a higher level than that on which the characters stand and at a distance that gives perspective. In no other way could your irony have been so immensely effective, nor the reader have been enabled so strongly to feel at times the strangeness of human circumstance in a vast heedless universe. In the eyes of Dr. Eckleberg various readers will see different significances; but their presence gives a superb touch to the whole thing: great unblinking eyes, expressionless, looking down upon the human scene. It's magnificent!

I could go on praising the book and speculating on its various elements, and means, but points of criticism are more important

[1] *The Great Gatsby*, Scribner's, 1925.
* Editor to Author: The Letters of Maxwell E. Perkins, ed. *John Hall Wheelock* (New York: Charles Scribner's Sons, 1950), pp. 38-41. Copyright 1950 by Charles Scribner's Sons. Reprinted by permission of the publisher.

173

now. I think you are right in feeling a certain slight sagging in chapters six and seven, and I don't know how to suggest a remedy. I hardly doubt that you will find one and I am only writing to say that I think it does need something to hold up here to the pace set, and ensuing. I have only two actual criticisms:

One is that among a set of characters marvelously palpable and vital—I would know Tom Buchanan if I met him on the street and would avoid him—Gatsby is somewhat vague. The reader's eyes can never quite focus upon him, his outlines are dim. Now everything about Gatsby is more or less a mystery, i.e. more or less vague, and this may be somewhat of an artistic intention, but I think it is mistaken. Couldn't *he* be physically described as distinctly as the others, and couldn't you add one or two characteristics like the use of that phrase "old sport"—not verbal, but physical ones, perhaps. I think that for some reason or other a reader—this was true of Mr. Scribner[2] and of Louise[3]—gets an idea that Gatsby is a much older man than he is, although you have the writer say that he is little older than himself. But this would be avoided if on his first appearance he was seen as vividly as Daisy and Tom are, for instance—and I do not think your scheme would be impaired if you made him so.

The other point is also about Gatsby: his career must remain mysterious, of course. But in the end you make it pretty clear that his wealth came through his connection with Wolfsheim. You also suggest this much earlier. Now almost all readers numerically are going to be puzzled by his having all this wealth and are going to feel entitled to an explanation. To give a distinct and definite one would be, of course, utterly absurd. It did occur to me, though, that you might here and there interpolate some phrases, and possibly incidents, little touches of various kinds, that would suggest that he was in some active way mysteriously engaged. You do have him called on the telephone, but couldn't he be seen once

---

[2] Charles Scribner, Senior (1854-1930), president of Charles Scribner's Sons.
[3] Mrs. Maxwell E. Perkins.

or twice consulting at his parties with people of some sort of mysterious significance, from the political, the gambling, the sporting world, or whatever it may be. I know I am floundering, but that fact may help you to see what I mean. The *total* lack of an explanation through so large a part of the story does seem to me a defect—or not of an explanation, but of the suggestion of an explanation. I wish you were here so I could talk about it to you, for then I know I could at least make you understand what I mean. What Gatsby did ought never to be definitely imparted, even if it could be. Whether he was an innocent tool in the hands of somebody else, or to what degree he was this, ought not to be explained. But if some sort of business activity of his were simply adumbrated, it would lend further probability to that part of the story.

There is one other point: in giving deliberately Gatsby's biography, when he gives it to the narrator, you do depart from the method of the narrative in some degree, for otherwise almost everything is told, and beautifully told, in the regular flow of it, in the succession of events or in accompaniment with them. But you can't avoid the biography altogether. I thought you might find ways to let the truth of some of his claims like "Oxford" and his army career come out, bit by bit, in the course of actual narrative. I mention the point anyway, for consideration in this interval before I send the proofs.

The general brilliant quality of the book makes me ashamed to make even these criticisms. The amount of meaning you get into a sentence, the dimensions and intensity of the impression you make a paragraph carry, are most extraordinary. The manuscript is full of phrases which make a scene blaze with life. If one enjoyed a rapid railroad journey I would compare the number and vividness of pictures your living words suggest, to the living scenes disclosed in that way. It seems, in reading, a much shorter book than it is, but it carries the mind through a series of experiences that one would think would require a book of three times its length.

176   Gertrude Stein

The presentation of Tom, his place, Daisy and Jordan, and the unfolding of their characters is unequaled so far as I know. The description of the valley of ashes adjacent to the lovely country, the conversation and the action in Myrtle's apartment, the marvelous catalogue of those who came to Gatsby's house—these are such things as make a man famous. And all these things, the whole pathetic episode, you have given a place in time and space, for with the help of T. J. Eckleberg and by an occasional glance at the sky, or the sea, or the city, you have imparted a sort of sense of eternity. You once told me you were not a *natural* writer —my God! You have plainly mastered the craft, of course; but you needed far more than craftsmanship for this.

As ever,

From GERTRUDE STEIN.*

Hotel Pernollet
Belley
(Ain)
Belley, le 22 May, 192-[1925]

My dear Fitzgerald:

Here we are and have read your book and it is a good book. I like the melody of your dedication and it shows that you have a background of beauty and tenderness and that is a comfort. The next good thing is that you write naturally in sentences and that too is a comfort. You write naturally in sentences and one can read all of them and that among other things is a comfort. You are creating the contemporary world much as Thackeray did his in *Pendennis* and *Vanity Fair* and this isn't a bad compliment. You make a modern world and a modern orgy strangely enough it was never done until you did it in *This Side of Paradise*. My

---

* From The Crack-Up, ed. Edmund Wilson (New York: New Directions, 1945), p. 308. Reprinted by permission of Donald Gallup, Literary Executor of the late Gertrude Stein.

belief in *This Side of Paradise* was alright. This is as good a book and different and older and that is what one does, one does not get better but different and older and that is always a pleasure. Best of good luck to you always, and thanks so much for the very genuine pleasure you have given me. We are looking forward to seeing you and Mrs. Fitzgerald when we get back in the Fall. Do please remember me to her and to you always

Gtde Stein

From EDITH WHARTON.*

Pavillon Colombe
St. Brice-Sous-Forêt (S&O)
Gare: Sarcelles

June 8, 1925

Dear Mr. Fitzgerald,

I have been wandering for the last weeks and found your novel—with its friendly dedication—awaiting me here on my arrival, a few days ago.

I am touched at your sending me a copy, for I feel that to your generation, which has taken such a flying leap into the future, I must represent the literary equivalent of tufted furniture & gas chandeliers. So you will understand that it is in a spirit of sincere deprecation that I shall venture, in a few days, to offer you in return the last product of my manufactory.

Meanwhile, let me say at once how much I like Gatsby, or rather His Book, & how great a leap I think you have taken this time—in advance upon your previous work. My present quarrel with you is only this: that to make Gatsby really Great, you ought to have given us his early career (not from the cradle—but from his visit to the yacht, if not before) instead of a short résumé of

* From *The Crack-Up*, ed. Edmund Wilson (*New York: New Directions, 1945*), pp. 309-310. Reprinted by permission of A. Watkins, Agents for the Estate of Edith Wharton.

it. That would have situated him, & made his final tragedy a tragedy instead of a "fait divers" for the morning papers.

But you'll tell me that's the old way, & consequently not *your* way; & meanwhile, it's enough to make this reader happy to have met your *perfect* Jew, & the limp Wilson, & assisted at that seedy orgy in the Buchanan flat, with the dazed puppy looking on. Every bit of that is masterly—but the lunch with Hildeshiem,[1] and his every appearance afterward, make me augur still greater things!— Thank you again.

> Yrs. Sincerely,
> Edith Wharton

I have left hardly space to ask if you & Mrs. Fitzgerald won't come to lunch or tea some day this week. Do call me up.

From T. S. ELIOT.*

FABER AND GWYER LTD.
Publishers

24 Russell Square,
London, W.C.1.
31st December, 1925

F. Scott Fitzgerald, Esqre.,
%Charles Scribners & Sons,
New York City.

Dear Mr. Scott Fitzgerald,

The Great Gatsby with your charming and overpowering inscription arrived the very morning that I was leaving in some haste for a sea voyage advised by my doctor. I therefore left it behind and only read it on my return a few days ago. I have, however, now read it three times. I am not in the least influenced by your remark about myself when I say that it has interested and excited me

---

[1] The name should be Wolfsheim. Hildesheim was misspelled Hildeshiem in the first edition of *The Great Gatsby*.
* From The Crack-Up, ed. Edmund Wilson (New York: New Directions, 1945), p. 310. Reprinted by permission of T. S. Eliot.

more than any new novel I have seen, either English or American, for a number of years.

When I have time I should like to write to you more fully and tell you exactly why it seems to me such a remarkable book. In fact it seems to me to be the first step that American fiction has taken since Henry James. . . .

By the way, if you ever have any short stories which you think would be suitable for the *Criterion* I wish you would let me see them.

With many thanks, I am,

Yours very truly,

T.S. Eliot

P.S. By a coincidence Gilbert Seldes in his New York Chronicle in the *Criterion* for January 14th has chosen your book for particular mention.

From THOMAS WOLFE, *July 26, 1937.* While this letter is not directly concerned with The Great Gatsby, it raises a number of very interesting questions about the writing of fiction, especially in terms of Fitzgerald's own letter to Wolfe, to which this is a reply. Wolfe's fiction, in every respect an instructive contrast to The Great Gatsby, serves as a point of departure.*

July 26, 1937

Mr. F. Scott Fitzgerald
c/o Charles Scribners' Sons
597 Fifth Avenue, N.Y.C.

Dear Scott:

I don't know where you are living and I'll be damned if I'll believe anyone lives in a place called "The Garden of Allah,"[1] which was what the address on your envelope said. I am sending this on to the old address we both know so well.

[1] This was Fitzgerald's real address, an apartment hotel, in Hollywood.
* From The Crack-Up, ed. Edmund Wilson (New York: New Directions, 1945), pp. 312-316. Reprinted by permission of Pincus Berner, Adm., Estate of Thomas Wolfe.

The unexpected loquaciouness of your letter struck me all of a heap. I was surprised to hear from you but I don't know that I can truthfully say I was delighted. Your bouquet arrived smelling sweetly of roses but cunningly concealing several large-sized brickbats. Not that I resented them. My resenter got pretty tough years ago; like everybody else I have at times been accused of "resenting criti[ci]sm" and although I have never been one of those boys who break out in a hearty and delighted laugh when someone tells them everything they write is lousy and agree enthusiastically, I think I have taken as many plain and fancy varieties as any American citizen of my age now living. I have not always smiled and murmured pleasantly "How true," but I have listened to it all, tried to profit from it where and when I could and perhaps been helped by it a little. Certainly I don't think I have been pig-headed about it. I have not been arrogantly contemptuous of it either, because one of my besetting sins, whether you know it or not, is a lack of confidence in what I do.

So I'm not sore at you or sore about anything you said in your letter. And if there is any truth in what you say—any truth for me—you can depend upon it I shall probably get it out. It just seems to me that there is not much in what you say. You speak of your "case" against me, and frankly I don't believe you have much case. You say you write these things because you admire me so much and because you think my talent unmatchable in this or any other country and because you are ever my friend. Well Scott I should not only be proud and happy to think that all these things are true but my respect and admiration for your own talent and intelligence are such that I should try earnestly to live up to them and to deserve them and to pay the most serious and respectful attention to anything you say about my work.

I have tried to do so. I have read your letter several times and I've got to admit it doesn't seem to mean much. I don't know what you are driving at or understand what you expect or hope me to do about it. Now this may be pig-headed but it isn't sore. I may be wrong but all I can get out of it is that you think I'd be a good writer if I were an altogether different writer from the writer that I am.

This may be true but I don't see what I'm going to do about it. And I don't think you can show me and I don't see what Flaubert and Zola have to do with it, or what I have to do with them. I wonder if you really think they have anything to do with it, or if this is just something you heard in college or read in a book somewhere. This either-or kind of criticism seems to me to be so meaningless. It looks so knowing and imposing but there is nothing in it. Why does it follow that if a man writes a book that is not like *Madame Bovary* it is inevitably like Zola. I may be dumb but I can't see this. You say that *Madame Bovary* becomes eternal while Zola already rocks with age. Well this may be true—but if it is true isn't it true because *Madame Bovary* may be a great book and those that Zola wrote may not be great ones? Wouldn't it also be true to say that *Don Quixote* or *Pickwick* or *Tristram Shandy* "become eternal" while already Mr. Galsworthy "rocks with age." I think it is true to say this and it doesn't leave much of your argument, does it? For your argument is based simply upon one *way*, upon one method instead of another. And have you ever noticed how often it turns out that what a man is really doing is simply rationalizing his own way of doing something, the way he has to do it, the way given him by his talent and his nature, into the only inevitable and right way of doing everything—a sort of classic and eternal art form handed down by Apollo from Olympus without which and beyond which there is nothing. Now you have your way of doing something and I have mine, there are a lot of ways, but you are honestly mistaken in thinking that there is a "way." I suppose I would agree with you in what you say about "the novel of selected incident" so far as it means anything. I say so far as it means anything because every novel, of course, is a novel of selected incident. There are no novels of unselected incident. You couldn't write about the inside of a telephone booth without selecting. You could fill a novel of a thousand pages with a description of a single room and yet your incidents would be selected. And I have mentioned *Don Quixote* and *Pickwick* and *The Brothers Karamazov* and *Tristram Shandy* to you in contrast to *The Silver Spoon* or *The White Monkey* as examples of books that have become "immortal" and that *boil* and *pour*. Just remember that although *Madame Bovary* in your opinion may be a great book, *Tristram Shandy is* indubitably a great book, and that it is great for quite different reasons. It is great because it *boils* and *pours*— for the *unselected* quality of its selection. You say that the great writer like Flaubert has consciously left out the stuff that Bill or Joe will come along presently and put in. Well, don't forget, Scott, that a great writer is not only a leaver-outer but also a putter-inner, and that Shakespeare and Cervantes and Dostoevsky were great putter-inners—greater putter-inners, in fact, than taker-outers and will be remembered for what they put in—remembered, I venture to say, as long as Monsieur Flaubert will be remembered for what he left out.

As to the rest of it in your letter about cultivating an alter ego, becoming a more conscious artist, my pleasantness or grief, exuberance or cynicism, and how nothing stands out in relief because everything is keyed at the same emotional pitch—this stuff is worthy of the great minds that review books nowadays—the Fadimans and De Votos—but not of you. For you are an artist and the artist has the only true critical intelligence. You have had to work and sweat blood yourself and you know what it is like to try to write a living word or create a living thing. So don't talk this foolish stuff to me about exuberance or being a conscious artist or not bringing things into emotional relief, or any of the rest of it. Let the Fadimans and De Votos do that kind of talking but not Scott Fitzgerald. You've got too much sense and you know too much. The little fellows who don't know may picture a man as a great "exuberant" six-foot-six clodhopper straight out of nature who bites off half a plug of apple tobacco, tilts the corn liquor jug and lets half of it gurgle down his throat, wipes off his mouth with the back of one hairy paw, jumps three feet in the air and clacks his heels together four times before he hits the floor again and yells "Whoopee, boys I'm a rootin, tootin, shootin son of a gun from Buncombe County—out of my way now, here I come!"—and then wads up three-hundred thousand words or so, hurls it back at a blank page, puts covers on it and says "Here's my book!" Now Scott, the boys who write book reviews in New York may think it's done that way; but the man who wrote *Tender Is the Night* knows better. You know you never did it that way, you know I never did, you know no one else who ever wrote a line worth reading ever did. So don't give me any of your guff, young fellow. And don't think I'm sore. But I get tired of guff—I'll take it from a fool or from a book reviewer but I won't take it from a friend who knows a lot better. I want to be a better artist. I want to be a more selective artist. I want to be a more restrained artist. I want to use such talent as I have, control such forces as I may own, direct such energy as I may use more cleanly, more surely and to better purpose. But Flaubert me no Flauberts, Bovary me no Bovarys. Zola me no Zolas. And exuberance me no exuberances. Leave this stuff for those who huckster in it and give me, I pray you, the benefits of your fine intelligence and your high creative faculties, all of which I so genuinely and profoundly admire. I am going into the woods for another two or three years. I am going to try to do the best, the most important piece of work I have ever done. I am going to have to do it alone. I am going to lose what little bit of reputation I may have gained, to have to hear and know and endure in silence again all of the doubt, the disparagement and ridicule, the post-mortems that they are so eager to read over you even before you are dead. I know what it means and so do you. We have both been through it before. We know it is the plain damn simple truth. Well, I've been through it once and I believe I can get through it again. I think I know a little more now than I did before, I certainly know what to expect and I'm going to try not to let it get me down. That is the reason why this time I shall look for intelligent understanding among some of my friends. I'm not ashamed to say that I shall need it. You say in your letter that you are ever my friend. I assure you that it is very good to hear this. Go for me with the gloves off if you think I need it. But don't De Voto me. If you do I'll call your bluff.

I'm down here for the summer living in a cabin in the country and I am enjoying it. Also I'm working. I don't know how long you are going to be in Hollywood or whether you have a job out there but I hope I shall see you before long and that all is going well with you. I still think as I always thought that *Tender Is the Night* had in it the best work you have ever done. And I believe you will surpass it in the future. Anyway, I send you my best wishes as always for health and work and success. Let me hear from you sometime. The address is Oteen, North Carolina, just a few miles from Asheville, Ham Basso, as you know, is not far away at Pisgah Forest and he is coming over to see me soon and perhaps we shall make a trip together to see Sherwood Anderson. And now this is all for the present—unselective, you see, as usual. Good bye Scott and good luck.

Ever Yours,
Tom Wolfe

THE METHOD OF *THE GREAT GATSBY*

SCENIC NARRATION: SELECTED QUOTATIONS*

James E. Miller in The Fictional Technique of Scott Fitzgerald,[1] points to the skill of the first three "presentation chapters," a "series of scenes dramatizing the important events of the story and connected by brief passages of interpretation and summary." (p. 100) Also, he comments shrewdly upon the manner in which Gatsby's past is constructed from several sources and presented in fragments which are placed each time at the proper moment of present action, for maximum effectiveness:

> Fitzgerald works "backwards and forwards" over his past until the complete portrait finally emerges at the end of the book. Just how much Fitzgerald has rearranged the events of Gatsby's life can be seen by tracing events through the book chronologically; the only glimpse of Gatsby's boyhood is in the last chapter; the account of Gatsby, at the age of seventeen, joining Dan Cody's yacht comes in Chapter VI; the important love affair between Gatsby and Daisy, which took place five years before the action in the book when Gatsby, then in the army, first met Daisy, is related three separate times (Chapters IV, VI, and VIII), but from various points of view and with various degrees of fullness; the

[1] The Hague, Martinus Nijhoff, 1957.
* F. Scott Fitzgerald, The Great Gatsby (New York: Charles Scribner's Sons, 1925), pp. 4-6, 6-7, 16-18, 23-26, 29, 39-40, 45-46. Copyright 1925 Charles Scribner's Sons; renewal copyright 1953 Frances Scott Fitzgerald Lanahan. Reprinted by permission of the publisher. The Scribner Library Edition of The Great Gatsby is the current source for the passages herein quoted.

account of Gatsby's war experiences and his trip, after discharge, back to Louisville to Daisy's home, is given in Chapter VIII; and Gatsby's entry into his present mysterious occupation through Wolfsheim is presented, briefly, in Chapter IX. The summer of 1922, the last summer of Gatsby's life, acts as a string on to which these varicolored "beads" of his past have been "haphazardly" strung.

A simple diagram of the sequence of events in *The Great Gatsby* is, perhaps, helpful. Allowing X to stand for the straight chronological account of the summer of 1922, and A, B, C, D, and E to represent the significant events of Gatsby's past, the nine chapters of *The Great Gatsby* may be charted: X, X, X, XCX, X, XBXCX, X, XCXDX, XEXAX. (p. 97)

This skill in method can be appreciated only through a careful reading of the entire novel. Yet certain scenes strike one as especially interesting; the quotations which follow are designed to illustrate Miller's suggestion concerning Fitzgerald's "scenic presentation."

The three houses:

It was a matter of chance that I should have rented a house in one of the strangest communities in North America. It was on that slender riotous island which extends itself due east of New York —and where there are, among other natural curiosities, two unusual formations of land. Twenty miles from the city a pair of enormous eggs, identical in contour and separated only by a courtesy bay, jut out into the most domesticated body of salt water in the Western hemisphere, the great wet barnyard of Long Island Sound. They are not perfect ovals—like the egg in the Columbus story, they are both crushed flat at the contact end—but their physical resemblance must be a source of perpetual confusion to the gulls that fly overhead. To the wingless a more arresting phenomenon is their dissimilarity in every particular except shape and size.

I lived at West Egg, the—well, the less fashionable of the two, though this is a most superficial tag to express the bizarre and not a little sinister contrast between them. My house was at the very tip of the egg, only fifty yards from the Sound, and squeezed between two huge places that rented for twelve or fifteen thousand a season. The one on my right was a colossal affair by any standard —it was a factual imitation of some Hôtel de Ville in Normandy, with a tower on one side, spanking new under a thin beard of raw ivy, and a marble swimming pool, and more than forty acres of lawn and garden. It was Gatsby's mansion. Or, rather, as I didn't know Mr. Gatsby, it was a mansion, inhabited by a gentleman of that name. My own house was an eyesore, but it was a small eyesore, and it had been overlooked, so I had a view of the water, a partial view of my neighbor's lawn, and the consoling proximity of millionaires—all for eighty dollars a month.

Across the courtesy bay the white palaces of fashionable East Egg glittered along the water, and the history of the summer really begins on the evening I drove over there to have dinner with the Tom Buchanans. Daisy was my second cousin once removed, and I'd known Tom in college. And just after the war I spent two days with them in Chicago. [4-6]

And so it happened that on a warm windy evening I drove over to East Egg to see two old friends whom I scarcely knew at all. Their house was even more elaborate than I expected, a cheerful red-and-white Georgian Colonial mansion, overlooking the bay. The lawn started at the beach and ran toward the front door for a quarter of a mile, jumping over sun-dials and brick walks and burning gardens—finally when it reached the house drifting up the side in bright vines as though from the momentum of its run. The front was broken by a line of French windows, glowing now with reflected gold and wide open to the warm windy afternoon, and Tom Buchanan in riding clothes was standing with his legs apart on the front porch.

He had changed since his New Haven years. Now he was a sturdy straw-haired man of thirty with a rather hard mouth and a supercilious manner. Two shining arrogant eyes had established dominance over his face and gave him the appearance of always leaning aggressively forward. Not even the effeminate swank of his riding clothes could hide the enormous power of that body—he seemed to fill those glistening boots until he strained the top lacing, and you could see a great pack of muscle shifting when his shoulder moved under his thin coat. It was a body capable of enormous leverage—a cruel body. [6-7]

The Buchanan world:

The telephone rang inside, startlingly, and as Daisy shook her head decisively at Tom the subject of the stables, in fact all subjects, vanished into air. Among the broken fragments of the last five minutes at table I remember the candles being lit again, pointlessly, and I was conscious of wanting to look squarely at every one, and yet to avoid all eyes. I couldn't guess what Daisy and Tom were thinking, but I doubt if even Miss Baker, who seemed to have mastered a certain hardy scepticism, was able utterly to put this fifth guest's shrill metallic urgency out of mind. To a certain temperament the situation might have seemed intriguing— my own instinct was to telephone immediately for the police.

The horses, needless to say, were not mentioned again. Tom and Miss Baker, with several feet of twilight between them, strolled back into the library, as if to a vigil beside a perfectly tangible body, while, trying to look pleasantly interested and a little deaf, I followed Daisy around a chain of connecting verandas to the porch in front. In its deep gloom we sat down side by side on a wicker settee.

Daisy took her face in her hands as if feeling its lovely shape, and her eyes moved gradually out into the velvet dusk. I saw that turbulent emotions possessed her, so I asked what I thought would be some sedative questions about her little girl.

"We don't know each other very well, Nick," she said suddenly. "Even if we are cousins. You didn't come to my wedding."

"I wasn't back from the war."

"That's true." She hesitated. "Well, I've had a very bad time, Nick, and I'm pretty cynical about everything."

Evidently she had reason to be. I waited but she didn't say any more, and after a moment I returned rather feebly to the subject of her daughter.

"I suppose she talks, and—eats, and everything."

"Oh, yes." She looked at me absently. "Listen, Nick; let me tell you what I said when she was born. Would you like to hear?"

"Very much."

"It'll show you how I've gotten to feel about—things. Well, she was less than an hour old and Tom was God knows where. I woke up out of the ether with an utterly abandoned feeling, and asked the nurse right away if it was a boy or a girl. She told me it was a girl, and so I turned my head away and wept. 'All right,' I said, 'I'm glad it's a girl. And I hope she'll be a fool—that's the best thing a girl can be in this world, a beautiful little fool.'

"You see I think everything's terrible anyhow," she went on in a convinced way. "Everybody thinks so—the most advanced people. And I *know*. I've been everywhere and seen everything and done everything." Her eyes flashed around her in a defiant way, rather like Tom's, and she laughed with thrilling scorn. "Sophisticated—God, I'm sophisticated!"

The instant her voice broke off ceasing to compel my attention, my belief, I felt the basic insincerity of what she had said. It made me uneasy, as though the whole evening had been a trick of some sort to exact a contributary emotion from me. I waited, and sure enough, in a moment she looked at me with an absolute smirk on her lovely face, as if she had asserted her membership in a rather distinguished secret society to which she and Tom belonged. [16-18]

The valley of ashes:

About half way between West Egg and New York the motor road hastily joins the railroad and runs beside it for a quarter of a mile, so as to shrink away from a certain desolate area of land. This is a valley of ashes—a fantastic farm where ashes grow like wheat into ridges and hills and grotesque gardens; where ashes take the forms of houses and chimneys and rising smoke and, finally, with a transcendent effort, of men who move dimly and already crumbling through the powdery air. Occasionally a line of gray cars crawls along an invisible track, gives out a ghastly creak, and comes to rest, and immediately the ash-gray men swarm up with leaden spades and stir up an impenetrable cloud, which screens their obscure operations from your sight.

But above the gray land and the spasms of bleak dust which drift endlessly over it, you perceive, after a moment, the eyes of Doctor T. J. Eckleburg. The eyes of Doctor T. J. Eckleburg are blue and gigantic—their retinas are one yard high. They look out of no face, but, instead, from a pair of enormous yellow spectacles which pass over a non-existent nose. Evidently some wild wag of an oculist set them there to fatten his practice in the borough of Queens, and then sank down himself into eternal blindness, or forgot them and moved away. But his eyes, dimmed a little by many paintless days under sun and rain, brood on over the solemn dumping ground.

The valley of ashes is bounded on one side by a small foul river, and, when the drawbridge is up to let barges through, the passengers on waiting trains can stare at the dismal scene for as long as half an hour. There is always a halt there of at least a minute, and it was because of this that I first met Tom Buchanan's mistress.

The fact that he had one was insisted upon wherever he was known. His acquaintances resented the fact that he turned up in popular restaurants with her and, leaving her at a table, sauntered about, chatting with whomsoever he knew. Though I was curious to see her, I had no desire to meet her—but I did. I went up to New York with Tom on the train one afternoon and when we stopped by the ashheaps he jumped to his feet and, taking hold of my elbow, literally forced me from the car.

"We're getting off," he insisted. "I want you to meet my girl."

I think he'd tanked up a good deal at luncheon, and his determination to have my company bordered on violence. The supercilious assumption was that on Sunday afternoon I had nothing better to do.

I followed him over a low whitewashed railroad fence, and we walked back a hundred yards along the road under Doctor Eckleburg's persistent stare. The only building in sight was a small block of yellow brick sitting on the edge of the waste land, a sort of compact Main Street ministering to it, and contiguous to absolutely nothing. One of the three shops it contained was for rent and another was an all-night restaurant, approached by a trail of ashes; the third was a garage—*Repairs.* GEORGE B. WILSON. *Cars bought and sold.*—and I followed Tom inside.

The interior was unprosperous and bare; the only car visible was the dust-covered wreck of a Ford which crouched in a dim corner. It had occurred to me that this shadow of a garage must be a blind, and that sumptuous and romantic apartments were concealed overhead, when the proprietor himself appeared in the door of an office, wiping his hands on a piece of waste. He was a blond, spiritless man, anæmic, and faintly handsome. When he saw us a damp gleam of hope sprang into his light blue eyes.

"Hello, Wilson, old man," said Tom, slapping him jovially on the shoulder. "How's business?"

"I can't complain," answered Wilson unconvincingly. "When are you going to sell me that car?"

"Next week; I've got my man working on it now."

"Works pretty slow, don't he?"

"No, he doesn't," said Tom coldly. "And if you feel that way about it, maybe I'd better sell it somewhere else after all."

"I don't mean that," explained Wilson quickly. "I just meant—"

His voice faded off and Tom glanced impatiently around the garage. Then I heard footsteps on a stairs, and in a moment the thickish figure of a woman blocked out the light from the office door. She was in the middle thirties, and faintly stout, but she carried her surplus flesh sensuously as some women can. Her face, above a spotted dress of dark blue crêpe-de-chine, contained no facet or gleam of beauty, but there was an immediately perceptible vitality about her as if the nerves of her body were continually smouldering. She smiled slowly and, walking through her husband as if he were a ghost, shook hands with Tom, looking him flush in the eye. Then she wet her lips, and without turning around spoke to her husband in a soft, coarse voice:

"Get some chairs, why don't you, so somebody can sit down."

"Oh, sure," agreed Wilson hurriedly, and went toward the little office mingling immediately with the cement color of the walls. A white ashen dust veiled his dark suit and his pale hair as it veiled everything in the vicinity—except his wife, who moved close to Tom. [23-26]

The apartment:

The apartment was on the top floor—a small living-room, a small dining-room, a small bedroom, and a bath. The living-room was crowded to the doors with a set of tapestried furniture entirely too large for it, so that to move about was to stumble continually over scenes of ladies swinging in the gardens of Versailles. The only picture was an over-enlarged photograph, apparently a hen sitting on a blurred rock. Looked at from a distance, however, the hen resolved itself into a bonnet, and the countenance of a stout old lady beamed down into the room. Several old copies of *Town Tattle* lay on the table together with a copy of *Simon Called Peter*, and some of the small scandal magazines of Broadway. Mrs. Wilson was first concerned with the dog. A reluctant elevator-boy went for a box full of straw and some milk, to which he added on his own initiative a tin of large, hard dog-biscuits—one of which decomposed apathetically in the saucer of milk all afternoon. Meanwhile Tom brought out a bottle of whiskey from a locked bureau door.

I have been drunk just twice in my life, and the second time was that afternoon; so everything that happened has a dim, hazy cast over it, although until after eight o'clock the apartment was full of cheerful sun. Sitting on Tom's lap Mrs. Wilson called up several people on the telephone; then there were no cigarettes, and I went out to buy some at the drugstore on the corner. When I came back they had disappeared, so I sat down discreetly in the living-room and read a chapter of *Simon Called Peter*—either it was terrible stuff or the whiskey distorted things, because it didn't make any sense to me. [29]

The preparations:

Every Friday five crates of oranges and lemons arrived from a fruiterer in New York—every Monday these same oranges and lemons left his back door in a pyramid of pulpless halves. There was a machine in the kitchen which could extract the juice of two hundred oranges in half an hour if a little button was pressed two hundred times by a butler's thumb.

At least once a fortnight a crop of caterers came down with several hundred feet of canvas and enough colored lights to make a Christmas tree of Gatsby's enormous garden. On buffet tables, garnished with glistening hors d'œuvres, spiced baked hams crowded against salads of harlequin designs and pastry pigs and turkeys bewitched to a dark gold. In the main hall a bar with a real brass rail was set up, and stocked with gins and liquors and with cordials so long forgotten that most of his female guests were too young to know one from another.

By seven o'clock the orchestra has arrived, no thin five-piece affair, but a whole pitful of oboes and trombones and saxophones and viols and cornets and piccolos, and low and high drums. The last swimmers have come in from the beach now and are dressing up-stairs; the cars from New York are parked five deep in the drive, and already the halls and salons and verandas are gaudy with primary colors, and hair shorn in strange new ways, and shawls beyond the dreams of Castile. The bar is in full swing, and floating rounds of cocktails permeate the garden outside, until the air is alive with chatter and laughter, and casual innuendo and introductions forgotten on the spot, and enthusiastic meetings between women who never knew each other's names.

The lights grow brighter as the earth lurches away from the sun, and now the orchestra is playing yellow cocktail music, and the opera of voices pitches a key higher. Laughter is easier minute by minute, spilled with prodigality, tipped out at a cheerful word. The groups change more swiftly, swell with new arrivals, dissolve and form in the same breath; already there are wanderers, confi-dent girls who weave here and there among the stouter and more stable, become for a sharp, joyous moment the center of a group, and then, excited with triumph, glide on through the sea-change of faces and voices and color under the constantly changing light. [39-40]

The high Gothic library:

The bar, where we glanced first, was crowded, but Gatsby was not there. She couldn't find him from the top of the steps, and he wasn't on the veranda. On a chance we tried an important-look-ing door, and walked into a high Gothic library, panelled with carved English oak, and probably transported complete from some ruin overseas.

A stout, middle-aged man, with enormous owl-eyed spectacles, was sitting somewhat drunk on the edge of a great table, staring with unsteady concentration at the shelves of books. As we entered he wheeled excitedly around and examined Jordan from head to foot.

"What do you think?" he demanded impetuously.

"About what?"

He waved his hand toward the book-shelves.

"About that. As a matter of fact you needn't bother to ascer-tain. I ascertained. They're real."

"The books?"

He nodded.

"Absolutely real—have pages and everything. I thought they'd be a nice durable cardboard. Matter of fact, they're absolutely real. Pages and—Here! Lemme show you."

Taking our scepticism for granted, he rushed to the bookcases and returned with Volume One of the "Stoddard Lectures."

"See!" he cried triumphantly. "It's a bona-fide piece of printed matter. It fooled me. This fella's a regular Belasco. It's a triumph. What thoroughness! What realism! Knew when to stop, too— didn't cut the pages. But what do you want? What do you expect?"

He snatched the book from me and replaced it hastily on its shelf, muttering that if one brick was removed the whole library was liable to collapse.

"Who brought you?" he demanded. "Or did you just come? I was brought. Most people were brought."

Jordan looked at him alertly, cheerfully, without answering.

"I was brought by a woman named Roosevelt," he continued. "Mrs. Claude Roosevelt. Do you know her? I met her somewhere last night. I've been drunk for about a week now, and I thought it might sober me up to sit in a library."

"Has it?"

"A little bit, I think. I can't tell yet. I've only been here an hour. Did I tell you about the books? They're real. They're—

"You told us."

We shook hands with him gravely and went back outdoors.
[45-46]

THE NARRATOR AND THE NARRATED: SELECTED QUOTATIONS*

These quotations are designed merely to highlight Carraway's nature and to suggest the problem of his understanding Gatsby. Some aspects of that problem are discussed on pp. 10-11, in the Introduction to this book.

The man of "interior rules":

. . . I'm inclined to reserve all judgments, a habit that has opened up many curious natures to me and also made me the victim of not a few veteran bores. The abnormal mind is quick to detect and attach itself to this quality when it appears in a normal person, and so it came about that in college I was unjustly accused of being a politician, because I was privy to the secret griefs of wild, unknown men. Most of the confidences were unsought— frequently I have feigned sleep, preoccupation, or a hostile levity when I realized by some unmistakable sign that an intimate revelation was quivering on the horizon; for the intimate revelations of young men, or at least the terms in which they express them, are usually plagiaristic and marred by obvious suppressions. Reserv-

* F. Scott Fitzgerald, The Great Gatsby (New York: Charles Scribner's Sons, 1925), pp. 1-2, 64-67, 99-100, 161-63. Copyright 1925 Charles Scribner's Sons; renewal copyright 1953 Frances Scott Fitzgerald Lanahan. Reprinted by permission of the publisher. The Scribner Library Edition of The Great Gatsby is the current source for the passage herein quoted.

ing judgments is a matter of infinite hope. I am still a little afraid of missing something if I forget that, as my father snobbishly suggested, and I snobbishly repeat, a sense of the fundamental decencies is parcelled out unequally at birth.

And, after boasting this way of my tolerance, I come to the admission that it has a limit. Conduct may be founded on the hard rock or the wet marshes, but after a certain point I don't care what it's founded on. When I came back from the East last autumn I felt that I wanted the world to be in uniform and at a sort of moral attention forever; I wanted no more riotous excursions with privileged glimpses into the human heart. Only Gatsby, the man who gives his name to this book, was exempt from my reaction—Gatsby, who represented everything for which I have an unaffected scorn. If personality is an unbroken series of successful gestures, then there was something gorgeous about him, some heightened sensitivity to the promises of life, as if he were related to one of those intricate machines that register earthquakes ten thousand miles away. This responsiveness had nothing to do with that flabby impressionability which is dignified under the name of the "creative temperament"—it was an extraordinary gift for hope, a romantic readiness such as I have never found in any other person and which it is not likely I shall ever find again. No—Gatsby turned out all right at the end; it is what preyed on Gatsby, what foul dust floated in the wake of his dreams that temporarily closed out my interest in the abortive sorrows and short-winded elations of men. [1-2]

The mysterious and legendary Gatsby:

I had talked with him perhaps six times in the past month and found, to my disappointment, that he had little to say. So my first impression, that he was a person of some undefined consequence, had gradually faded and he had become simply the proprietor of an elaborate road-house next door.

And then came that disconcerting ride. We hadn't reached West

Egg Village before Gatsby began leaving his elegant sentences unfinished and slapping himself indecisively on the knee of his caramel-colored suit.

"Look here, old sport," he broke out surprisingly, "what's your opinion of me, anyhow?"

A little overwhelmed, I began the generalized evasions which that question deserves.

"Well, I'm going to tell you something about my life," he interrupted. "I don't want you to get a wrong idea of me from all these stories you hear."

So he was aware of the bizarre accusations that flavored conversation in his halls.

"I'll tell you God's truth." His right hand suddenly ordered divine retribution to stand by. "I am the son of some wealthy people in the Middle West—all dead now. I was brought up in America but educated at Oxford, because all my ancestors have been educated there for many years. It is a family tradition."

He looked at me sideways—and I knew why Jordan Baker had believed he was lying. He hurried the phrase "educated at Oxford," or swallowed it, or choked on it, as though it had bothered him before. And with this doubt, his whole statement fell to pieces, and I wondered if there wasn't something a little sinister about him, after all.

"What part of the Middle West?" I inquired casually.

"San Francisco."

"I see."

"My family all died and I came into a good deal of money."

His voice was solemn, as if the memory of that sudden extinction of a clan still haunted him. For a moment I suspected that he was pulling my leg, but a glance at him convinced me otherwise.

"After that I lived like a young rajah in all the capitals of Europe—Paris, Venice, Rome—collecting jewels, chiefly rubies, hunting big game, painting a little, things for myself only, and trying to forget something very sad that had happened to me long ago."

With an effort I managed to restrain my incredulous laughter. The very phrases were worn so threadbare that they evoked no image except that of a turbaned "character" leaking sawdust at every pore as he pursued a tiger through the Bois de Boulogne.

"Then came the war, old sport. It was a great relief, and I tried very hard to die, but I seemed to bear an enchanted life. I accepted a commission as first lieutenant when it began. In the Argonne Forest I took two machine-gun detachments so far forward that there was a half mile gap on either side of us where the infantry couldn't advance. We stayed there two days and two nights, a hundred and thirty men with sixteen Lewis guns, and when the infantry came up at last they found the insignia of three German divisions among the piles of dead. I was promoted to be a major, and every Allied government gave me a decoration—even Montenegro, little Montenegro down on the Adriatic Sea!"

Little Montenegro! He lifted up the words and nodded at them—with his smile. The smile comprehended Montenegro's troubled history and sympathized with the brave struggles of the Montenegrin people. It appreciated fully the chain of national circumstances which had elicited this tribute from Montenegro's warm little heart. My incredulity was submerged in fascination now; it was like skimming hastily through a dozen magazines.

He reached in his pocket, and a piece of metal, slung on a ribbon, fell into my palm.

"That's the one from Montenegro."

To my astonishment, the thing had an authentic look. "Orderi de Danilo," ran the circular legend, "Montenegro, Nicolas Rex."

"Turn it."

"Major Jay Gatsby," I read, "For Valour Extraordinary."

"Here's another thing I always carry. A souvenir of Oxford

days. It was taken in Trinity Quad—the man on my left is now the Earl of Doncaster."

It was a photograph of half a dozen young men in blazers loafing in an archway through which were visible a host of spires. There was Gatsby, looking a little, not much, younger—with a cricket bat in his hand.

Then it was all true. I saw the skins of tigers flaming in his palace on the Grand Canal; I saw him opening a chest of rubies to ease, with their crimson-lighted depths, the gnawings of his broken heart. [64-67]

The "son of God":

James Gatz who had been loafing along the beach that afternoon in a torn green jersey and a pair of canvas pants, but it was already Jay Gatsby who borrowed a rowboat, pulled out to the *Tuolomee,* and informed Cody that a wind might catch him and break him up in half an hour.

I suppose he'd had the name ready for a long time, even then. His parents were shiftless and unsuccessful farm people—his imagination had never really accepted them as his parents at all. The truth was that Jay Gatsby of West Egg, Long Island, sprang from his Platonic conception of himself. He was a son of God—a phrase which, if it means anything, means just that—and he must be about His Father's business, the service of a vast, vulgar, and meretricious beauty. So he invented just the sort of Jay Gatsby that a seventeen-year-old boy would be likely to invent, and to this conception he was faithful to the end.

For over a year he had been beating his way along the south shore of Lake Superior as a clam-digger and a salmon-fisher or in any other capacity that brought him food and bed. His brown, hardening body lived naturally through the half-fierce, half-lazy work of the bracing days. He knew women early, and since they spoiled him he became contemptuous of them, of young virgins because they were ignorant, of the others because they were hysterical about things which in his overwhelming self-absorption he took for granted.

But his heart was in a constant, turbulent riot. The most grotesque and fantastic conceits haunted him in his bed at night. A universe of ineffable gaudiness spun itself out in his brain while the clock ticked on the washstand and the moon soaked with wet light his tangled clothes upon the floor. Each night he added to the pattern of his fancies until drowsiness closed down upon some vivid scene with an oblivious embrace. For a while these reveries provided an outlet for his imagination; they were a satisfactory hint of the unreality of reality, a promise that the rock of the world was founded securely on a fairy's wing.

An instinct toward his future glory had led him, some months before, to the small Lutheran college of St. Olaf's in southern Minnesota. He stayed there two weeks, dismayed at its ferocious indifference to the drums of his destiny, to destiny itself, and despising the janitor's work with which he was to pay his way through. Then he drifted back to Lake Superior, and he was still searching for something to do on the day that Dan Cody's yacht dropped anchor in the shallows alongshore. [99-100]

The "foul dust":

At two o'clock Gatsby put on his bathing-suit and left word with the butler that if any one phoned word was to be brought to him at the pool. He stopped at the garage for a pneumatic mattress that had amused his guests during the summer, and the chauffeur helped him pump it up. Then he gave instructions that the open car wasn't to be taken out under any circumstances— and this was strange, because the front right fender needed repair.

Gatsby shouldered the mattress and started for the pool. Once he stopped and shifted it a little, and the chauffeur asked him if he needed help, but he shook his head and in a moment disappeared among the yellowing trees.

No telephone message arrived, but the butler went without

his sleep and waited for it until four o'clock—until long after there was any one to give it to if it came. I have an idea that Gatsby himself didn't believe it would come, and perhaps he no longer cared. If that was true he must have felt that he had lost the old warm world, paid a high price for living too long with a single dream. He must have looked up at an unfamiliar sky through frightening leaves and shivered as he found what a grotesque thing a rose is and how raw the sunlight was upon the scarcely created grass. A new world, material without being real, where poor ghosts, breathing dreams like air, drifted fortuitously about . . . like that ashen, fantastic figure gliding toward him through the amorphous trees.

The chauffeur—he was one of Wolfsheim's protégés—heard the shots—afterward he could only say that he hadn't thought anything much about them. I drove from the station directly to Gatsby's house and my rushing anxiously up the front steps was the first thing that alarmed any one. But they knew then, I firmly believe. With scarcely a word said, four of us, the chauffeur, butler, gardener, and I, hurried down to the pool.

There was a faint, barely perceptible movement of the water as the fresh flow from one end urged its way toward the drain at the other. With little ripples that were hardly the shadows of waves, the laden mattress moved irregularly down the pool. A small gust of wind that scarcely corrugated the surface was enough to disturb its accidental course with its accidental burden. The touch of a cluster of leaves revolved it slowly, tracing, like the leg of transit, a thin red circle in the water.

It was after we started with Gatsby toward the house that the gardener saw Wilson's body a little way off in the grass, and the holocaust was complete. [161-163]

BEYOND WEST EGG: THE END OF
*THE GREAT GATSBY**

The concluding paragraphs of the novel suggest two principal extensions of the events on Long Island, July of 1922: one is the fact that the characters "were all Westerners," which makes the problem especially acute of suggesting that Gatsby is a novel that poses a Midwestern point of view against the East; the other is the association of Gatsby's "dream" with American history and with the "American promise." Both of these are discussed above, in the Introduction.

How it looked from the Midwest:

That's my Middle West—not the wheat or the prairies or the lost Swede towns, but the thrilling returning trains of my youth, and the street lamps and sleigh bells in the frosty dark and the shadows of holly wreaths thrown by lighted windows on the snow. I am part of that, a little solemn with the feel of those long winters, a little complacent from growing up in the Carraway house in a city where dwellings are still called through decades by a family's name. I see now that this has been a story of the

* F. Scott Fitzgerald, The Great Gatsby (New York: Charles Scribner's Sons, 1925), pp. 177-78, 181-82. Copyright 1925 Charles Scribner's Sons; renewal copyright 1953 Frances Scott Fitzgerald Lanahan. Reprinted by permission of the publisher. The Scribner Library Edition of The Great Gatsby is the current source for the passage herein quoted.

West, after all—Tom and Gatsby, Daisy and Jordan and I, were all Westerners, and perhaps we possessed some deficiency in common which made us subtly unadaptable to Eastern life.

Even when the East excited me most, even when I was most keenly aware of its superiority to the bored, sprawling, swollen towns beyond the Ohio, with their interminable inquisitions which spared only the children and the very old—even then it had always for me a quality of distortion. West Egg, especially, still figures in my more fantastic dreams. I see it as a night scene by El Greco: a hundred houses, at once conventional and grotesque, crouching under a sullen, overhanging sky and a lustreless moon. In the foreground four solemn men in dress suits are walking along the sidewalk with a stretcher on which lies a drunken woman in a white evening dress. Her hand, which dangles over the side, sparkles cold with jewels. Gravely the men turn in at a house— the wrong house. But no one knows the woman's name, and no one cares.

After Gatsby's death the East was haunted for me like that, distorted beyond my eyes' power of correction. So when the blue smoke of brittle leaves was in the air and the wind blew the wet laundry stiff on the line I decided to come back home. [177-178]

The green world and the green light:

On the last night, with my trunk packed and my car sold to the grocer, I went over and looked at that huge incoherent failure of a house once more. On the white steps an obscene word, scrawled by some boy with a piece of brick, stood out clearly in the moonlight, and I erased it, drawing my shoe raspingly along the stone. Then I wandered down to the beach and sprawled out on the sand.

Most of the big shore places were closed now and there were hardly any lights except the shadowy, moving glow of a ferryboat across the Sound. And as the moon rose higher the inessential houses began to melt away until gradually I became aware of the old island here that flowered once for Dutch sailors' eyes—a fresh, green breast of the new world. Its vanished trees, the trees that had made way for Gatsby's house, had once pandered in whispers to the last and greatest of all human dreams; for a transitory enchanted moment man must have held his breath in the presence of this continent, compelled into an æsthetic contemplation he neither understood nor desired, face to face for the last time in history with something commensurate to his capacity for wonder.

And as I sat there brooding on the old, unknown world, I thought of Gatsby's wonder when he first picked out the green light at the end of Daisy's dock. He had come a long way to this blue lawn, and his dream must have seemed so close that he could hardly fail to grasp it. He did not know that it was already behind him, somewhere back in that vast obscurity beyond the city, where the dark fields of the republic rolled on under the night.

Gatsby believed in the green light, the orgiastic future that year by year recedes before us. It eluded us then, but that's no matter—tomorrow we will run faster, stretch out our arms farther. . . . And one fine morning—

So we beat on, boats against the current, borne back ceaselessly into the past. [181-182]

The permanence of THE GREAT GATSBY

part *4*

AFTER THE first glow of reviews and complimentary letters, Fitzgerald saw The Great Gatsby become an established, successful novel, more in his lifetime a succès d'estime than a popular novel, though it has since become both. Critical issues about which discussions of it have revolved include these: the strategy of Carraway as a "modified first-person narrator"; the suitability of Carraway as judge of the "Egg" world; the significance of the novel's parallels with contemporary visions of the world, notably Eliot's The Waste Land; the novel as a criticism of American society and its history.

The first two of the essays included here (they are arranged in order of dates of publication) are concerned with the general area of Fitzgerald's work and his literary consciousness. The others treat directly with The Great Gatsby, with some excursions into critical generality.

THE MORAL OF SCOTT FITZGERALD*

Glenway Wescott

This article was originally published in the New Republic of February 17, 1941, a few weeks after Fitzgerald's death in December, 1940.

F. Scott Fitzgerald is dead, aged forty-four. *Requiescat in pace; ora pro nobis.* In the twenties, his heyday, he was a kind of king of our American youth; and as the news of his end appeared in the papers there were strange coincidences along with it. A number of others—a younger writer who was somewhat of his school and, like him, had committed his talent unfortunately to Hollywood, and that writer's pretty, whimsical wife, and another young woman who was a famous horse-trainer, and the young leader of a popular jazz-band—also met sudden deaths that week. I was reminded of the holocausts by which primitive rulers were provided with an escort, servants and pretty women and boon companions, for eternity. The twenties were heaven, so to speak, often enough; might not heaven be like the twenties? If it were, in one or two particulars, Scott Fitzgerald would be sorry; sorry once more.

His health failed, and with a peculiar darkness and dead-weight

* Glenway Wescott, "The Moral of Scott Fitzgerald," The Crack-Up, ed. Edmund Wilson (New York: New Directions, 1945), pp. 323-37. Reprinted by permission of the author.

in mind and heart, some five years ago. Then in a wonderful
essay entitled *The Crack-Up* he took stock of himself, looking
twenty years back for what flaws were in him or in the day and age,
what early damage had been done, and how. Thanks to that, one
can speak of his weaknesses without benefit of gossip, without
impertinence. And so I do, asking for charity toward him and
clarity about him; and a little on my own mortal account; and
for certain innocent immature American writers' benefit.

My theme is as usual personality rather than esthetics; but my
sentiment on this occasion is not personal. Aside from our Midwestern birth and years of foreign residence, you could scarcely
find two men of the same generation less alike than we two.
Neither our virtues nor our vices appeared to overlap at all. I did
not have the honor of his particular friendship. I have only one
vivid memory of conversation with him, which was on a Mediterranean beach. Across the Bay of Angels and over the big good-
for-nothing city of Nice, some of the Alps hung in the air as pearly
as onions; and that air and that sea, which has only delicate tides,
quivered with warm weather. It was before the publication of *The
Sun Also Rises*, the summer of 1925 or 1926, and Hemingway was
what he wanted to talk to me about. He came abruptly and drew
me a little apart from our friends and relations, into the shade
of a rock.

Hemingway had published some short stories in the dinky
de-luxe way in Paris; and I along with all the literary set had discovered him, which was fun; and when we returned to New York
we preached the new style and peculiar feeling of his fiction as
if it were evangel. Still, that was too slow a start of a great
career to suit Fitzgerald. Obviously Ernest was the one true genius
of our decade, he said; and yet he was neglected and misunderstood and, above all, insufficiently remunerated. He thought I
would agree that *The Apple of the Eye* and *The Great Gatsby*
were rather inflated market values just then. What could I do to
help launch Hemingway? Why didn't I write a laudatory essay

on him? With this questioning, Fitzgerald now and then impatiently grasped and shook my elbow.

There was something more than ordinary art-admiration about it, but on the other hand it was no mere matter of affection for Hemingway; it was so bold, unabashed, lacking in sense of humor. I have a sharp tongue and my acquaintances often underestimate my good nature; so I was touched and flattered by Fitzgerald's taking so much for granted. It simply had not occurred to him that unfriendliness or pettiness on my part might inhibit my enthusiasm about the art of a new colleague and rival. As a matter of fact, my enthusiasm was not on a par with his; and looking back now, I am glad for my sake that it was not. He not only said but, I believe, honestly felt that Hemingway was inimitably, essentially superior. From the moment Hemingway began to appear in print, perhaps it did not matter what he himself produced or failed to produce. He felt free to write just for profit, and to live for fun, if possible. Hemingway could be entrusted with the graver responsibilities and higher rewards such as glory, immortality. This extreme of admiration—this excuse for a morbid belittlement and abandonment of himself—was bad for Fitzgerald, I imagine. At all events he soon began to waste his energy in various hack-writing.

I was told last year that another talented contemporary of ours had grown so modest in the wage-earning way, fallen so far from his youthful triumph, that he would sign a friend's stories and split the payment. Under the friend's name it would have been hundreds of dollars, and under his, a thousand or thousands. Perhaps this was not true gossip, but it is a good little exemplary tale, and of general application. It gives me goose-flesh. A signature which has been so humiliated is apt never to be the same again, in the signer's own estimation. As a rule the delicate literary brain, the aching creative heart, cannot stand that sort of thing. It is better for a writer even to fancy himself a Messiah, against the day when writing or life goes badly. And there is more to this than the matter of esthetic integrity. For if his opinion of himself is divided by disrespect—sheepish, shameful, cynical—he usually finds his earning capacity as well as his satisfaction falling off. The vast public, which appears to have no taste, somehow senses when it is being scornfully talked down to. The great hacks are innocent, and serenely class themselves with Tolstoy and Dickens. Their getting good enough to compare with P. G. Wodehouse or Zane Grey may depend upon that benign misapprehension.

Probably Fitzgerald never fell into any abuse of his reputation as unwise and unwholesome as the above-mentioned confrères. His standard of living did seem to the rest of us high. Publishers in the twenties made immense advances to novelists who had and could lend prestige; and when in the thirties Fitzgerald's popularity lapsed, movies had begun to be talkies, which opened up a new lucrative field of literary operation. Certainly he did write too much in recent years with his tongue in his cheek; his heart in his boots if not in his pocket. And it was his opinion in 1936 that the competition and popular appeal of the films—"a more glittering, a grosser power," as he put it—had made the God-given form of the novel archaic; a wrong thought indeed for a novelist.

This is not the ideal moment to reread and appraise his collectable works. With the mind at a loss, muffled like a drum— the ego a little inflamed as it always is by presentness of death— we may exaggerate their merit or their shortcomings. I remember thinking, when the early best sellers were published, that his style was a little too free and easy; but I was a fussy stylist in those days. His phrasing was almost always animated and charming; his diction excellent. He wrote very little in slang or what I call baby-talk: the pitfall of many who specialized in American contemporaneity after him. But for other reasons—obscurity of sentiment, facetiousness—a large part of his work may not endure, as readable reading matter for art's sake. It will be precious as documentary evidence, instructive example. That is not, in the way of immortality, what the writer hopes; but it is much more than most writers of fiction achieve.

This Side of Paradise haunted the decade like a song, popular but perfect. It hung over an entire youth-movement like a banner, somewhat discolored and wind-worn now; the wind has lapsed out of it. But a book which college boys really read is a rare thing, not to be dismissed idly or in a moment of severe sophistication. Then there were dozens of stories, some delicate and some slapdash; one very odd, entitled *Head and Shoulders*. I love *The Great Gatsby*. Its very timeliness, as of 1925, gave it a touch of the old-fashioned a few years later; but I have reread it this week and found it all right; pleasure and compassion on every page. A masterpiece often seems a period-piece for a while; then comes down out of the attic, to function anew and to last. There is a great deal to be said for and against his final novel, *Tender Is the Night*. On the whole I am warmly for it. To be sane or insane is a noble issue, and very few novels take what might be called an intelligent interest in it; this does, and gives a fair picture of the entertaining expatriate habit of life besides.

In 1936, in three issues of *Esquire*, he published the autobiographical essay, *The Crack-Up*, as it were swan-song. I first read it at my barber's, which, I suppose, is according to the editorial devices of that magazine, a medium of advertising for men's ready-made clothing. There is very little in world literature like this piece: Max Jacob's *Defense de Tartuffe*; the confidential chapter of *The Seven Pillars of Wisdom*, perhaps; Sir Walter Raleigh's verse-epistle before his beheading, in a way. Fitzgerald's theme seems more dreadful, plain petty stroke by stroke; and of course his treatment lacks the good grace and firmness of the old and old-style authors. Indeed it is cheap here and there, but in embarrassment rather than in crudity or lack of courage. Or perhaps Fitzgerald as he wrote was too sensitive to what was to appear along with it in the magazine: the jokes, the Petty girls, the haberdashery. He always suffered from an extreme environmental sense. Still it is fine prose and naturally his timeliest piece today: self-autopsy and funeral sermon. It also, with an innocent air, gravely indicts our native idealism in some respects, our common code, our college education.

And in general—for ailing civilization as well as one dead Fitzgerald—this is a day of wrath.

   He had made a great recovery from a seemingly mortal physical
illness; then found everything dead or deadish in his psyche, his
thought all broken, and no appetite for anything on earth. It was
not from alcohol, he said, evidently proud of the fact that he had
not had any for six months, not even beer. We may be a little
doubtful of this protestation; for protestation indeed is a kind of
sub-habit of the alcoholic. Six months is no time at all, in terms of
the things that kill us. Alcohol in fact never exclusively causes anything. Only, just as it will heighten a happy experience, it will
deepen a rut or a pit, in the way of fatigue chiefly. Who cares,
when a dear one is dying of a chest-cold or an embolism, whether
he is a drunkard or a reformed ex-drunkard?—Yes, I know, the
dying one himself cares! But when Fitzgerald wrote his essay he
still had five years to live, quite a long time. It was not about ill
health, and of course he was as sane as an angel. His trouble just
then and his subject was only his lassitude of imagination; his
nauseated spirit; that self-hypnotic state of not having any will-
power; and nothing left of the intellect but inward observation and
dislike. Why, he cried, why was I "identified with the objects of
my horror and compassion"? He said it was the result of "too much
anger and too many tears." That was his snap-judgment; blunt
sentimentality of a boy or ex-boy. But since he was a story-teller
above all, he did not stop at that; he proceeded to tell things about
the past in which the mystery showed extraordinarily.

   The Crack-Up has never been issued in book form; and perhaps
because the pretty pictures in Esquire are so exciting to thumb-tack
up on the wall, back numbers of it are not easy to come by. So I
am tempted to try to summarize it all; but no, it must be published.
Especially the first half is written without a fault: brief easy fiery
phrases—the thinking that he compared to a "moving about of
great secret trunks," and "the heady villainous feeling"—one quick
and thorough paragraph after another, with so little shame and so

little emphasis that I have wondered if he himself knew how much he was confessing.

He still regretted his bad luck in not getting abroad into the trenches as an army officer in 1918, and even his failure at football in 1913 or 1914. On certain of those unlucky days of his youth he felt as badly as in 1936, and badly in the same way; he makes a point of the similarity. Perhaps the worst of the early crises came in his junior year, when he lost the presidency of one of the Princeton clubs. Immediately afterward, as an act of desperation and consolation, he made love for the first time; and also that year, not until then, he turned to literary art, as the best of a bad bargain. Ominous! Fantastic, too, that a man who is dying or at least done with living—one who has had practically all that the world affords, fame and prosperity, work and play, love and friendship, and lost practically all—should still think seriously of so much fiddledeedee of boyhood! Very noble convictions underlay Fitzgerald's entire life, and he explains them nobly. But when he comes to the disillusionment, that too is couched in alumnal imagery; it is along with "the shoulder-pads worn for one day on the Princeton freshman football field and the overseas cap never worn overseas" that his ideals are relegated to the junk-heap, he says. It is strange and baroque; like those large bunches of battle-trappings which appear decoratively in seventeenth-century architecture, empty helmets and empty cuirasses and firearms laid crossways, sculptured up on the lintels of barracks and on the lids of tombs. Those condemned old European societies which have been too much militarized, too concerned with glory and glorious death, scarcely seem more bizarre than this: a kind of national consciousness revolving to the bitter end around college; and the latter also seems a precarious basis for a nation.

Aside from his literary talent—literary genius, self-taught—I think Fitzgerald must have been the worst educated man in the world. He never knew his own strength; therefore nothing inspired him very definitely to conserve or budget it. When he was a freshman, did the seniors teach him a manly technique of drinking, with the price and penalty of the several degrees of excess of it? If they had, it might never have excited him as a vague, fatal moral issue. The rest of us, his writing friends and rivals, thought that he had the best narrative gift of the century. Did the English department at Princeton try to develop his admiration of that fact about himself, and make him feel the burden and the pleasure of it? Apparently they taught him rather to appreciate this or that other writer, to his own disfavor. Did any worldly-wise critic ever remind him that beyond a certain point, writing for profit becomes unprofitable; bad business as well as bad art? Another thing: my impression is that only as he wrote, or just before writing, *Tender Is the Night*, did he discover certain causes and gradations of mental illness which, nowadays, every boy ought to be taught as soon as he has mastered the other facts of life.

Even the army failed to inculcate upon Lieutenant Fitzgerald one principle that a good army man must accept: heroism is a secondary virtue in an army. Lieutenant Fitzgerald had no business pining for the front-line trenches in advance of his superior officers' decision that it was the place for him. The point of soldiering is to kill; not a mere willingness to be killed. This seems important today, as we prepare again for perhaps necessary war, and again too much is made of the spirit of self-sacrifice and embattlement of ideals; and not enough of the mere means of victory. And with reference to literature, too, as Fitzgerald drops out of our insufficient little regiment, we writers particularly blame him for that all-out idealism of his. No matter what he died for—if he died *for* anything—it was in too great a hurry; it was not worth it at his age.

In several of the obituary notices of Fitzgerald I detect one little line of mistaken moralizing, which I think is not uncommon; and his example and his fiction may have done something to propagate it. They seem to associate all rebellious morality somehow with a state of poor health. This is an unfair attack, and on the other hand a too easy alibi. Bad behavior is not always a feeble, pitiful, fateful thing. Malice of mind, strange style, offensive subject matter, do not always derive from morbid psyche or delicate physique. Wickedness is not necessarily weakness; and *vice versa*. For there is will-power in humanity. Its genuine manifestation is only in the long run; but, with knowledge, it can have the last word. Modern psychology does not deny it. Whether one is a moralist or an immoralist—a vengeful daily preacher like Mr. Westbrook Pegler, or an occasional devil's advocate like myself, or the quietest citizen—these little distinctions ought to be kept clear.

Fitzgerald was weak; we have the proof of it now in his demise. Fitzgerald, the outstanding aggressor in the little warfare which divided our middle classes in the twenties—warfare of moral emancipation against moral conceit, flaming youth against old guard—definitely has let his side down. The champion is as dead as a doornail. Self-congratulatory moral persons may crow over him if they wish.

There is bound to be a slight anger at his graveside; curse-words amid our written or spoken obsequies. The whole school of writers who went to France has been a bit maligned while the proletarian novelists and the politico-critics have enjoyed the general applause. Some of us are reckless talkers, and no doubt we have maligned each other and each himself as well. It was the beautiful, talented Miss Stein in her Paris salon who first called us "the lost generation." It was Hemingway who took up the theme and made it a popular refrain. The twenties were in fact a time of great prosperity and liberty, a spendthrift and footloose time; and especially in France you got your American money's worth of everything if you were clever. Still I doubt whether, in dissipation and unruly emotion, we strayed much farther out of the way than young Americans ordinarily do, at home as abroad. I think we were somewhat extraordinarily inclined to make youthful rebelliousness, imprudent pursuit of pleasure or ambition, a little easier for our young brothers. Heaven knows how it will be for our sons.

In any case, time is the real moralist; and a great many of the so-called lost are still at hand, active and indeed conspicuous: Bishop and Hemingway and Bromfield and Cummings and V. Thomson and Tate, Gordon and Porter and Flanner and others, the U. S. A.'s odd foreign legion. We were a band of toughs in fact, indestructible, which perhaps is the best thing to be said for us at this point. For the next step is to age well. Relatively speaking, I think we are aging well; giving evidence of toughness in the favorable sense as well: tenacity and hardiness, and a kind of worldly wisdom that does not have to change its platform very often, and skepticism mixed in with our courage to temper it and make it last. Sometimes we are still spoken of as the young or youngish or "younger" writers, but there can be no sense in that, except by lack of competition; every last one of us is forty. That is the right age to give advice to the immature and potential literary generation. For their sake, lest they feel unable to take our word for things, it seems worth while to protest against the strange bad name we have had.

In any case we are the ones who know about Fitzgerald. He was our darling, our genius, our fool. Let the young people consider his untypical case with admiration but great caution; with qualms and a respect for fate, without fatalism. He was young to the bitter end. He lived and he wrote at last like a scapegoat, and now has departed like one. As you might say, he was Gatsby, a greater Gatsby. Why not? Flaubert said, "*Madame Bovary, c'est moi!*" On the day before Christmas, in a sensible bitter obituary, *The New York Times* quoted a paragraph from *The Crack-Up* in which the deceased likened himself to a plate. "Sometimes, though, the cracked plate has to be kept in service as a household necessity. It can never be warmed up on the stove nor shuffled with the other plates in the dishpan; it will not be brought out for company but it will do to hold crackers late at night or to go into the ice-box with the left-overs." A deadly little prose-poem! No doubt the ideals Fitzgerald acquired in college and in the army—and put to

the test on Long Island and in the Alpes-Maritimes and in Hollywood—always were a bit second-hand, fissured, cracked, if you like.
But how faithfully he reported both idealization and ordeal; and
how his light smooth earthenware style dignifies it!

The style in which others have written of him is different. On
the day after Christmas, in his popular column in *The New York
World-Telegram*, Mr. Westbrook Pegler remarked that his death
"recalls memories of a queer bunch of undisciplined and self-
indulgent brats who were determined not to pull their weight in the
boat and wanted the world to drop everything and sit down and
bawl with them. A kick in the pants and a clout over the scalp
were more like their needing. . . ." With a kind of expert politeness
throughout this *in memoriam*, Mr. Pegler avoids commenting upon
the dead man himself exactly. His complaint is of anonymous
persons: the company Fitzgerald kept, readers who let themselves
be influenced by him, and his heroes and heroines: "Sensitive
young things about whom he wrote and with whom he ran to
fires not only because he could exploit them for profit in print but
because he found them congenial. . . ." I suppose Mr. Pegler's
column is profitable too; and if I were doing it I should feel easier
in my mind, surer of my aim, if I knew and liked my exploitees.
Joking aside, certainly this opinion of his does not correspond in
the least to my memory of the gay twenties. Certainly if sensitive
young men and women of the thirties believe Pegler, they will not
admire Fitzgerald or like the rest of us much.

Too bad; there should be peace between the generations now,
at least among the literary. Popularity or no popularity, we have
none too many helpful friends; and in a time of world war there
may be panic and conservatism and absent-mindedness and neglect
of literature in general, and those slight acts of obscure vengeance
so easy to commit when fellow citizens have begun to fear and
imagine and act as a mass. There should not be any quarrel between literature and journalism either. Modernly conceived and well
done—literary men sticking to the truth and newspapermen using

imagination—they relate to each other very closely, and may sustain and inspire each other back and forth. In a time of solemn subject matter it is more and more needful that they should.

In any case Mr. Pegler's decade is out as well as ours; the rude hard-working thirties as well as the wild twenties. The forties have come. Those of us who have been youthful too long—which, I suppose, is the real point of his criticism—now certainly realize our middle age; no more time to make ready or dawdle, nor energy to waste. That is one universal effect of war on the imagination: time, as a moral factor, instantly changes expression and changes pace. Everyman suddenly has a vision of sudden death.

What is the difference, from the universal angle? Everyone has to die once; no one has to die twice. But now that mortality has become the world's worst worry once more, there is less sophistication of it. Plain as day we see that the bull in the arena is no more fated than the steer in the slaughterhouse. The glamorous gangster's cadaver with bellyful of bullets is no deader than the commonplace little chap overcome by pernicious anemia. Napoleon III at the battle of Sedan, the other battle of Sedan, rouged his cheeks in order not to communicate his illness and fright to his desperate army. An unemployed young actor, a friend of a friend of mine, lately earned a living for a while by rouging cheeks of well-off corpses at a smart mortician's. All this equally—and infinitude of other things under the sun—is jurisdiction of death. The difference between a beautiful death and an ugly death is in the eye of the beholder, the heart of the mourner, the brain of the survivor.

The fact of Scott Fitzgerald's end is as bad and deplorable as could be; but the moral of it is good enough, and warlike. It is to enliven the rest of the regiment. Mere tightening the belt, stiffening the upper lip, is not all I mean; nor the simple delight of being alive still, the dance on the grave, the dance between holocausts. As we have it—documented and prophesied by his best work, commented upon in the newspaper with other news of the day—it is a deep breath of knowledge, fresh air, and an incitement to particular literary virtues.

For the private life and the public life, literary life and real life, if you view them in this light of death—and now we have it also boding on all the horizon, like fire—are one and the same. Which brings up another point of literary criticism; then I have done. The great thing about Fitzgerald was his candor; verbal courage; simplicity. One little man with eyes really witnessing; objective in all he uttered, even about himself in a subjective slump; arrogant in just one connection, for one purpose only, to make his meaning clear. The thing, I think, that a number of recent critics have most disliked about him is his confessional way, the personal tone, the *tête-à-tête* or man-to-man style, first person singular. He remarked it himself in *The Crack-Up*: "There are always those to whom all self-revelation is contemptible."

I on the other hand feel a real approval and emulation of just that; and I recommend that all our writers give it serious considera-tion. It might be the next esthetic issue and new mode of Ameri-can letters. It is American enough; our greatest fellows, such as Franklin and Audubon and Thoreau and Whitman, were self-expressers in so far as they knew themselves. This is a time of greater knowledge, otherwise worse; an era which has as many evil earmarks as, for example, the Renaissance: awful political genius running amok and clashing, migrations, races whipped together as it were by a titanic egg-beater, impatient sexuality and love of stimulants and cruelty, sacks, burnings and plagues. Fine things eventually may be achieved amid all this, as in that other century. I suggest revelation of man as he appears to himself in his mirror —not as he poses or wishes or idealizes—as one thing to try a re-vival of, this time. Naked truth about man's nature in unmistak-able English.

In the Renaissance they had anatomy: Vesalius in Paris at mid-night under the gallows-tree, bitten by the dogs as he disputed with them the hanged cadavers which they wanted to eat and he wanted to cut up. They had anatomy and we have psychology. The throws of dice in our world—at least the several dead-weights with which the dice appear to be loaded against us—are moral matters; and no one ever learns much about all that except in his own person, at any rate in private. In public, in the nation and the inter-nation and the anti-nation, one just suffers the weight of the morality of others like a dumb brute. This has been a dishonest century above all: literature lagging as far behind modern habits as behind modern history; democratic statesmanship all vitiated by good form, understatement, optimism; and the nations which could not afford democracy, finally developing their supremacy all on a basis of the deliberate lie. And now is the end, or another beginning.

Writers in this country still can give their little examples of truth-telling; little exercises for their fellow citizens, to develop their ability to distinguish truth from untruth in other connections when it really is important. The importance arises as desperately in the public interest as in private life. Even light fiction can help a society get together and agree upon its vocabulary; little strokes of the tuning-fork, for harmony's sake. And for clarity's sake, let us often use, and sanction the use of, words of one syllable. The shortest and most potent is the personal pronoun: I. The sanctified priest knows that, he says *credo*; and the trustworthy physician only gives his opinion, not a panacea. The witness in the courtroom does not indulge in the editorial we; the judge and the lawyers will not allow it; and indeed, if the case is important, if there is life or liberty or even a large amount of money at stake, not even supposition or hearsay is admitted as evidence. Our worldwide case is important.

Not only is Anglo-Saxondom all at war with the rest of the world in defense of its accustomed power and prosperity, and of the luxuries of the spirit such as free speech, free publication, free faith—for the time being, the United States is the likeliest place for the preservation of the Mediterranean and French ideal of fine art and writing: which puts a new, peculiar obligation upon us ex-expatriates. The land of the free should become and is becoming a city of refuge; but there is cultural peril even in that. France has merely committed her tradition to our keeping, by default;

whereas Germany has exiled to us her most important professors and brilliant writers. Perhaps the latter are bound to introduce into our current literature a little of that mystically philosophic, obscurely scientific mode which somewhat misled or betrayed them as a nation. Therefore we must keep up more strictly and energetically than ever, our native specific skeptical habit of mind; our plainer and therefore safer style.

In any consideration of the gravity of the work of art and letters—and upon any solemn occasion such as the death of a good writer like Scott Fitzgerald—I think of Faust, and that labor he dreamed of when he was blind and dying, keeping the devil waiting. It was the drainage of a stinking sea-marsh and the construction of a strong dyke. Fresh fields amid the eternally besieging sea: room for a million men to live, not in security—Goethe expressly ruled out that hope of which we moderns have been too fond— but free to do the best they could for themselves. Does it seem absurd to compare a deceased best seller with that mythic man: former wholesome Germany's demigod? There must always be some pretentiousness about literature, or else no one would take its pains or endure its disappointments. Throughout this article I have mixed bathos with pathos, joking with tenderness, in order to venture here and there a higher claim for literary art than is customary now. I am in dead earnest. Bad writing is in fact a rank feverish unnecessary slough. Good writing is a dyke, in which there is a leak for every one of our weary hands. And honestly I do see the very devil standing worldwide in the decade to come, bound to get some of us. I realize that I have given an exaggerated impression of Fitzgerald's tragedy in recent years: all the above is based on his confession of 1936, and he was not so nearly finished as he thought. But fear of death is one prophecy that never fails; and now his strength is only in print, and his weakness of no account, except for our instruction.

SCOTT FITZGERALD—THE AUTHORITY
OF FAILURE*

William Troy

Of course, in any absolute sense, Scott Fitzgerald was not a failure at all; he has left one short novel, passages in several others, and a handful of short stories which stand as much chance of survival as anything of their kind produced in this country during the same period. If the tag is so often attached to his name, it has been largely his own fault. It is true that he was the victim, among a great number of other influences in American life, of that paralyzing high-pressure by which the conscientious American writer is hastened to premature extinction as artist or as man. Upon the appearance of *The Crack-Up*, a selection by Edmund Wilson of Fitzgerald's letters, notebooks and fugitive pieces, it was notable that all the emptiest and most venal elements in New York journalism united to crow amiably about his literary corpse to this same tune of insufficient production. Actually their reproaches betrayed more of their own failure to estimate what was good and enduring in his writing than his acknowledgeable limitations as an artist. If Fitzgerald had turned out as much as X or Y or Z, he would have been a different kind of writer—undoubtedly more

* William Troy, "Scott Fitzgerald—the Authority of Failure," Accent, VI (Autumn, 1945), 56-60. Reprinted by permission of the Estate of William Troy.

admirable from the standpoint of the quasi-moral American *ethos* of production at any cost, but possibly less worth talking about five years after his death. And it might be said that Fitzgerald never hovered so close to real failure as when he listened from time to time, with too willing an ear, to these same reproaches.

But Fitzgerald brought most of it on himself by daring to make failure the consistent theme of his work from first to last. (Similarly Virginia Woolf used to be accused by the reviewers of being a sterile writer because she made sterility her principal theme.) It is perhaps only adumbrated in *This Side of Paradise*; for the discovery of its hero Amory Blaine that the world is not altogether his oyster is hardly the stuff of high tragedy. The book is interesting today as a document of the early Twenties; nobody who would know what it was like to be young and privileged and self-centered in that bizarre epoch can afford to neglect it. But it can also be read as a preliminary study in the kind of tortured narcissism that was to plague its author to the end of his days. (See the article called "Early Success" in the Wilson collection.) *The Beautiful and Damned* is a more frayed and pretentious museum-piece, and the muddiest in conception of all the longer books. It is not so much a study in failure as in the *atmosphere* of failure—that is to say, of a world in which no moral decisions can be made because there are no values in terms of which they may be measured. Hardly is it a world suited to the purposes of the novelist, and the characters float around in it as in some aquamarine region comfortably shot through with the soft colors of self-pity and romantic irony. Not until *The Great Gatsby* did Fitzgerald hit upon something like Mr. Eliot's "objective correlative" for the intermingled feeling of personal insufficiency and disillusionment with the world out of which he had unsuccessfully tried to write a novel.

Here is a remarkable instance of the manner in which adoption of a special form or technique can profoundly modify and define a writer's whole attitude toward his world. In the earlier books author and hero tended to melt into one because there was no internal principle of differentiation by which they might be separated; they respired in the same climate, emotional and moral; they were tarred with the same brush. But in *Gatsby* is achieved a dissociation, by which Fitzgerald was able to isolate one part of himself, the spectatorial or aesthetic, and also the more intelligent and responsible, in the person of the ordinary but quite sensible narrator, from another part of himself, the dream-ridden romantic adolescent from St. Paul and Princeton, in the person of the legendary Jay Gatsby. It is this which makes the latter one of the few truly mythological creations in our recent literature—for what is mythology but this same process of projected wish-fulfillment carried out on a larger scale and by the whole consciousness of a race? Indeed, before we are quite through with him, Gatsby becomes much more than a mere exorcizing of whatever false elements of the American dream Fitzgerald felt within himself: he becomes a symbol of America itself, dedicated to "the service of a vast, vulgar and meretricious beauty."

Not mythology, however, but a technical device which had been brought to high development by James and Conrad before him, made this dissociation possible for Fitzgerald. The device of the intelligent but sympathetic observer situated at the center of the tale, as James never ceases to demonstrate in the Prefaces, makes for some of the most priceless values in fiction—economy, suspense, intensity. And these values *The Great Gatsby* possesses to a rare degree. But the same device imposes on the novelist the necessity of tracing through in the observer or narrator himself some sort of growth in general moral perception, which will constitute in effect *his* story. Here, for example, insofar as the book is Gatsby's story it is a story of failure—the prolongation of the adolescent incapacity to distinguish between dream and reality, between the terms demanded of life and the terms offered. But insofar as it is the narrator's story it is a successful transcendence of a particularly bitter and harrowing set of experiences, localized in the sinister, distorted, El Greco-like Long Island atmosphere of the later 'Twenties, into a world of restored sanity and calm, symbolized by the bracing winter nights of the Middle Western prairies. "Conduct may be founded on the hard rock or the wet marshes," he writes, "but after a certain point I don't care what it's founded on. When I came back from the East last autumn I felt that I wanted the world to be in uniform and at a sort of moral attention forever; I wanted no more riotous excursions with privileged glimpses into the human heart ever recurring." By reason of its enforced perspective the book takes on the pattern and the meaning of a Grail-romance—or of the initiation ritual on which it is based. Perhaps this will seem a far-fetched suggestion to make about a work so obviously modern in every respect; and it is unlikely that Fitzgerald had any such model in mind. But like *Billy Budd*, *The Red Badge of Courage*, or *A Lost Lady*—to mention only a few American stories of similar length with which it may be compared—it is a record of the strenuous passage from deluded youth to maturity.

Never again was Fitzgerald to repeat the performance. *Tender Is the Night* promises much in the way of scope but it soon turns out to be a backsliding into the old ambiguities. Love and money, fame and youth, youth and money—however one shuffles the antitheses they have a habit of melting into each other like the blue Mediterranean sky and sea of the opening background. To Dick Diver, with a mere change of pronoun, may be applied Flaubert's analysis of Emma Bovary: "*Elle confondait, dans son désir, les sensualités du luxe avec les joies du coeur, l'élégance des habitudes et les délicatesses du sentiment.*" And it is this Bovaryism on the part of the hero, who as a psychiatrist should conceivably know more about himself, which in rendering his character so suspect prevents his meticulously graded deterioration from assuming any real significance. Moreover, there is an ambiguous treatment of the problem of guilt. We are never certain whether Diver's predicament is the result of his own weak judgment or of the behavior of his neurotic wife. At the end we are strangely unmoved by his down-fall because it has been less a tragedy of will than of circumstance.

Of *The Last Tycoon* we have only the unrevised hundred and thirty-three pages, supported by a loose collection of notes and synopses. In an unguarded admission Fitzgerald describes the book as "an escape into a lavish, romantic past that perhaps will not come again into our time." Its hero, suggested by a well-known Hollywood prodigy of a few years ago, is another one of those poor boys betrayed by "a heightened sensitivity to the promises of life." When we first meet him he is already a sick and disillusioned man, clutching for survival at what is advertised in the notes as "an immediate, dynamic, unusual, physical love affair." This is nothing less than "the meat of the book." But as much of it as is rendered includes some of the most unfortunate writing which Fitzgerald has left; he had never been at his best in the approach to the physical. Nor is it clear in what way the affair is related to the other last febrile gesture of Stahr—his championship of the Hollywood underdog in a struggle with the racketeers and big producers. Fortuitously the sense of social guilt of the mid-Thirties creeps into the fugue, although in truth this had been a strong undertone in early short-stories like "May Day" and "The Rich Boy." It is evident that Stahr is supposed to be some kind of symbol— but of what it would be hard to determine. From the synopses he is more like a receptacle for all the more familiar contradictions of his author's own sensibility—his arrogance and generosity, his fondness for money and his need for integrity, his attraction toward the fabulous in American life and his repulsion by its waste and terror. "Stahr is miserable and embittered toward the end," Fitzgerald writes, in one of his own last notes for the book. "Before death, thoughts from *Crack-Up*." Apparently it was all to end in a flare-up of sensational and not too meaningful irony: Stahr, on his way to New York to call off a murder which he had ordered for the best of motives, is himself killed in an airplane crash, and his possessions are rifled by a group of schoolchildren on a mountain.

If there is anything symbolic in this situation, could it be the image of the modern Icarus soaring to disaster in that "universe of ineffable gaudiness" which was Fitzgerald's vision of the America of his time?

Inquiry into what was the real basis of Fitzgerald's long pre-occupation with failure will not be helped too much by the auto-biographical sketches in *The Crack-Up*. The reasons there offered are at once too simple and too complicated. No psychologist is likely to take very seriously the two early frustrations described—inability to make a Princeton football team and to go overseas in the last war. In the etiology of the Fitzgerald case, as the psychologists would say, the roots run much deeper, and nobody cares to disturb them at this early date. His unconscionable good looks were indeed a public phenomenon, and their effect on his total personality was something which he himself would not decline to admit. The *imago* of the physical self had a way of eclipsing at times the more important *imago* of the artist. But even this is a delicate enough matter. Besides, there were at work elements of a quite different order—racial and religious. For some reason he could never accept the large and positive influence of his Celtic inheritance, especially in his feeling for language, and his hearkening back to the South has a little too nostalgic a ring to be convincing. Closely related to this was the never resolved attitude toward money and social position in relation to individual worth. But least explored of all by his critics were the permanent effects of his early exposure to Catholicism, which are no less potent because rarely on the surface of his work. (The great exception is "Absolution," perhaps the finest of the short stories.) Indeed, it may have been the old habit of the confession which drove him, pathetically, at the end, to the public *examen de conscience* in the garish pages of *Esquire* magazine.

To add to his sense of failure there was also his awareness of distinct intellectual limitations, which he shared with the majority of American novelists of his time. "I had done very little think-

ing," he admits, "save within the problems of my craft." Whatever
he received at Princeton was scarcely to be called an education;
in later years he read little, shrank from abstract ideas, and was
hardly conscious of the historical events that were shaping up
around him. Perhaps it is not well for the novelist to encumber
himself with too much knowledge, although one cannot help recalling the vast cultural apparatus of a Tolstoi or a Joyce, or the
dialectical intrepidity of a Dostoievski or a Mann. And recalling
these Europeans, none of whom foundered on the way, one won-
ders whether a certain coyness toward the things of the mind is
not one reason for the lack of development in most American
writers. Art is not intellect alone; but without intellect art is not
likely to emerge beyond the plane of perpetual immaturity.

Lastly, there was Fitzgerald's exasperation with the *multiplicity*
of modern human existence—especially in his own country. "It's
under you, over you, and all around you," he protested, in the
hearing of the present writer, to a young woman who had connived at the slow progress of his work. "And the problem is to get
hold of it somehow." It was exasperating because for the writer,
whose business is to extract the unique quality of his time, what
Baudelaire calls the quality of *modernité*, there was too much to
be sensed, to be discarded, to be reconciled into some kind of
order. Yet for the writer this was the first of obligations, without
it he was nothing—"Our passion is our task, and our task is our
passion." What was the common problem of the American novelist
was intensified for him by his unusually high sense of vocation.

In the last analysis, if Fitzgerald failed, it was because the only
standard which he could recognize, like the Platonic conception
of himself forged by young Jay Gatsby in the shabby bedroom in
North Dakota, was too much for him to realize. His failure was
the defect of his virtues. And this is perhaps the greatest meaning
of his career to the younger generation of writers.

"I talk with the authority of failure," he writes in the note-
books, "Ernest with the authority of success. We could never sit

across the same table again." It is a great phrase. And the statement as a whole is one neither of abject self-abasement nor of false humility. What Fitzgerald implies is that the stakes for which he played were of a kind more difficult and more unattainable than "Ernest" or any of his contemporaries could even have imagined. And his only strength is in the consciousness of this fact.

F. SCOTT FITZGERALD*

Lionel Trilling

This essay was originally published in the Nation (April 25, 1945) and later as an introduction to the New Directions edition of The Great Gatsby (1945). The following selection—a combination and revision of the two essays—appeared in The Liberal Imagination.

" 'So be it! I die content and my destiny is fulfilled,' said Racine's Orestes; and there is more in his speech than the insanely bitter irony that appears on the surface. Racine, fully conscious of this tragic grandeur, permits Orestes to taste for a moment before going mad with grief the supreme joy of a hero; to assume his *exemplary* role." The heroic awareness of which André Gide speaks in his essay on Goethe was granted to Scott Fitzgerald for whatever grim joy he might find in it. It is a kind of seal set upon his heroic quality that he was able to utter his vision of his own fate publicly and aloud and in *Esquire* with no lessening of his dignity, even with an enhancement of it. The several essays in which Fitzgerald examined his life in crisis have been gathered together by Edmund Wilson—who is for many reasons the most appropriate editor possible—and published, together with Fitz-

* Lionel Trilling, "F. Scott Fitzgerald," The Liberal Imagination (New York: The Viking Press, 1950), pp. 243-54. Copyright 1945 by Lionel Trilling. Reprinted by permission of The Viking Press, Inc.

gerald's notebooks and some letters, as well as certain tributes and memorabilia, in a volume called, after one of the essays, *The Crack-Up*. It is a book filled with the grief of the lost and the might-have-been, with physical illness and torture of mind. Yet the heroic quality is so much here, Fitzgerald's assumption of the "exemplary role" is so proper and right that it occurs to us to say, and not merely as a piety but as the most accurate expression of what we really do feel, that

> *Nothing is here for tears, nothing to wail*
> *Or knock the breast, no weakness, no contempt,*
> *Dispraise, or blame, nothing but well and fair,*
> *And what may quiet us in a death so noble.*

This isn't what we may fittingly say on all tragic occasions, but the original occasion for these words has a striking aptness to Fitzgerald. Like Milton's Samson, he had the consciousness of having misused the power with which he had been endowed. "I had been only a mediocre caretaker . . . of my talent," he said. And the parallel carries further, to the sojourn among the Philistines and even to the maimed hero exhibited and mocked for the amusement of the crowd—on the afternoon of September 25, 1936, the New York *Evening Post* carried on its front page a feature story in which the triumphant reporter tells how he managed to make his way into the Southern nursing home where the sick and distracted Fitzgerald was being cared for and there "interviewed" him, taking all due note of the contrast between the present humiliation and the past glory. It was a particularly gratuitous horror, and yet in retrospect it serves to augment the moral force of the poise and fortitude which marked Fitzgerald's mind in the few recovered years that were left to him.

The root of Fitzgerald's heroism is to be found, as it sometimes is in tragic heroes, in his power of love. Fitzgerald wrote much about love, he was preoccupied with it as between men and women, but it is not merely where he is being explicit about it that his power appears. It is to be seen where eventually all a writer's

qualities have their truest existence, in his style. Even in Fitzgerald's early, cruder books, or even in his commercial stories, and
even when the style is careless, there is a tone and pitch to the
sentences which suggest his warmth and tenderness, and, what is
rare nowadays and not likely to be admired, his gentleness without
softness. In the equipment of the moralist and therefore in the
equipment of the novelist, aggression plays an important part,
and although it is of course sanctioned by the novelist's moral intention and by whatever truth of moral vision he may have, it is
often none the less fierce and sometimes even cruel. Fitzgerald
was a moralist to the core and his desire to "preach at people in
some acceptable form" is the reason he gives for not going the
way of Cole Porter and Rodgers and Hart—we must always remember in judging him how many real choices he was free and
forced to make—and he was gifted with the satiric eye; yet we
feel that in his morality he was more drawn to celebrate the good
than to denounce the bad. We feel of him, as we cannot feel of all
moralists, that he did not attach himself to the good because this
attachment would sanction his fierceness toward the bad—his first
impulse was to love the good, and we know this the more surely
because we perceive that he loved the good not only with his mind
but also with his quick senses and his youthful pride and desire.

He really had but little impulse to blame, which is the more
remarkable because our culture peculiarly honors the act of blam-
ing, which it takes as the sign of virtue and intellect. "Forbearance,
good word," is one of the jottings in his notebook. When it came
to blame, he preferred, it seems, to blame himself. He even did
not much want to blame the world. Fitzgerald knew where "the
world" was at fault. He knew that it was the condition, the field,
of tragedy. He is conscious of "what preyed on Gatsby, what
foul dust floated in the wake of his dreams." But he never made
out that the world imposes tragedy, either upon the heroes of his
novels, whom he called his "brothers," or upon himself. When he
speaks of his own fate, he does indeed connect it with the nature
of the social world in which he had his early flowering, but he

never finally lays it upon that world, even though at the time when he was most aware of his destiny it was fashionable with minds more pretentious than his to lay all personal difficulty whatever at the door of the "social order." It is, he feels, *his* fate—and as much as to anything else in Fitzgerald, we respond to the delicate tension he maintained between his idea of personal free will and his idea of circumstance: we respond to that moral and intellectual energy. "The test of a first-rate intelligence," he said, "is the ability to hold two opposed ideas in the mind, at the same time, and still retain the ability to function."

The power of love in Fitzgerald, then, went hand in hand with a sense of personal responsibility and perhaps created it. But it often happens that the tragic hero can conceive and realize a love that is beyond his own prudence or beyond his powers of dominance or of self-protection, so that he is destroyed by the very thing that gives him his spiritual status and stature. From Proust we learn about a love that is destructive by a kind of corrosiveness, but from Fitzgerald's two mature novels, *The Great Gatsby* and *Tender Is the Night*, we learn about a love—perhaps it is peculiarly American—that is destructive by reason of its very tenderness. It begins in romance, sentiment, even "glamour"—no one, I think, has remarked how innocent of mere "sex," how charged with sentiment is Fitzgerald's description of love in the jazz age—and it takes upon itself reality, and permanence, and duty discharged with an almost masochistic scrupulousness of honor. In the bright dreams begins the responsibility which needs so much prudence and dominance to sustain; and Fitzgerald was anything but a prudent man and he tells us that at a certain point in his college career "some old desire for personal dominance was broken and gone." He connects that loss of desire for dominance with his ability to write; and he set down in his notebook the belief that "to record one must be unwary." Fitzgerald, we may say, seemed to feel that both love and art needed a sort of personal defenselessness.

The phrase from Yeats, the derivation of the "responsibility" from the "dreams," reminds us that we must guard against dismissing, with easy words about its immaturity, Fitzgerald's preoccupation with the bright charm of his youth. Yeats himself, a wiser man and wholly fulfilled in his art, kept to the last of his old age his connection with his youthful vanity. A writer's days must be bound each to each by his sense of his life, and Fitzgerald the undergraduate was father of the best in the man and the novelist.

His sojourn among the philistines is always much in the mind of everyone who thinks about Fitzgerald, and indeed it was always much in his own mind. Everyone knows the famous exchange between Fitzgerald and Ernest Hemingway—Hemingway refers to it in his story, "The Snows of Kilimanjaro" and Fitzgerald records it in his notebook—in which, to Fitzgerald's remark, "The very rich are different from us," Hemingway replied, "Yes, they have more money." It is usually supposed that Hemingway had the better of the encounter and quite settled the matter. But we ought not be too sure. The novelist of a certain kind, if he is to write about social life, may not brush away the reality of the differences of class, even though to do so may have the momentary appearance of a virtuous social avowal. The novel took its rise and its nature from the radical revision of the class structure in the eighteenth century, and the novelist must still live by his sense of class differences, and must be absorbed by them, as Fitzgerald was, even though he despise them, as Fitzgerald did.

No doubt there was a certain ambiguity in Fitzgerald's attitude toward the "very rich"; no doubt they were for him something more than the mere object of his social observation. They seem to have been the nearest thing to an aristocracy that America could offer him, and we cannot be too simple about what a critic has recently noted, the artist's frequent "taste for aristocracy, his need —often quite open—of a superior social class with which he can make some fraction of common cause—enough, at any rate, to account for his own distinction." Every modern reader is by definition wholly immune from all ignoble social considerations, and, no matter what his own social establishment or desire for it may be, he knows that in literature the interest in social position must never be taken seriously. But not all writers have been so simple and virtuous—what are we to make of those risen gentlemen, Shakespeare and Dickens, or those fabricators of the honorific "de," Voltaire and Balzac? Yet their snobbery—let us call it that—is of a large and generous kind and we are not entirely wrong in connecting their peculiar energies of mind with whatever it was they wanted from gentility or aristocracy. It is a common habit of writers to envision an actuality of personal life which shall have the freedom and the richness of detail and the order of form that they desire in art. Yeats, to mention him again, spoke of the falseness of the belief that the "inherited glory of the rich" really holds richness of life. This, he said, was a mere dream; and yet, he goes on, it is a necessary illusion—

> Yet Homer had not sung
> Had he not found it certain beyond dreams
> That out of life's own self-delight had sprung
> The abounding glittering jet. . . .

And Henry James, at the threshold of his career, allegorized in his story "Benvolio" the interplay that is necessary for some artists between their creative asceticism and the bright, free, gay life of worldliness, noting at the same time the desire of worldliness to destroy the asceticism.[1]

With a man like Goethe the balance between the world and his asceticism is maintained, and so we forgive him his often absurd feelings—but perhaps absurd as well as forgivable only in the light of our present opinion of his assured genius—about aristocracy. Fitzgerald could not always keep the balance true; he was not, as we know, a prudent man. And no doubt he deceived

[1] George Moore's comment on Æ's having spoken in reproof of Yeats's pride in a quite factitious family line is apposite; "Æ, who is usually quick-witted, should have guessed that Yeats's belief in his lineal descent from the great Duke of Ormonde was part of his poetic equipment."

himself a good deal in his youth, but certainly his self-deception was not in the interests of vulgarity, for aristocracy meant to him a kind of disciplined distinction of personal existence which, presumably, he was so humble as not to expect from his art. What was involved in that notion of distinction can be learned from the use which Fitzgerald makes of the word "aristocracy" in one of those serious moments which occur in his most frivolous *Saturday Evening Post* stories; he says of the life of the young man of the story, who during the war was on duty behind the lines, that "it was not so bad—except that when the infantry came limping back from the trenches he wanted to be one of them. The sweat and mud they wore seemed only one of those ineffable symbols of aristocracy that were forever eluding him." Fitzgerald was perhaps the last notable writer to affirm the Romantic fantasy, descended from the Renaissance, of personal ambition and heroism, of life committed to, or thrown away for, some ideal of self. To us it will no doubt come more and more to seem a merely boyish dream; the nature of our society requires the young man to find his distinction through cooperation, subordination, and an expressed piety of social usefulness, and although a few young men have made Fitzgerald into a hero of art, it is likely that even to these admirers the whole nature of his personal fantasy is not comprehensible, for young men find it harder and harder to understand the youthful heroes of Balzac and Stendhal, they increasingly find reason to blame the boy whose generosity is bound up with his will and finds its expression in a large, strict, personal demand upon life.

I am aware that I have involved Fitzgerald with a great many great names and that it might be felt by some that this can do him no service, the disproportion being so large. But the disproportion will seem large only to those who think of Fitzgerald chiefly through his early public legend of heedlessness. Those who have a clear recollection of the mature work or who have read *The Crack-Up* will at least not think of the disproportion as one of kind. Fitzgerald himself did not, and it is by a man's estimate of himself that we must begin to estimate him. For all the engaging self-depreciation which was part of his peculiarly American charm, he put himself, in all modesty, in the line of greatness, he judged himself in a large way. When he writes of his depression, of his "dark night of the soul" where "it is always three o'clock in the morning," he not only derives the phrase from St. John of the Cross but adduces the analogous black despairs of Wordsworth, Keats, and Shelley. A novel with Ernest Hemingway as the model of its hero suggests to him Stendhal portraying the Byronic man, and he defends *The Great Gatsby* from some critical remark of Edmund Wilson's by comparing it with *The Brothers Karamazov.* Or again, here is the stuff of his intellectual pride at the very moment that he speaks of giving it up, as years before he had given up the undergraduate fantasies of valor: "The old dream of being an entire man in the Goethe-Byron-Shaw tradition . . . has been relegated to the junk heap of the shoulder pads worn for one day on the Princeton freshman football field and the overseas cap never worn overseas." And was it, that old dream, unjustified? To take but one great name, the one that on first thought seems the least relevant of all—between Goethe at twenty-four the author of *Werther,* and Fitzgerald, at twenty-four the author of *This Side of Paradise,* there is not really so entire a difference as piety and textbooks might make us think; both the young men so handsome, both winning immediate and notorious success, both rather more interested in life than in art, each the spokesman and symbol of his own restless generation.

It is hard to overestimate the benefit which came to Fitzgerald from his having consciously placed himself in the line of the great. He was a "natural," but he did not have the contemporary American novelist's belief that if he compares himself with the past masters, or if he takes thought—which, for a writer, means really knowing what his predecessors have done—he will endanger the integrity of his natural gifts. To read Fitzgerald's letters to his daughter—they are among the best and most affecting letters I know—and to catch the tone in which he speaks about the literature of the past, or to read the notebooks he faithfully kept, indexing them as Samuel Butler had done, and to perceive how continuously he thought about literature, is to have some clue to the secret of the continuing power of Fitzgerald's work.

The Great Gatsby, for example, after a quarter-century is still as fresh as when it first appeared; it has even gained in weight and relevance, which can be said of very few American books of its time. This, I think, is to be attributed to the specifically intellectual courage with which it was conceived and executed, a courage which implies Fitzgerald's grasp—both in the sense of awareness and of appropriation—of the traditional resources available to him. Thus, The Great Gatsby has its interest as a record of contemporary manners, but this might only have served to date it, did not Fitzgerald take the given moment of history as something more than a mere circumstance, did he not, in the manner of the great French novelists of the nineteenth century, seize the given moment as a moral fact. The same boldness of intellectual grasp accounts for the success of the conception of its hero—Gatsby is said by some to be not quite credible, but the question of any literal credibility he may or may not have becomes trivial before the large significance he implies. For Gatsby, divided between power and dream, comes inevitably to stand for America itself. Ours is the only nation that prides itself upon a dream and gives its name to one, "the American dream." We are told that "the truth was that Jay Gatsby of West Egg, Long Island, sprang from his Platonic conception of himself. He was a son of God— a phrase which, if it means anything, means just that—and he must be about His Father's business, the service of a vast, vulgar, and meretricious beauty." Clearly it is Fitzgerald's intention that our mind should turn to the thought of the nation that has sprung from its "Platonic conception" of itself. To the world it is anomalous in America, just as in the novel it is anomalous in Gatsby, that so much raw power should be haunted by envisioned romance. Yet in that anomaly lies, for good or bad, much of the truth of our national life, as, at the present moment, we think about it.

Then, if the book grows in weight of significance with the years, we can be sure that this could not have happened had its form and style not been as right as they are. Its form is ingenious—with the ingenuity, however, not of craft but of intellectual intensity. The form, that is, is not the result of careful "plotting"—the form of a good novel never is—but is rather the result of the necessities of the story's informing idea, which require the sharpness of radical foreshortening. Thus, it will be observed, the characters are not "developed": the wealthy and brutal Tom Buchanan haunted by his "scientific" vision of the doom of civilization, the vaguely guilty, vaguely homosexual Jordan Baker, the dim Wolfsheim, who fixed the World Series of 1919, are treated, we might say, as if they were ideographs, a method of economy that is reinforced by the ideographic use that is made of the Washington Heights flat, the terrible "valley of ashes" seen from the Long Island Railroad, Gatsby's incoherent parties, and the huge sordid eyes of the oculist's advertising sign. (It is a technique which gives the novel an affinity with *The Waste Land*, between whose author and Fitzgerald there existed a reciprocal admiration.) Gatsby himself, once stated, grows only in the understanding of the narrator. He is allowed to say very little in his own person. Indeed, apart from the famous "Her voice is full of money," he says only one memorable thing, but that remark is overwhelming in its intellectual audacity: when he is forced to admit that his lost Daisy did perhaps love her husband, he says, "In any case it was just personal." With that sentence he achieves an insane greatness, convincing us that he really is a Platonic conception of himself, really some sort of Son of God.

What underlies all success in poetry, what is even more important than the shape of the poem or its wit of metaphor, is the poet's voice. It either gives us confidence in what is being said or

it tells us that we do not need to listen; and it carries both the
modulation and the living form of what is being said. In the novel
no less than in the poem, the voice of the author is the decisive
factor. We are less consciously aware of it in the novel, and, in
speaking of the elements of a novel's art, it cannot properly be
exemplified by quotation because it is continuous and cumulative.
In Fitzgerald's work the voice of his prose is of the essence of his
success. We hear in it at once the tenderness toward human desire that modifies a true firmness of moral judgment. It is, I would
venture to say, the normal or ideal voice of the novelist. It is characteristically modest, yet it has in it, without apology or self-
consciousness, a largeness, even a stateliness, which derives from
Fitzgerald's connection with tradition and with mind, from his
sense of what has been done before and the demands which this
past accomplishment makes. ". . . I became aware of the old island
here that flowered once for Dutch sailors' eyes—a fresh green
breast of the new world. Its vanished trees, the trees that had
made way for Gatsby's house, had once pandered in whispers to
the last and greatest of all human dreams; for a transitory and enchanted moment man must have held his breath in the presence of
this continent, compelled into an aesthetic contemplation he
neither understood nor desired, face to face for the last time in
history with something commensurate to his capacity for wonder."
Here, in the well-known passage, the voice is a little dramatic, a
little *intentional*, which is not improper to a passage in climax and
conclusion, but it will the better suggest in brief compass the
habitual music of Fitzgerald's seriousness.

Fitzgerald lacked prudence, as his heroes did, lacked that blind
instinct of self-protection which the writer needs and the American writer needs in double measure. But that is all he lacked—and
it is the generous fault, even the heroic fault. He said of his Gatsby,
"If personality is an unbroken series of successful gestures, there
was something gorgeous about him, some heightened sensitivity
to the promises of life, as if he were related to one of those in-

tricate machines that register earthquakes ten thousand miles away. This responsiveness had nothing to do with that flabby impressionability which is dignified under the name of 'the creative temperament'—it was an extraordinary gift for hope, a romantic readiness such as I have never found in any other person and which it is not likely I shall ever find again." And it is so that we are drawn to see Fitzgerald himself as he stands in his exemplary role.

FITZGERALD'S BRAVE NEW WORLD*

Edwin Fussell

Think of the lost ecstasy of the Elizabethans. "Oh my America, my new found land," think of what it meant to them and of what it means to us.

(T. E. Hulme, *Speculations*)

I

The source of Fitzgerald's excellence is an uncanny ability to juxtapose the sensibilities implied by the phrase "romantic wonder" with the most conspicuous, as well as the most deeply significant, phenomena of American civilization, and to derive from that juxtaposition a moral critique of human nature. None of our major writers is more romantically empathic than this avatar of Keats in the era of Harding; none draws a steadier bead on the characteristic shortcomings, not to say disasters, of the most grandiose social experiment of modern times. Thence the implacable moralist with stars (Martinis) in his eyes: worshipper, analyst, judge, and poet. But it is not very illuminating to say that Fitzgerald wrote the story of his own representative life, unless we are prepared to read his confessions—and then his evaluation of those confessions—as American history; and unless we reciprocally

* Edwin Fussell, "Fitzgerald's Brave New World," revision of an article from English Literary History, XIX (December, 1952), 291-306. Reprinted by permission of the author.

learn to read American history as the tale of the romantic imagination in the United States.

Roughly speaking, Fitzgerald's basic plot is the history of the
New World (ironic *double entendre* here and throughout); more
precisely, of the human imagination in the New World. It
shows itself in two predominant patterns, quest and seduction.
The quest is the search for romantic wonder (a kind of febrile
secular beatitude), in the terms proposed by contemporary America; the seduction represents capitulation to these terms. Obversely,
the quest is a flight: from reality, from normality, from time, fate,
death, and the conception of *limit*. In the social realm, the pattern
of desire may be suggested by such phrases as "the American
dream" and "the pursuit of happiness." Fitzgerald begins by ex-
posing the corruption of that dream in industrial America; he ends
by discovering that the pursuit is universally seductive and perpetually damned. Driven by inner forces that compel him towards
the personal realization of romantic wonder, the Fitzgerald hero
is destroyed by the materials which the American experience
offers as objects and criteria of passion; or, at best, he is purged
of these unholy fires, chastened, and reduced.

In general, this quest has two symptomatic goals. There is, for
one, the search for eternal youth and beauty, what might be
called the historic myth of Ponce de Leon. ("Historic" because
the man was really looking for a fountain; "myth" because no
such fountain ever existed).[1] The essence of romantic wonder
appears to reside in the illusion of perennial youth and grace and
happiness surrounding the leisure class of which Fitzgerald customarily wrote; thus the man of imagination in America, searching for
the source of satisfaction of his deepest aesthetic needs, is seduced

---

[1] It is a curious but far from meaningless coincidence that Frederick Jackson
Turner used the image of "a magic fountain of youth" to evoke the creative
and restorative powers of the unexhausted Western frontier. I am inclined to
think Fitzgerald knew what he was about when he called *The Great Gatsby*
"a story of the West." Traditionally in American writing "the West" means
both the Western part of the United States and the New World, and
especially the first as synecdoche of the other.

by the delusion that these qualities are actually to be found in people who, in sober fact, are vacuous and irresponsible. But further, this kind of romantic quest, which implies both escape and destruction, is equated on the level of national ideology with a transcendental and Utopian contempt for time and history, and on the religious level, which Fitzgerald (whose Catholic apostasy was about half genuine and half imagined) persistently but hesitantly approaches, with a blasphemous rejection of the very conditions of human existence.

The second goal is, simply enough, money. The search for wealth is the familiar Anglo-Saxon Protestant ideal of personal material success, most succinctly embodied for our culture in the saga of young Benjamin Franklin. It is the romantic assumption of this aspect of the "American dream" that all the magic of the world can be had for money. Both from a moral, and from a highly personal and idiosyncratic Marxist standpoint, Fitzgerald examines and condemns the plutocratic ambitions of American life and the ruinous price exacted by their lure. But the two dreams are, of course, so intimately related as to be for all practical purposes one: the appearance of eternal youth and beauty centers in a particular social class whose glamor is made possible by social inequality and inequity. Beauty, the presumed object of aesthetic contemplation, is commercialized, love is bought and sold. Money is the means to the violent recovery or specious arrest of an enchanting youth.

In muted contrast, Fitzgerald repeatedly affirms his faith in an older, simpler America, generally identified as pre-Civil War; the emotion is that of pastoral, the social connotations agrarian and democratic. In such areas he continues to find fragments of basic human value, social, moral, and religious. But these affirmations are for the most part subordinate and indirect; Fitzgerald's attention was chiefly directed upon the merchandise of romantic wonder proffered by his own time and place. Like the narrator in *Gatsby*, he was always "within and without, simultaneously enchanted and repelled by the inexhaustible variety of life." Through a delicate and exact imagery, he was able to extend this attitude of simultaneous enchantment and repulsion over the whole of the American civilization he knew. His keenest perception, and the one that told most heavily for his fiction, was the universal quality of the patterns he was tracing, his greatest discovery that there was nothing new about the Lost Generation except its particular toys. The quest for romantic wonder and the inevitable failure were only the latest in a long series.

Fitzgerald approached this major theme slowly and more by intuition than design. Or perhaps he had to live it, and then understand it, before he could write it. In a hazy form it is present in such early stories as "The Offshore Pirate" and "Dalyrimple Goes Wrong." It is allegorized in "The Diamond as Big as the Ritz" and fumbled in *The Beautiful and Damned*.

"May Day," significantly motivated by his first sharp awareness of class cleavages in American society, together with important cleavages of period in American history, is for the reader tracing Fitzgerald's gradual realization of this major theme the most rewarding production of his early career. Its formal construction on social principles ("Mr. In" and "Mr. Out") is obvious enough; what usually goes unnoticed is the way Fitzgerald's symbolic method extends his critique from the manners of drunken undergraduates to the pervasive malaise of an entire civilization. The hubris with which these characters fade from the story in a parody of the Ascension dramatically and comically pinpoints the materialistic hedonism, along with its traditional counterpart, a vulgar idealism, which Fitzgerald is already identifying as his culture's fatal flaw:

> Then they were in an elevator bound skyward.
> "What floor, please?" said the elevator man.
> "Any floor," said Mr. In.
> "Top floor," said Mr. Out.
> "This is the top floor," said the elevator man.
> "Have another floor put on," said Mr. Out.
> "Higher," said Mr. In.
> "Heaven," said Mr. Out.

Set against the story's controlling symbol, the universal significance of this passage frames its particular historical implications.
The scene is an all-night restaurant, and the preliminary description emphasizes social and economic inequality, the brutalizations
of poverty, the sick insouciance of unmerited riches. As a Yale
junior is ejected for throwing hash at the waiters, "the great
plate-glass front had turned to a deep creamy blue . . . Dawn had
come up in Columbus Circle, magical, breathless dawn, silhouet-
ting the great statue of the immortal Christopher [Christ-bearer],
and mingling in a curious and uncanny manner with the fading
yellow electric light inside." The final significance of this symbol
can only be established after considering the conclusion of *The
Great Gatsby* (and perhaps not even then; what, for example,
about that oceanic "blue," or the failing efficacy of man-made
illumination against the light of day, prior in time to the light
it supersedes?). But the general intention is clear enough: Fitzgerald is measuring the behavior and attitudes of the Lost Generation with a symbol of romantic wonder extensive enough to com-
prehend all American experience, as far back as 1492. The contrast involves the ironic rejection of all that this present generation
believes in, the immaturity and triviality of its lust for pleasure.
But then, by a further turn of irony, the voyage of Columbus and
his discovery of the Western Hemisphere is also the actual event
forming the first link in the chain leading to the butt-end of contemporary folly. There is the further implication that some sort
of conscious search is at the heart of American experience, but had
never before taken so childish a form. What Fitzgerald is almost
certainly trying to say with this image is: we are the end of Columbus' dream, and this is our brave new world.

II

With *The Great Gatsby* (1925), Fitzgerald first brought his
vision to full and mature realization. Gatsby is essentially the
man of imagination in America, given specificity and solidity and

precision by the materials American society offers him. "If personality is an unbroken series of successful gestures, then there was something gorgeous about him, some heightened sensitivity to the promises of life, as if he were related to one of those intricate machines that register earthquakes ten thousand miles away." It is Gatsby's capacity for romantic wonder that Fitzgerald is insisting upon in this preliminary exposition, a capacity he goes on to define as "an extraordinary gift for hope, a romantic readiness" (the first phrase suggesting the central theological virtue, the second implying its parodic counterpart). With the simile of the seismograph, a splendid image of the human sensibility in a mechanized age, Fitzgerald has in effect already introduced the vast back-drop of American civilization against which Gatsby's gestures are to be interpreted. The image is as integral as intricate; for if Gatsby is to be taken as the product and manifestation of the seductive and corrupting motivations involved in "the American dream," he is also the instrument by means of which Fitzgerald will register the tremors that point to its self-contained possibilities of destruction, its *fault* (flaw), in the geological sense. "What preyed on Gatsby, what foul dust floated in the wake of his dreams" is the stuff of the novel, the social content of Fitzgerald's fictional world. But it is equally essential to realize that Gatsby, too, has been derailed by values and attitudes held in common with the society that destroys him. How else, indeed, might he be destroyed? Certainly, in such a world, the novel assures us, a dream like Gatsby's cannot possibly remain pristine, given the materials with which the original impulse toward wonder must invest itself. In short, Gatsby is somewhat more than pathetic, a sad figure preyed upon by the American leisure class. The novel is neither melodramatic nor bathetic, but critical. The unreal values of the world of Tom and Daisy Buchanan, to a very considerable degree, are Gatsby's values too, inherent in his dream. Gatsby from the beginning lives in an imaginary world, where "a universe of ineffable gaudiness spun itself out in his brain"; negatively, this quality manifests itself in a dangerous, and frequently vulgar, tendency toward sentimental idealizations: his reveries "were a satisfactory hint of the unreality of reality, a promise that the rock of the world was founded securely on a fairy's wing." (A variety of religious overtones emanates from the word "rock"). Gatsby's capacity for wonder is obviously corrupted by the meager and vicious nature of American culture. Potentially, he constitutes a tentative and limited indictment of that culture; actually, he is that culture's thoroughly appropriate scapegoat and victim. "He was a son of God . . . and he must be about His Father's business, the service of a vast, vulgar, and meretricious beauty." God the Father, or the Founding Fathers? In such ambiguity lurk the novel's deepest ironies.

Daisy finally becomes for Gatsby the iconic manifestation of this dubious vision of beauty. Little enough might have been possible for Gatsby at best, but once he "wed his unutterable visions to her perishable breath, his mind would never romp again like the mind of God." (Parody of the Incarnation). Steadily and surreptitiously, Fitzgerald continues to suggest the idea of blasphemy in connection with Gatsby's Titanic imaginative lusts. But of course the focus of the novel must be sexual and social, for the implication *of* the religious implication is that Gatsby (that is to say American culture) provides mainly secular objects for the religious imagination to feed on, as it also provides tawdry images for the aesthetic imagination. After concentrating Gatsby's wonder on Daisy, Fitzgerald proceeds to an explicit statement of her thematic significance. Gatsby was "overwhelmingly aware of the *youth* and mystery that *wealth* imprisons and *preserves*, of the freshness of many clothes, and of Daisy, gleaming like silver, safe and proud above the hot struggles of the poor" (my italics). Her voice is mysteriously enchanting, the typifying feature of her role as *la belle dame sans merci*, and throughout the action serves to suggest her loveliness and desirability. But only Gatsby, in a rare moment of insight, is able to identify the causes of its subtle and elusive magic, upon which Nick Carraway meditates: "It was full of money—that was the inexhaustible charm that rose and fell in it, the jingle of it, the cymbals' song of it . . . High in a white palace the king's daughter, the golden girl . . ."

Possession of an image like Daisy is all that Gatsby can finally conceive as "success"; and Gatsby is meant to be a very representative American in the intensity of his yearning for success, as well as in the symbols which he equates with it. Gatsby is a contemporary variation on an old American pattern, the rags-to-riches story exalted by American legend as early as Crèvecoeur's *Letters from an American Farmer* (most mawkishly in the "History of Andrew, the Hebridian," significantly appended to the famous Letter III, "What is an American"), and primarily fixed in the popular mind by Benjamin Franklin. Franklin's youthful resolutions are parodied in those that the adolescent Gatsby writes on the back flyleaf of his copy of *Hopalong Cassidy*, a conjunction of documents as eloquently expressive of American continuities as of the progress of civilization in the new world.

The connection between Gatsby's individual tragedy and the tragedy of American civilization is also made, and again through symbol, with respect to historical attitudes. Gatsby's philosophy of history is summed up in his devotion to the green light burning on Daisy's dock. Nick first sees Gatsby in an attitude of supplication, a gesture that pathetically travesties the traditional gestures of worship. He finally discerns that the object of that trembling piety is precisely this green light which, until his disillusion, remains one of Gatsby's "enchanted objects." But only in the novel's concluding passage, toward which all action and symbol relentlessly tend, is the reader given the full implications of the green light as the historically-corrupted religious symbol ("Gatsby believed in the green light, the orgiastic future"). With no historical sense whatever, yet trapped in the detritus of American history, Gatsby is the superbly effective fictional counterpart of that native philistine maxim that "history is bunk." For those interested in such comparisons, he may also recall the more crowing moods of Emerson and Thoreau and the alleged "time-lessness" of their idealistic visions and exhortations, now, alas, like Daisy who gleamed like silver, somewhat tarnished. For Fitz-gerald, this contemptuous repudiation of tradition, historical neces-sity, and moral accountability, was deluded and hubristic. When he finally came to see—as he clearly did in *Gatsby*—that in this irresponsibility lay the real meaning behind the obsessive youth-worship of popular culture in his own day, he was able to identify Gatsby as at once the man of his age and the man of the ages, a miserable twentieth-century Ponce de Leon. His fictional world was no longer simply the Jazz Age, the Lost Generation, but the whole of American civilization as it culminated in his own time.

In the final symbol of the novel, Fitzgerald pushes the personal equation to national, even universal scope, in a way that recalls the method of "May Day." Fitzgerald is commenting on Gatsby's state of disillusion immediately before his death:

> He must have felt that he had lost the old warm world, paid a high price for living too long with a single dream. He must have looked up at an unfamiliar sky through frightening leaves and shivered as he found what a grotesque thing a rose is and how raw the sunlight was upon the scarcely created grass. A new world, ma-terial without being real, where poor ghosts, breathing dreams like air, drifted fortuitously about . . .

Such was the romantic perception of wonder, when finally strip-ped of its pleasing and falsifying illusions. Such was Fitzgerald's maturest vision of the United States of America, perhaps the most magnificent statement in all our literature of the cruel modernity of the "new world," its coldness, unreality, and absurdity nour-ished (if one may use so inappropriate a word) by that great mass neurosis known as "the American Dream." So Fitzgerald, the quintessential outsider-insider, moves to his final critique:

> And as the moon rose higher the inessential houses began to melt away until gradually I became aware of the old island here that

flowered once for Dutch sailors' eyes—a fresh, green breast of the new world. Its vanished trees, the trees that had made way for Gatsby's house, had once pandered in whispers to the last and greatest of all human dreams; for a transitory enchanted moment man must have held his breath in the presence of this continent, compelled into an aesthetic contemplation he neither understood nor desired, face to face for the last time in history with something commensurate to his capacity for wonder.

The most obvious point to be made about this passage is its insistence that Gatsby's insatiable capacity for wonder could have, in the modern world, no proper objective. The emotion lingered on, generations of Americans had translated it into one or another set of inadequate terms, but Gatsby, like all his ancestors, though increasingly, was doomed by demanding the impossible. There is also the ironic contrast between the wonder of the New World (to its Old World discoverers) and what Americans (who all came from the Old World in the first place) have made of it; the same point Fitzgerald made in similar fashion with the Columbus image in "May Day." Finally, there is a more universal, an extra-historical meaning implicit in the language of this passage —the hope that the new world could possibly satisfy man's inordinate, secular lusts (displaced religious emotions from the very outset) was "the last and greatest of all human dreams," seductive and unreal. The most impressive associations cluster around the word "pander," which implies the illicit commercial traffic among love, youth, and beauty, and which thus effectually subsumes most of the central meanings of the novel. In a later essay, Fitzgerald repeated with variations the "panders in whispers" phrase: New York City "no longer whispers of fantastic success and eternal youth," a fine instance of how the myths of Benjamin Franklin and Ponce de Leon came to be blended in his mind. The two parallel themes do, of course, meet in *The Great Gatsby*; indeed, they are tangled at the heart of the plot, for the most outrageous irony in Gatsby's tragedy is his belief that he can buy his dream, which is, precisely, to recapture the past. Unfortunately for this all too representative American, his dream "was already behind him, somewhere back in that vast obscurity beyond the city, where the dark fields of the republic rolled on under the night." It hardly needs saying that Fitzgerald chooses his language carefully, and that every word is loaded.

III

Tender Is the Night (1934) restates the essential theme and complicates it. If this novel seems somehow less successful than *Gatsby*, that is perhaps because the greater proliferation of thematic statement is not matched by a corresponding gain in clarity and control. But beneath the additional richness, and apparent confusion, the same general story can be made out. Dick Diver is like Gatsby the American as man of imagination. His chief difference from Gatsby is that he dispenses romantic wonder to others, in addition to living by and for it himself. Gatsby tries to purvey dreams, but doesn't know how. But to Rosemary Hoyt (of whom, more later) Dick's "voice promised that he would . . . open up whole *new worlds* for her, unroll an endless succession of magnificent possibilities" (my italics). Diver is the man with the innate capacity for romantic wonder, temporarily a member of the American leisure class of the 'twenties, an "organizer of private gaiety, curator of richly incrusted happiness." His intellectual and imaginative energies have been diverted from normal creative and functional channels and expended on the effort to prevent, for a handful of the very rich, the American dream from revealing its nightmarish realities.

Although Dick is given a more specific background than Gatsby, he is equally a product of his civilization and shares its characteristic deficiencies: "the illusions of eternal strength and health, and of the essential goodness of people; illusions of a nation, the lies of generations of frontier mothers who had to croon falsely that there were no wolves outside the cabin door." (The lies also of generations of American politicians, historians, publicists, fireside poets, and similar confidence-men, who had no such easy excuse). This inherent romantic has been further weakened, though not quite destroyed, by the particular forms of sentimentality of his own generation: "he must press on toward the Isles of Greece, the cloudy waters of unfamiliar ports, the lost girl on shore, the moon of popular songs. A part of Dick's mind was made up of the tawdry souvenirs of his boyhood. Yet in that somewhat littered Five-and-Ten, he had managed to keep alive the low painful fire of intelligence."

Such is the man, potentially noble like Gatsby, but with the fatal flaw of imagination common to and conditioned by the superficial symbols and motivations of his culture, who is brought against the conditions of temptation represented by Nicole. She is the granddaughter of a "self-made American capitalist" and of a German Count, and her family is placed in perspective by Fitzgerald's frequent analogies with feudal aristocracy. "Her father would have it on almost any clergyman," such as Dick's father; "they were an American ducal family without a title—the very name . . . caused a psychological metamorphosis in people." Yet behind this facade of glamor and power lies unnatural lust and perversion. Nicole's father, this "fine American type," has committed incest with his daughter—the very incarnation of the American vision of youth, beauty, and wealth—and made of her a psychotic for young Dr. Diver to cure. As Nicole says, " 'I'm a crook by heritage.' "

Through Nicole Fitzgerald conveys, as he had with Daisy, all that is sexually and socially desirable in youth and beauty: "there were all the potentialities for romantic love in that lovely body and in the delicate mouth. . . . Nicole had been a beauty as a young girl and she would be a beauty later." Apparently she is eternally youthful, and only at the end of the novel is it discernible that she has aged. Her face, which corresponds in sensuous utility to Daisy's voice, is lovely and hard, "her eyes brave and watchful, looking straight ahead toward nothing." She is an empty child, representative of her social class, of the manners and morals of the 'twenties, and of the world of values for which America, like Diver, was once more selling its soul. But it is chiefly Nicole's semblance of perpetual youth that allows Fitzgerald to exploit her as a central element in the narrative correlative he is constructing for his vision of American life. Occasionally he handles her in a way that goes beyond social criticism, entering, if obliquely and implicitly, the realm of religious apprehension:

> The only physical disparity between Nicole at present and the Nicole of five years before was simply that she was no longer a young girl. But she was enough ridden by the current youth worship, the moving pictures with their myriad faces of girl-children, blandly represented as carrying on the work and wisdom of the world, to feel a jealousy of youth.
>
> She put on the first ankle-length day dress that she had owned for many years, and crossed herself reverently with Chanel Sixteen.

(So Diver, at the end of the novel, but with full consciousness of the blasphemy, "blesses" the Riviera beach "with a papal cross," immediately before returning to the obscurity of small-town America. The malediction may by a later generation of readers be taken as Fitzgerald's also, whose equally obscure end was ironically to come in the most notorious of American small towns, Hollywood.) But while Fitzgerald could upon occasion thus extend the significance of his narrative, he never neglected to keep it firmly grounded in a specific social and economic world, and it is in this realm that most of his correspondences are established:

> Nicole was the product of much ingenuity and toil. For her sake trains began their run at Chicago and traversed the round belly of the continent to California; chicle factories fumed and link belts grew link by link in factories; men mixed toothpaste in vats and drew mouthwash out of copper hogsheads; girls canned tomatoes quickly in August or worked rudely at the Five-and-Tens on Christmas Eve; half-breed Indians toiled on Brazilian coffee plantations and dreamers were muscled out of patent rights in new tractors— these were some of the people who gave a tithe to Nicole, and

as the whole system swayed and thundered onward it lent a feverish bloom to such processes of hers as wholesale buying, like the
flush of a fireman's face holding his post before a spreading blaze.
She illustrated very simple principles, containing in herself her own
doom, but illustrated them so accurately that there was grace in the
procedure.[2]

Yet even here religious nuance continues ("Christmas Eve,"
"tithe"); the simple principles Nicole illustrates are not only
Marxian but also Christian. Still, if her principles are simple, their
illustration is epic in scope and intention. The social ramifications
of Fitzgerald's great novels are broad indeed; at their base are
criminal injustice and inhuman waste, on a world-wide scale, and
at their apex the American girl, the king's daughter, beautiful,
forever young, and insane.

In the central scenes of temptation (Book II, chapter V, in
the original form), Fitzgerald quite deliberately allows Nicole
to assume her full symbolic significance, thereby revealing un-
mistakably that the central action of *Tender Is the Night* must be
read against the broadest background of American life. Throughout this chapter runs the *leitmotif* of the author's generalizing
commentary, beginning with the passage: "the impression of her
youth and beauty grew on Dick until it welled up inside him
in a compact paroxysm of emotion. She smiled, a moving childish
smile that was like all the lost youth in the world." This mood of
pathetic nostalgia is quickly objectified in the talk of Dick and
Nicole about American popular songs; soon Dick feels that "there
was that excitement about her that seemed to reflect all the excitement of the world." So ends the first of the two scenes that
comprise this chapter. The second meeting opens on a similar
key: "Dick wished she had no background, that she was just a
girl lost with no address save the night from which they had
come." This time they play the songs they had mentioned the

---

[2] Cf. Gatsby as seismograph. Probably it is dangerous to take too literally
Fitzgerald's remark that he was "essentially Marxian"; it seems to me equally
dangerous to ignore it altogether.

week before: "they were in America now." And Fitzgerald drives the point home in his last sentence: "Now there was this scarcely saved waif of disaster bringing him the essence of a continent. . ."

At first Dick laughs off the notion that Nicole's family has purchased him, but he gradually succumbs, "inundated by a trickling of goods and money." Once again, Nicole is the typifying object of her class and society, especially in the terms she proposes for the destruction of her victim's moral and intellectual integrity: "Naturally Nicole, *wanting to own him, wanting him to stand still forever,* encouraged any slackness on his part" (my italics). Although the pattern is more complex than in *Gatsby*, practically the same controlling lines of theme can be observed. The man of imagination, fed on the emotions of romantic wonder, is tempted and seduced and (in this case, nearly) destroyed by that American dream which customarily takes two forms: the escape from time and the materialistic pursuit of a purely hedonistic happiness. On the historical level, the critique is of the error of American romanticism in attempting to transcend and thus escape historical responsibility. On the economic level, the critique is of the fatal beauty of American capitalism, its destructive charm and recklessness. Thematically, the lines come together when Nicole attempts to own Dick and therefore to escape time—keeping him clear of it, too—as when Gatsby tries to buy back the past. On the religious level, if indeed there is one, the critique must be defined more cautiously: perhaps one can say that Fitzgerald intermittently insinuates the possibility that human kind are inveterately prone to befuddle themselves with the conspicuous similarities between the city of man and the city of God, paying scant attention to their more radical difference.

In Rosemary Hoyt, who brings from Hollywood to Europe the latest American version of the dream of youthful innocence, Fitzgerald has still another important center of consciousness. It is through her eyes, for instance, that Fitzgerald gives us his first elaborate glimpses of the Divers, and their hangers-on, at the

Americanized Riviera. Because of Rosemary's acute but undisciplined perceptions, Fitzgerald can insist perpetually on the ironic tensions between the richest texture of social appearance and the hidden reality of moral agony: her "naïveté responded wholeheartedly to the expensive simplicity of the Divers, unaware of its complexity and its lack of innocence, unaware that it was all a selection of quality rather than quantity from the run of the world's bazaar; and that the simplicity of behavior also, the nursery-like peace and good-will, the emphasis on the simpler virtues, was part of a desperate bargain with the gods and had been attained through struggles she could not have guessed at." ("Nursery-like peace and good will" is a good example of how Fitzgerald's subtly paradoxical prose style incessantly supplies the kind of religious-secular befuddlement alluded to above).

Rosemary manifests the effects of Hollywood sentimentality and meretriciousness on the powers of American perception and imagination. The image-patterns that surround her movements are largely concerned with childhood; she is "as dewy with belief as a child from one of Mrs. Burnett's vicious tracts." Immature and egocentric, she provides one more symbol of the corruption of imagination in American civilization; both deluded and deluding, she is without resources for escape such as are available to Nick Carroway and, to a considerably lesser extent, Dick Diver. It is Diver who sounds the last important note about her: " 'Rosemary didn't grow up.' " That she is intended as a representative figure Fitzgerald makes amply clear in his embittered account of her picture "Daddy's Girl": "There she was—so young and innocent—the product of her mother's loving care . . . embodying all the immaturity of the race, cutting a new cardboard paper doll to pass before its empty harlot's mind."

Nicole and Rosemary are for this novel the objectified images of Fitzgerald's "brave new world." Only occasionally, and only in pathos, does Dick Diver escape the limits of this terrifying world. Once, the three of them are sitting in a restaurant, and Dick notices a group of "gold star mothers": "in their happy faces, the dignity that surrounded and pervaded the party, he perceived all the maturity of an older America. For a while the sobered women who had come to mourn for their dead, for something they could not repair, made the room beautiful. Momentarily, he sat again on his father's knee, riding with Moseby while the old loyalties and devotions fought on around him. Almost with an effort he turned back to his two women at the table and faced the whole new world in which he believed." Only as this illusion fades, to the accompaniment of an almost unbearable "interior laughter," does Dick Diver achieve a minimal and ambiguous salvation, a few shattered fragments of reality, including the anonymity of professional and social failure.

IV

For purposes of corroboration, one can add a certain amount of documentation from Fitzgerald's non-fictional writings, as collected in the posthumous volume *The Crack-Up* (1945). The point that most needs buttressing, probably, is that Fitzgerald saw in the quest for romantic wonder a recurrent pattern of American behavior. Such an attitude seems strongly implied by the works of fiction, but of course it is additionally reassuring to find Fitzgerald writing his daughter: "You speak of how good your generation is, but I think they share with every generation since the Civil War in America the sense of being somehow about to inherit the earth. You've heard me say before that I think the faces of most American women over thirty are relief maps of petulant and bewildered unhappiness" (p. 306). A brief sketch of a "typical product of our generation" in the *Note-Books* indicates further what qualities were involved in this "sense of being about to inherit the earth": "her dominant idea and goal is freedom without responsibility, which is like gold without metal, spring without winter, youth without age, one of those maddening, coo-coo mirages of wild riches" (p. 166). That this personal attitude, translated into the broader terms of a whole culture, represented a negation of historical responsibility, is made sufficiently clear in another *Note-Book* passage: "Americans, he liked to say, should be born with fins, and perhaps they were—perhaps money was a form of fin. In England, property begot a strong place sense, but Americans, restless and with shallow roots, needed fins and wings. There was even a recurrent idea in America about an education that would leave out history and the past, that should be a sort of equipment for aerial adventure, weighed down by none of the stowaways of inheritance or tradition" (p. 109). Still another passage, this time from one of the "Crack-Up" essays, makes it equally clear that Fitzgerald habitually saw the universal applicability of all he was saying about the ruling passions of America: "This is what I think now: that the natural state of the sentient adult is a qualified unhappiness. I think also that in an adult the desire to be finer in grain than you are, 'a constant striving' (as those people say who gain their bread by saying it) only adds to this unhappiness in the end—that end that comes to our youth and hope" (p. 84).

Fortunately, by some kind of unexplained miracle (perhaps nothing more mysterious than his deep-seated integrity as a writer), Fitzgerald did not have it in himself to be a cynic. For all the failure and futility he found in the American experience, his attitude was an attitude of acceptance, remarkably free of that sense of despair which Kierkegaard correctly prophesied as the typical sin of the moderns. There was always in him something of Jimmy Gatz's "extraordinary gift of hope," which enabled him to touch the subjects he touched without being consumed by them. (The tragedies of his personal life are another matter; I am speaking only of his heroism and integrity as an artist.) The exhaustion of the frontier and the rebound of the post-war expatriate movement marked for him the end of a long period in human history and it was really this entire period, the history of the post-Renaissance man in America, that he made the substance of his works. After exploring his materials to their limits Fitzgerald knew, at his greatest moments, that he had discovered a universal pattern of desire and belief and behavior, and that in it was compounded the imaginative history of modern, especially American, civilization. Thus (again from the *Note-Books*):

> He felt then that if the pilgrimage eastward of the rare poisonous flower of his race was the end of the adventure which had started westward three hundred years ago, if the long serpent of the curiosity had turned too sharp upon itself, cramping its bowels, bursting its shining skin, at least there had been a journey; like to the satisfaction of a man coming to die—one of those human things that one can never understand unless one has made such a journey and heard the man give thanks with the husbanded breath. The frontiers were gone—there were no more barbarians. The short gallop of the last great race, the polyglot, the hated and the despised, the crass and scorned, had gone—at least it was not a meaningless extinction up an alley (p. 199).

There are dozens more such passages, in the non-fictional prose as in the fictional; naturally, for Fitzgerald's subject, however broadly he came to understand it, was in the first instance his own journey. He was by nature almost incredibly sympathetic. He was also more knowledgeable—both morally and intellectually—than he is generally credited with being. To such an extent that his more enthusiastic readers are almost tempted to say: if the polyglot gallop is not a meaningless cancellation of itself, that is chiefly because Fitzgerald—and the few Americans who by virtue of their imaginative grasp of our history can rightly be called his peers—interposed a critical distance between his matter and his expression of it. There is perhaps more difference between an ordinary understanding of America and Fitzgerald's than between the gaudy idealizations of the Elizabethans and the equally comfortable cynicism of twentieth-century London.

SCOTT FITZGERALD'S CRITICISM OF AMERICA*

Marius Bewley

This essay was slightly changed and enlarged in The Eccentric Design (Columbia University Press, 1959), pp. 259-87. Since the added material is not concerned with The Great Gatsby, I am using the earlier version as the text here.

Critics of Scott Fitzgerald tend to agree that *The Great Gatsby* is somehow a commentary on that elusive phrase, the American dream. The assumption seems to be that Fitzgerald approved. On the contrary, it can be shown that *The Great Gatsby* offers some of the severest and closest criticism of the American dream that our literature affords. Read in this way, Fitzgerald's masterpiece ceases to be a pastoral documentary of the Jazz Age and takes its distinguished place among those great national novels whose profound corrective insights into the nature of American experience are not separable from the artistic form of the novel itself. That is to say, Fitzgerald—at least in this one book—is in a line with the greatest masters of American prose. *The Great Gatsby* embodies a criticism of American experience—not of manners, but of a basic historic attitude to life—more radical than any-

* Marius Bewley, "Scott Fitzgerald's Criticism of America," The Sewanee Review, LXII (Spring, 1954), 223-46. Reprinted with the permission of the author.

thing in James's own assessment of the deficiencies of his country. The theme of *Gatsby* is the withering of the American dream.

Essentially, this phrase represents the romantic enlargement of the possibilities of life on a level at which the material and the spiritual have become inextricably confused. As such, it led inevitably toward the problem that has always confronted American artists dealing with American experience—the problem of determining the hidden boundary in the American vision of life at which the reality ends and the illusion begins. Historically, the American dream is anti-Calvinistic, and believes in the goodness of nature and man. It is accordingly a product of the frontier and the West rather than of the Puritan Tradition. The simultaneous operation of two such attitudes in American life created a tension out of which much of our greatest art has sprung. Youth of the spirit—perhaps of the body as well—is a requirement of its existence; limit and deprivation are its blackest devils. But it shows an astonishing incapacity to believe in them:

> I join you . . . in branding as cowardly the idea that the human mind is incapable of further advances. This is precisely the doctrine which the present despots of the earth are inculcating, and their friends here re-echoing; and applying especially to religion and politics; "that it is not probable that anything better will be discovered than what was known to our fathers." . . . But thank heaven the American mind is already too much opened to listen to these impostures, and while the art of printing is left to us, science can never be retrograde. . . . To preserve the freedom of the human mind . . . every spirit should be ready to devote itself to martyrdom. . . . But that the enthusiasm which characterizes youth should lift its parricide hands against freedom and science would be such a monstrous phenomenon as I could not place among the possible things in this age and country.

That is the hard kernel, the seed from which the American dream would grow into unpruned luxuriance. Jefferson's voice is not remote from many European voices of his time, but it stands in unique relation to the country to whom he spoke. That attitude was bred into the bone of America, and in various, often distorted, ways, it has lasted. Perhaps that is where the trouble begins, for if these virtues of the American imagination have the elements of greatness in them, they call immediately for discriminating and practical correctives. The reality in such an attitude lies in its faith in life; the illusion lies in the undiscriminating multiplication of its material possibilities.

The Great Gatsby is an exploration of the American dream as it exists in a corrupt period, and it is an attempt to determine that concealed boundary that divides the reality from the illusions. The illusions seem more real than the reality itself. Embodied in the subordinate characters in the novel, they threaten to invade the whole of the picture. On the other hand, the reality is embodied in Gatsby; and as opposed to the hard, tangible illusions, the reality is a thing of the spirit, a promise rather than the possession of a vision, a faith in the half-glimpsed, but hardly understood, possibilities of life. In Gatsby's America, the reality is undefined to itself. It is inarticulate and frustrated. Nick Carraway, Gatsby's friend and Fitzgerald's narrator, says of Gatsby:

> Through all he said, even through his appalling sentimentality, I was reminded of something—an elusive rhythm, a fragment of lost words, that I had heard somewhere a long time ago. For a moment a phrase tried to take shape in my mouth and my lips parted like a dumb man's, as though there was more struggling upon them than a wisp of startled air. But they made no sound, and what I had almost remembered was incommunicado forever.

This is not pretentious phrase-making performing a vague gesture towards some artificial significance. It is both an evocative and an exact description of that unholy cruel paradox by which the conditions of American history have condemned the grandeur of the aspiration and vision to expend itself in a waste of shame and silence. But the reality is not entirely lost. It ends by redeeming the human spirit, even though it live in a wilderness of illusions, from the cheapness and vulgarity that encompass it. In this novel, the illusions are known and condemned at last simply by the rank complacency with which they are content to be themselves. On the other hand, the reality is in the energy of the spirit's resistance, which may not recognize itself as resistance at all, but which can neither stoop to the illusions nor abide with them when they are at last recognized. Perhaps it is really nothing more than ultimate immunity from the final contamination, but it encompasses the difference between life and death. Gatsby never succeeds in seeing through the sham of his world or his acquaintances very clearly. It is of the essence of his romantic American vision that it should lack the seasoned powers of discrimination. But it invests those illusions with its own faith, and thus it discovers its projected goodness in the frauds of its crippled world. *The Great Gatsby* becomes the acting out of the tragedy of the American vision. It is a vision totally untouched by the scales of values that order life in a society governed by traditional manners; and Fitzgerald knows that although it would be easy to condemn and "place" the illusions by invoking these outside values, to do so would be to kill the reality that lies beyond them, but which can sometimes only be reached through them.

For example, Fitzgerald perfectly understood the inadequacy of Gatsby's romantic view of wealth. But that is not the point. He presents it in Gatsby as a romantic baptism of desire for a reality that stubbornly remains out of his sight. It is as if a savage islander, suddenly touched with Grace, transcended in his prayers and aspirations the grotesque little fetish in which he imagined he discovered the object of his longing. The scene in which Gatsby shows his piles of beautiful imported shirts to Daisy and Nick has been mentioned as a failure of Gatsby's, and so of Fitzgerald's, critical control of values. Actually, the shirts are sacramentals, and it is clear that Gatsby shows them, neither in vanity nor in pride, but with a reverential humility in the presence of some inner vision he cannot consciously grasp, but toward which he desperately struggles in the only way he knows.

In an essay called "Myths for Materialists" Mr. Jacques Barzun once wrote that figures, whether of fact or fiction, insofar as they express destinies, aspirations, attitudes typical of man or particular groups, are invested with a mythical character. In this sense Gatsby is a "mythic" character, and no other word will define him. Not only is he an embodiment (as Fitzgerald makes clear at the outset) of that conflict between illusion and reality at the heart of American life; he is an heroic personification of the American romantic hero, the true heir of the American dream. "There was something gorgeous about him," Nick Carraway says, and although "gorgeous" was a favorite word with the 'twenties, Gatsby wears it with an archetypal American elegance.

One need not look far in earlier American literature to find his forebears. Here is the description of a young bee hunter from *Col. David Crockett's Exploits and Adventures in Texas*, published in 1836:

> I thought myself alone in the street, where the hush of morning was suddenly broken by a clear, joyful, and musical voice, which sang. . . .
> I turned toward the spot whence the sounds proceeded, and discovered a tall figure leaning against the sign post. His eyes were fixed on the streaks of light in the east, his mind was absorbed, and he was clearly unconscious of anyone being near him. He continued his song in so full and clear a tone, that the street re-echoed. . . .
> I now drew nigh enough to see him distinctly. He was a young man, not more than twenty-two. His figure was light and graceful at the same time that it indicated strength and activity. He was dressed in a hunting shirt, which was made with uncommon neatness, and ornamented tastily with fringe. He held a highly finished rifle in his right hand, and a hunting pouch, covered with Indian ornaments, was slung across his shoulders. His clean shirt collar was open, secured only by a black riband around his neck. His boots were polished, without a soil upon them; and on his head was a neat fur cap, tossed on in a manner which said, "I don't give a d—n," just as plainly as any cap could speak it. I thought it must be some popinjay on a lark, until I took a look at his countenance.

It was handsome, bright, and manly. There was no mistake in that face. From the eyes down to the breast he was sunburnt as dark as mahogany while the upper part of his high forehead was as white and polished as marble. Thick clusters of black hair curled from under his cap. I passed on unperceived, and he continued his song. . . .

This young dandy of the frontier, dreaming in the dawn and singing to the morning, is a progenitor of Gatsby. It is because of such a traditional American ancestry that Gatsby's romanticism transcends the limiting glamor of the Jazz Age.

But such a romanticism is not enough to "mythicize" Gatsby. Gatsby, for all his shimmer of representative surfaces, is never allowed to become soiled by the touch of realism. In creating him, Fitzgerald observed as high a decorum of character as a Renaissance playwright: for Gatsby's parents were shiftless and unsuccessful farm people, Gatsby really "sprang from his Platonic conception of himself. He was a son of God—a phrase which, if it means anything, means just that—and he must be about His Father's business, the service of a vast, vulgar, meretricious beauty."

Fitzgerald created Gatsby with a sense of his own election; but the beauty it was in his nature to serve had already been betrayed by history. Even in the midst of the blighted earthly paradise of West Egg, Long Island, Gatsby bore about him the marks of his birth. He is a kind of exiled Duke in disguise. We know him by his bearing, the decorous pattern of his speech. Even his dress invariably touches the imagination: "Gatsby in a white flannel suit, silver shirt, and gold colored tie. . . ." There is something dogmatically Olympic about the combination. After Gatsby's death when his pathetic old father journeys east for the funeral, one feels that he is only the kindly shepherd who once found a baby on the cold hillside.

But so far I have been talking in general terms. This beautiful control of conventions can be studied more closely in the description of Gatsby's party at which (if we except that distant glimpse of him at the end of Chapter I, of which I shall speak later) we encounter him for the first time. We are told later that Gatsby was gifted with a "hint of the unreality of reality, a promise that the rock of the world was founded securely on a fairy's wing." Fitzgerald does not actually let us meet Gatsby face to face until he has concretely created this fantastic world of Gatsby's vision, for it is the element in which we must meet Gatsby if we are to understand his impersonal significance:

> There was music from my neighbor's house through the summer nights. In his blue gardens men and girls came and went like moths among the whisperings and the champagne and the stars. At high tide in the afternoon I watched his guests diving from the tower of his raft, or taking the sun on the hot sand of his beach while his two motor-boats slit the waters of the Sound, drawing aquaplanes over cataracts of foam. On week-ends his Rolls-Royce became an omnibus, bearing parties to and from the city between nine in the morning and long past midnight, while his station wagon scampered like a brisk yellow bug to meet all trains. And on Mondays eight servants, including an extra gardener, toiled all day with mops and scrubbing-brushes and hammers and garden-shears, repairing the ravages of the night before.

The nostalgic poetic quality, which tends to leave one longing for sterner stuff, is, in fact, deceptive. It is Gatsby's ordeal that he must separate the foul dust that floated in the wake of his dreams from the reality of the dream itself: that he must find some vantage point from which he can bring the responsibilities and the possibilities of life into a single focus. But the "ineffable gaudiness" of the world to which Gatsby is committed is a fatal deterrent. Even within the compass of this paragraph we see how the focus has become blurred: how the possibilities of life are conceived of in material terms. But in that heroic list of the vaster luxury items—motor-boats, aquaplanes, private beaches, Rolls-Royces, diving towers—Gatsby's vision maintains its gigantic unreal stature. It imposes a rhythm on his guests which they accept in terms of their own tawdry illusions, having no conception of the compulsion that drives him to offer them the hospitality of his fabulous wealth. They come for their weekends as George Dane in Henry James's *The Great Good Place* went into his dream retreat. But the result is not the same: "on Mondays eight servants, including an extra gardener, toiled all day with mops and scrubbing-brushes and hammers and garden-shears, repairing the ravages of the night before." That is the most important sentence in the paragraph, and despite the fairy-story overtone, it possesses an ironic nuance that rises toward the tragic. And how fine that touch of the extra gardener is—as if Gatsby's guests had made a breach in nature. It completely qualifies the over-fragility of the moths and champagne and blue gardens in the opening sentences.

This theme of the relation of his guests to Gatsby is still further pursued in Chapter IV. The cataloging of American proper names with poetic intention has been an ineffectual cliché in American writing for many generations. But Fitzgerald uses the convention magnificently:

> Once I wrote down on the empty spaces of a time-table the names of those who came to Gatsby's house that summer. It is an old time-table now, disintegrating at its folds, and headed "This schedule in effect July 5th, 1922." But I can still read the gray names, and they will give you a better impression than my generalities of those who accepted Gatsby's hospitality and paid him the subtle tribute of knowing nothing about him.

The names of these guests could have been recorded nowhere else as appropriately as in the margins of a faded timetable. The embodiments of illusions, they are as ephemeral as time itself; but because their illusions represent the distortions and shards of some shattered American dream, the timetable they adorn is "in effect July 5th"—the day following the great national festival when the exhausted holiday crowds, as spent as exploded firecrackers, return to their homes. The list of names which Fitzgerald proceeds to enumerate conjures up with remarkable precision an atmosphere of vulgar American fortunes and vulgar American destinies. Those

who are familiar with the social registers, business men's direc-
tories, and movie magazines of the 'twenties might be able to
analyze the exact way in which Fitzgerald achieves his effect, but
it is enough to say here that he shares with Eliot a remarkable
clairvoyance in seizing the cultural implications of proper names.
After two pages and more, the list ends with the dreamily elegiac
close: "All these people came to Gatsby's house in the summer."

Why did they come? There is the answer of the plotted story
—the free party, the motor-boats, the private beach, the endless
flow of cocktails. But in the completed pattern of the novel one
knows that they came for another reason—came blindly and instinctively—illusions in pursuit of a reality from which they have
become historically separated, but by which they might alone be
completed or fulfilled. And why did Gatsby invite them? As contrasted with them, he alone has a sense of the reality that hovers
somewhere out of sight in this nearly ruined American dream;
but the reality is unintelligible until he can invest it again with
the tangible forms of his world, and relate it to the logic of history.
Gatsby and his guests feel a mutual need of each other, but
the division in American experience has widened too far, and no
party, no hospitality however lavish, can heal the breach. The illusions and the reality go their separate ways. Gatsby stands at
the door of his mansion, in one of the most deeply moving and
significant paragraphs of the novel, to wish his guests good-bye:

> The caterwauling horns had reached a crescendo and I turned
> away and cut across the lawn toward home. I glanced back once.
> A wafer of a moon was shining over Gatsby's house, making the
> night fine as before, and surviving the laughter and the sound
> of his still glowing garden. A sudden emptiness seemed to flow now
> from the windows and the great doors, endowing with complete
> isolation the figure of the host, who stood on the porch, his hand up
> in a formal gesture of farewell.

If one turns back to Davy Crockett's description of the elegant
young bee hunter, singing while the dawn breaks in the east, and
thinks of it in relation with this midnight picture of Gatsby,

"his hand up in a formal gesture of farewell," while the last guests depart through the debris of the finished party, the quality of the romanticism seems much the same, but the situation is exactly reversed; and from the latter scene there opens a perspective of profound meaning. Suddenly Gatsby is not merely a likable, romantic hero; he is a creature of myth in whom is incarnated the aspiration and the ordeal of his race.

"Mythic" characters are impersonal. There is no distinction between their public and their private lives. Because they share their meaning with everyone, they have no secrets and no hidden corners into which they can retire for a moment, unobserved. An intimacy so universal stands revealed in a ritual pattern for the inspection and instruction of the race. The "mythic" character can never withdraw from that air which is his existence—that is to say, from that area of consciousness (and hence of publicity) which every individual shares with the members, both living and dead, of his group or race. Gatsby is a "mythic" character in this sense— he has no private life, no meaning or significance that depends on the fulfillment of his merely private destiny, his happiness as an individual in a society of individuals. In a transcendent sense he touches our imaginations, but in this smaller sense—which is the world of the realistic novel—he even fails to arouse our curiosity. At this level, his love affair with Daisy is too easily "placed," a tawdry epic "crush" of no depth or interest in itself. But Gatsby not only remains undiminished by what is essentially the meanness of the affair: his stature grows, as we watch, to the proportions of a hero. We must inquire how Fitzgerald managed this extraordinary achievement.

Daisy Buchanan exists at two well-defined levels in the novel. She is what she is—but she exists also at the level of Gatsby's vision of her. The intelligence of no other important novelist has been as consistently undervalued as Fitzgerald's, and it is hardly surprising that no critic has ever given Fitzgerald credit for his superb understanding of Daisy's vicious emptiness. Even Fitzgerald's admirers regard Daisy as rather a good, if somewhat silly, little thing; but Fitzgerald knew that at its most depraved levels the American dream merges with the American debutante's dream—a thing of deathly hollowness. Fitzgerald faces up squarely to the problem of telling us what Daisy has to offer in a human relationship. At one of Gatsby's fabulous parties—the one to which Daisy brings her husband, Tom Buchanan—Gatsby points out to Daisy and Tom, among the celebrated guests, one particular couple:

> "Perhaps you know that lady," Gatsby indicated a gorgeous, scarcely human orchid of a woman who sat in state under a white-plum tree. Tom and Daisy stared, with that peculiarly unreal feeling that accompanies the recognition of a hitherto ghostly celebrity of the movies.
> "She's lovely," said Daisy.
> "The man bending over her is her director."

Superficially, the scene is highly civilized. One fancies one has seen it in Manet. But in the context we know that it has no reality whatever—the star and her director can get no nearer reality than by rehearsing a scene. Our attention is then taken up by other scenes at the party, but by suddenly returning to this couple after an interval of two pages to make his point, Fitzgerald achieves a curious impression of static or arrested action. We have the feeling that if we walked behind the white-plum tree we should only see the back of a canvas screen:

> Almost the last thing I remember was standing with Daisy and watching the moving-picture director and his Star. They were still under the white-plum tree and their faces were touching except for a pale, thin ray of moonlight between. It occurred to me that he had been very slowly bending toward her all evening to attain this proximity, and even while I watched I saw him stoop one ultimate degree and kiss at her cheek.
> "I like her," said Daisy, "I think she's lovely."
> But the rest offended her—and inarguably, because it wasn't a gesture but an emotion.

Daisy likes the moving-picture actress because she has no substance. She is a gesture that is committed to nothing more real than her own image on the silver screen. She has become a gesture divorced forever from the tiresomeness of human reality. In effect, this passage is Daisy's confession of faith. She virtually announces here what her criteria of human emotions and conduct are. Fitzgerald's illustration of the emptiness of Daisy's character —an emptiness that we see curdling into the viciousness of a monstrous moral indifference as the story unfolds—is drawn with a fineness and depth of critical understanding, and communicated with a force of imagery so rare in modern American writing, that it is almost astonishing that he is often credited with giving in to those very qualities which *The Great Gatsby* so effectively excoriates.

But what is the basis for the mutual attraction between Daisy and Gatsby? In Daisy's case the answer is simple. We remember that Nick Carraway has described Gatsby's personality as an "unbroken series of successful gestures." Superficially, Daisy finds in Gatsby, or thinks she finds, that safety from human reality which the empty gesture implies. What she fails to realize is that Gatsby's gorgeous gesturings are the reflex of an aspiration toward the possibilities of life, and this is something entirely different from those vacant images of romance and sophistication that fade so easily into the nothingness from which they came. But in a sense, Daisy is safe enough from the reality she dreads. The true question is not what Gatsby sees in Daisy, but the direction he takes from her, what he sees *beyond* her; and that has, despite the immaturity intrinsic in Gatsby's vision, an element of grandeur in it. For Gatsby, Daisy does not exist in herself. She is the green light that signals him into the heart of his ultimate vision. *Why* she should have this evocative power over Gatsby is a question Fitzgerald faces beautifully and successfully as he recreates that milieu of uncritical snobbishness and frustrated idealism—monstrous fusion—which is the world in which Gatsby is compelled to live.

Fitzgerald, then, has a sure control when he defines the quality of this love affair. He shows it in itself as vulgar and specious. It has no possible interest in its own right, and if it did have the pattern of the novel would be ruined. Our imaginations would be fettered in those details and interests which would detain us on the narrative level where the affair works itself out as human history, and Gatsby would lose his "mythic" quality. But the economy with which Gatsby is presented, the formal and boldly drawn structural lines of his imagination lead us at once to a level where it is obvious that Daisy's significance in the story lies in her failure to represent the objective correlative of Gatsby's vision. And at the same time, Daisy's wonderfully representative quality as a creature of the Jazz Age relates her personal failure to the larger failure of Gatsby's society to satisfy his need. In fact, Fitzgerald never allows Daisy's failure to become a human or personal one. He maintains it with sureness on a symbolic level where it is identified with and reflects the failure of Gatsby's decadent American world. There is a famous passage in which Gatsby sees Daisy as an embodiment of the glamor of wealth. Nick Carraway is speaking first to Gatsby:

"She's got an indiscreet voice," I remarked. "It's full of—" I hesitated.
"Her voice is full of money," he said suddenly. That was it. I'd never understood before. It was full of money—that was the inexhaustible charm that rose and fell in it, the jingle of it, the cymbals' song of it. . . . High in a white palace the king's daughter, the golden girl . . .

Gatsby tries to build up the inadequacy of each value by the support of the other; but united they fall as wretchedly short of what he is seeking as each does singly. Gatsby's gold and Gatsby's girl belong to the fairy story in which the Princess spins whole rooms of money from skeins of wool. In the fairy story, the value never lies in the gold but in something beyond. And so it is in this story. For Gatsby, Daisy is only the promise of fulfillment that lies beyond the green light that burns all night on her dock.

This green light that is visible at night across the bay from the windows and lawn of Gatsby's house is the central symbol in the book. Significantly, our first glimpse of Gatsby at the end of Chapter I is related to it. Nick Carraway, whose modest bungalow in West Egg stands next to Gatsby's mansion, returning from an evening at the Buchanans', while lingering on the lawn for a final moment under the stars, becomes aware that he is not alone:

> . . . fifty feet away a figure had emerged from the shadow of my neighbor's mansion and was standing with his hands in his pockets regarding the silver pepper of the stars. Something in his leisurely movements and the secure position of his feet upon the lawn suggested that it was Mr. Gatsby himself, come out to determine what share was his of our local heavens.
>
> I decided to call to him. . . . But I didn't . . . for he gave a sudden intimation that he was content to be alone—he stretched out his arms toward the dark water in a curious way, and, as far as I was from him, I could have sworn he was trembling. Involuntarily I glanced seaward—and distinguished nothing except a single green light, minute and far away, that might have been the end of a dock. When I looked once more for Gatsby he had vanished, and I was alone again in the unquiet darkness.

It is hardly too much to say that the whole being of Gatsby exists only in relation to what the green light symbolizes. This first sight we have of Gatsby is a ritualistic tableau that literally contains the meaning of the completed book, although the full meaning of what is implicit in the symbol reveals itself slowly, and is only finally rounded out on the last page. We have a fuller definition of what the green light means in its particular, as opposed to its universal, signification in Chapter V. Gatsby is speaking to Daisy as they stand at one of the windows of his mansion:

"If it wasn't for the mist we could see your home across the bay," said Gatsby. "You always have a green light that burns all night at the end of your dock."

Daisy put her arm through his abruptly, but he seemed absorbed in what he had just said. Possibly it had occurred to him that the colossal significance of that light had now vanished forever. Compared to the great distance that had separated him from Daisy it had seemed very near to her, almost touching her. It had seemed as close as a star to the moon. Now it was again a green light on a dock. His count of enchanted objects had diminished by one.

Some might object to this symbolism on the grounds that it is easily vulgarized—as A. J. Cronin has proved. But if studied carefully in its full context it represents a convincing achievement. The tone or pitch of the symbol is exactly adequate to the problem it dramatizes. Its immediate function is that it signals Gatsby into his future, away from the cheapness of his affair with Daisy which he has vainly tried (and desperately continues trying) to create in the image of his vision. The green light is successful because, apart from its visual effectiveness as it gleams across the bay, it embodies the profound naiveté of Gatsby's sense of the future, while simultaneously suggesting the historicity of his hope. This note of historicity is not fully apparent at this point, of course. The symbol occurs several times, and most notably at the end:

Gatsby believed in the green light, the orgiastic future that year by year recedes before us. It eluded us then, but that's no matter —tomorrow we will run faster, stretch out our arms farther. . . . And one fine morning—

So we beat on, boats against the current, borne back ceaselessly into the past.

Thus the American dream, whose superstitious valuation of the future began in the past, gives the green light through which alone the American returns to his traditional roots, paradoxically retreating into the pattern of history while endeavoring to exploit the possibilities of the future. There is a suggestive echo of the past in Gatsby's sense of Daisy. He had known her, and fallen in love with her, five years before the novel opens. During that long interval while they had disappeared from each other's sight, Daisy has become a legend in Gatsby's memory, a part of his private past through which (as a "mythic" character) he assimilates into the pattern of that historic past through which he would move into the historic future. But the legendary Daisy, meeting her after five years, has dimmed a little in luster:

> "And she doesn't understand," he said. "She used to be able to understand. We'd sit for hours—"
> He broke off and began to walk up and down a desolate path of fruit rinds and discarded favors and crushed flowers.
> "I wouldn't ask too much of her," I ventured. "You can't repeat the past."
> "Can't repeat the past?" he cried incredulously. "Why of course you can!"
> He looked around him wildly, as if the past were lurking here in the shadow of his house, just out of reach of his hand.

By such passages Fitzgerald dramatizes Gatsby's symbolic role. The American dream, stretched between a golden past and a golden future, is always betrayed by a desolate present—a moment of fruit rinds and discarded favors and crushed flowers. Imprisoned in his present, Gatsby belongs even more to the past than to the future. His aspirations have been rehearsed, and his tragedy suffered, by all the generations of Americans who have gone before. His sense of the future, of the possibilities of life, he has learned from the dead.

If we return to the passage in which, linked arm in arm, Gatsby and Daisy stand at the window looking toward the green light across the bay, it may be possible to follow a little more sympathetically that quality of disillusion which begins to creep into Gatsby's response to life. It does not happen because of the impoverished elements of his practical romance: it happens because Gatsby is incapable of compromising with his inner vision.

The imagery of this particular passage, as I suggested, is gauged to meet the requirements of Gatsby's young romantic dream. But two pages later Fitzgerald takes up the theme of Gatsby's struggle against disenchantment once again, and this time in an imagery that suggests how much he had learned from *The Waste Land:*

> When Klipspringer had played "The Love Nest" he turned around on the bench and searched unhappily for Gatsby in the gloom.
> "I'm all out of practice, you see. I told you I couldn't play. I'm all out of prac—"
> "Don't talk so much, old sport," commanded Gatsby. "Play!"
>
> > *In the morning,*
> > *In the evening,*
> > *Ain't we got fun—*
>
> Outside the wind was loud and there was a faint flow of thunder along the Sound. All the lights were going on in West Egg now; the electric trains, men-carrying, were plunging home through the rain from New York. It was the hour of a profound human change, and excitement was generating on the air.
>
> > *One thing's sure and nothing's surer*
> > *The rich get richer and the poor get—children.*
> > *In the meantime,*
> > *In between time—*
>
> As I went over to say good-by I saw that the expression of bewilderment had come back into Gatsby's face, as though a faint doubt had occurred to him as to the quality of his present happiness. Almost five years! There must have been moments even that afternoon when Daisy tumbled short of his dreams—not through her own fault, but because of the colossal vitality of his illusion. It had gone beyond her, beyond everything. He had thrown himself into it with a creative passion, adding to it all the time, decking it out with every bright feather that drifted his way. No amount of fire or freshness can challenge what a man can store up in his ghostly heart.

In view of such writing it is absurd to argue that Fitzgerald's art was a victim of his own attraction to the Jazz Age. The snatches of song that Klipspringer sings evoke the period with an immediacy that is necessary if we are to understand the peculiar poignancy of Gatsby's ordeal. But the songs are more than evocative. They provide the ironic musical prothalamion for Gatsby's romance, and as Gatsby listens to them an intimation of the practical truth presses in on him. The recognition is heightened poetically by that sense of the elements, the faint flow of thunder along the Sound, which forms the background of those artificial little tunes. And it is not odd that this evocation of the outdoor scene, while Klipspringer pounds at the piano inside, sustains in the imagination the image of that green light, symbol of Gatsby's faith, which is burning across the bay. This scene draws on the "violet hour" passage from "The Fire Sermon" in which "the human engine waits/Like a taxi throbbing waiting. . . ." It is the hour of a profound human change, and in the faint stirrings of Gatsby's recognition there is for a moment, perhaps, a possibility of his escape. But the essence of the American dream whose tragedy Gatsby is enacting is that it lives in a past and a future that never existed, and is helpless in the present that does.

Gatsby's opposite number in the story is Daisy's husband, Tom Buchanan, and Gatsby's stature—his touch of doomed but imperishable spiritual beauty, if I may call it so—is defined by his contrast with Tom. In many ways they are analogous in their characteristics—just sufficiently so to point up the differences. For example, their youth is an essential quality of them both. But Tom Buchanan was "one of those men who reach such an acute limited excellence at twenty-one that everything afterward savors of anti-climax." Even his body—"a body capable of enormous leverage"—was "a cruel body." In the description of Tom we are left physically face to face with a scion of those ruthless generations who raised up the great American fortunes, and who now live in uneasy arrogant leisure on their brutal acquisitions. But Gatsby's youth leaves an impression of interminability. Its climax is always in the future, and it gives rather than demands. Its energy is not in its body, but in its spirit, and meeting Gatsby for the first time, one seizes, as Nick Carraway did, this impression in his smile:

> It was one of those rare smiles with a quality of eternal re-assurance in it, that you may come across four or five times in life. It faced—or seemed to face—the whole eternal world for an instant, and then concentrated on *you* with an irresistible prejudice in your favor. It understood you just as far as you wanted to be understood, believed in you as you would like to believe in yourself, and assured you that it had precisely the impression of you that, at your best, you hoped to convey. Precisely at that point it vanished— and I was looking at an elegant young rough-neck, a year or two over thirty, whose elaborate formality of speech just missed being absurd.

This passage is masterly in the way in which it presents Gatsby to us less as an individual than as a projection, or mirror, of our ideal selves. To do that is the function of all "mythic" characters. Gatsby's youth is not simply a matter of three decades that will quickly multiply themselves into four or five. It is a quality of faith and hope that may be betrayed by history, may be killed by society, but that no exposure to the cynical turns of time can reduce to the compromises of age.

Again, Gatsby and Tom are alike in the possession of a certain sentimentality, but Tom Buchanan's is based on depraved self-pity. He is never more typical than when coaxing himself to tears over a half-finished box of dog biscuits that recalls a drunken and illicit day from his past, associated in memory with his dead mistress. His self-pity is functional. It is sufficient to condone his most criminal acts in his own eyes as long as the crimes are not imputable. But Gatsby's sentimentality exists in the difficulty of expressing, in the phrases and symbols provided by his decadent society, the reality that lies at the heart of his aspiration. "So he waited, listening for a moment longer to the tuning fork that had been struck upon a star"—Gatsby's sentimentality (if it *is* sentimentality, and I rather doubt it) is as innocent as that. It has nothing of self-pity or indulgence in it—it is all aspiration and goodness; and it must be remembered that Fitzgerald himself is *outside* Gatsby's vocabulary, using it with great mastery to convey the poignancy of the situation.

Tom Buchanan and Gatsby represent antagonistic but historically related aspects of America. They are related as the body and the soul when a mortal barrier has risen up between them. Tom Buchanan is virtually Gatsby's murderer in the end, but the crime that he commits by proxy is only a symbol of his deeper spiritual crime against Gatsby's inner vision. Gatsby's guilt, insofar as it exists, is radical failure—a failure of the critical faculty that seems to be an inherent part of the American dream—to understand that Daisy is as fully immersed in the destructive element of the American world as Tom himself. After Daisy, while driving Gatsby's white automobile, has killed Mrs. Wilson and, implicitly at least, left Gatsby to shoulder the blame, Nick Carraway gives us a crucial insight into the spiritual affinity of the Buchanan couple, drawing together in their callous selfishness in a moment of guilt and crisis:

> Daisy and Tom were sitting opposite each other at the kitchen table, with a plate of cold fried chicken between them, and two bottles of ale. He was talking intently across the table at her, and in his earnestness his hand had fallen upon and covered her own. Once in a while she looked up at him and nodded in agreement.
> They weren't happy, and neither of them had touched the chicken or the ale—and yet they weren't unhappy either. There was an unmistakable air of natural intimacy about the picture, and anybody would have said that they were conspiring together.

They instinctively seek out each other because each recognizes the other's strength in the corrupt spiritual element they inhabit.

There is little point in tracing out in detail the implications of the action any further, although it could be done with an exactness approaching allegory. That it is not allegory is owing to the fact that the pattern emerges from the fullness of Fitzgerald's living experience of his own society and time. In the end the most that can be said is that *The Great Gatsby* is a dramatic affirmation in fictional terms of the American spirit in the midst of an American world that denies the soul. Gatsby exists in, and for, that affirmation alone.

When, at the end, not even Gatsby can hide his recognition of the speciousness of his dream any longer, the discovery is made in universalizing terms that dissolve Daisy into the larger world she has stood for in Gatsby's imagination:

> He must have looked up at an unfamiliar sky through frightening leaves and shivered as he found what a grotesque thing a rose is and how raw the sunlight was upon the scarcely created grass. A new world, material without being real, where poor ghosts, breathing dreams like air, drifted fortuitously about. . . .

"A new world, material without being real." Paradoxically, it was Gatsby's dream that conferred reality upon the world. The reality was in his faith in the goodness of creation, and in the possibilities of life. That these possibilities were intrinsically related to such romantic components limited and distorted his dream, and finally left it helpless in the face of the Buchanans, but it did not corrupt it. When the dream melted, it knocked the prop of reality from under the universe, and face to face with the physical substance at last, Gatsby realized that the illusion was *there*—there where Tom and Daisy, and generations of small-minded, ruthless Americans had found it—in the dreamless, visionless complacency of mere matter, substance without form. After this recognition, Gatsby's death is only a symbolic formality, for the world into which his mere body had been born rejected the gift he had been created to embody—the traditional dream from which alone it could awaken into life.

As the novel closes, the experience of Gatsby and his broken dream explicitly becomes the focus of that historic dream for which he stands. Nick Carraway is speaking:

Most of the big shore places were closed now and there were hardly any lights except the shadowy, moving glow of a ferryboat across the Sound. And as the moon rose higher the inessential houses began to melt away until gradually I became aware of the old island here that flowered once for Dutch sailors' eyes—a fresh, green breast of the new world. Its vanished trees, the trees that had once made way for Gatsby's house, had once pandered in whispers to the last and greatest of all human dreams; for a transitory enchanted moment man must have held his breath in the presence of this continent, compelled into an aesthetic contemplation he neither understood nor desired, face to face for the last time in history with something commensurate to his capacity for wonder.

It is fitting that this, like so many of the others in *Gatsby*, should be a moonlight scene, for the history and the romance are one. Gatsby fades into the past forever to take his place with the Dutch sailors who had chosen their moment in time so much more happily than he.

We recognize that the great achievement of this novel is that it manages, while poetically evoking a sense of the goodness of that early dream, to offer the most damaging criticism of it in American literature. The astonishing thing is that the criticism—if indictment wouldn't be the better word—manages to be part of the tribute. Gatsby, the "mythic" embodiment of the American dream, is shown to us in all his immature romanticism. His insecure grasp of social and human values, his lack of critical intelligence and self-knowledge, his blindness to the pitfalls that surround him in American society, his compulsive optimism, are realized in the text with rare assurance and understanding. And yet the very grounding of these deficiencies is Gatsby's goodness and faith in life, his compelling desire to realize all the possibilities of existence, his belief that we can have an Earthly Paradise populated by Buchanans. A great part of Fitzgerald's achievement is that he suggests effectively that these terrifying deficiencies are not so much the private deficiencies of Gatsby, but are deficiencies inherent in contemporary manifestations of the American vision itself—a vision no doubt admirable, but stupidly defenseless before the equally American world of Tom and Daisy. Gatsby's deficiencies of intelligence and judgment bring him to his tragic death— a death that is spiritual as well as physical. But the more important question that faces us through our sense of the immediate tragedy is where they have brought America.

THE THEME AND THE NARRATOR OF
'THE GREAT GATSBY'*

Thomas Hanzo

Of the two most prominent careers which figure in F. Scott Fitzgerald's *The Great Gatsby*, Jay Gatsby's is a variation of the American success story, and Nick Carraway's is an example, differing
from others in locale and therefore also in implication, of the
provincial American's career in a society more sophisticated than
his own.[1] Fitzgerald was able to combine the types through the
convention of the first person narration, but Nick's fate has been
generally ignored in detailed criticisms of the book. Gatsby and
his dream, in these interpretations, are Fitzgerald's subjects, and
through them is seen his ultimate subject, "fundamentally, the
heterogeneous nature of American culture," as a recent article has
it.[2] Lionel Trilling has suggested a use of this conception by Fitzgerald which, by a slight distortion, I should like to develop for

[1] The Americans of Henry James' novels are examples of the type; James dealt,
according to Yvor Winters, "with the American, uprooted from his native
usages, and confronted with the alien usages of a subtle and ancient society."
"Maule's Well, or Henry James and the Relation of Morals to Manners,"
In Defense of Reason (New York, 1947), p. 312.
[2] W. M. Frohock, "Morals, Manners and Scott Fitzgerald," *Southwest Review*, XL (Summer, 1955), p. 224.
* Thomas Hanzo, "The Theme and the Narrator of 'The Great Gatsby',"
Modern Fiction Studies II (Winter, 1956-1957), 183-90. Reprinted with the
permission of the author and Modern Fiction Studies.

my own purposes: "He [Fitzgerald] exaggerated the idea of society and his dependence upon it in order, we may say, to provide a field for the activity of his conscience, for the trial of his self."[3] Gatsby surely represents one of Fitzgerald's trials of self, an incomplete one, however, in contrast with the less dramatic experience of Nick Carraway. Fitzgerald's intention cannot be clarified, nor the significance of his achievement grasped, without our sharing with Nick the trial of his self and the activity of his conscience in that society of which Gatsby is only the most notable part.

When Carraway's voice introduces and concludes the action, Fitzgerald makes us conscious of the narrator, whose role may first be outlined by a comparison in which he acts the foil to Gatsby. We may begin with a difference which Fitzgerald would rightly have approved: Gatsby is rich, Nick relatively poor. Gatsby is alone, mysterious, obsessed; Nick makes friends easily, his life is ordinary, and he is quite sane. Gatsby is without conscience except perhaps where Daisy is concerned, and Nick subjects every act and motive to the scrutiny of a lively moral sense. Gatsby learns nothing in the course of the novel, or at least until his doom has been secured, for he decided too early what he wanted and strove for it with a determination which subordinated all other demands. Although Nick is thirty years old in the summer of 1922, the time of the novel, he is still an adolescent when he settles on Long Island, with an adolescent's memory of the war, and he comes to New York to enter the bondselling business chiefly because other restless young men are doing the same thing. Nick has no purposes, he thinks of no powers to realize, and only very gradually, not until sometime in 1924, does he come to understand what his New York interlude has meant.

I cannot presume that this view of Carraway's part in the novel constitutes a revolutionary interpretation of *The Great Gatsby*. Arthur Mizener, whose analysis of *The Great Gatsby* has appeared in several forms and is undoubtedly the most widely distributed,

[3] "Fitzgerald Plain," *The New Yorker*, 26:4 (February 3, 1951), p. 80.

approves Fitzgerald's choice of form and recognizes the structural importance of the first-person convention: "By means of this narrator he [Fitzgerald] was able to focus his story."[4] But the novel is the story of Gatsby, "a poor boy from the Middle West," and when Mr. Mizener classifies *The Great Gatsby* as a "tragic pastoral," it is Gatsby who illustrates the difference between the "simple virtue" of the West, and the "sophistication" and "corruption" of the East.[5] The moral distance between the two localities may be measured in more profound ways if we take Nick Carraway as our example and his sensibility and intelligence as the recognizable determinants which inform the story with its meaning. Such a reading of *The Great Gatsby* must also be compared, and at several points, with the interpretation of R. W. Stallman, who, in "Gatsby and the Hole in Time," characterizes Nick as a "defunct arch-priest" and regards the notion that Nick is to be seen as the "moral center of the book" as possible only to the "duped reader."[6] Fitzgerald's intention that we understand clearly what happens to Carraway may be appreciated in the first part of the first chapter. The novel's extraordinary economy requires, at least in its best parts, an attentive reading of detail, and since there are barely two pages in the first section, a close following of the text will not be intolerable.

Nick Carraway begins his story with the recollection that his father advised him to reserve his judgment of others because they may not have had the same "advantages." Nick's tolerance has made him the confidant of some and the victim of others, but to preserve his caution he has always reminded himself that "a sense of the fundamental decencies is parcelled out unequally at birth." Carraway's father has warned him about the difficulties of moral

[4] "F. Scott Fitzgerald: The Poet of Borrowed Time," *Critiques and Essays on Modern Fiction*, p. 295. Mr. Mizener, an acute reader of Fitzgerald, is well aware of Nick's moral involvement in the action of *The Great Gatsby*. I can hope to complement his analysis by a fullness of treatment he did not judge necessary.
[5] *Ibid.*, p. 296.
[6] *Modern Fiction Studies*, I (November, 1955), p. 7.

judgment, a difficulty originating in circumstances of origin and inheritance. But conduct, Nick observes, must be principled in some fashion. There is a "limit" to toleration. "Conduct may be founded on the hard rock or on the wet marshes, but after a certain point I don't care what it's founded on." That is, while it may be impossible to fix moral responsibility or to determine derelictions from that responsibility, Nick insists that action reveal some principle and that toleration does not permit indifference. His criticism of the standards and conduct of his Long Island friends has tired him, he concludes; he can wish the world "to stand at a sort of moral attention forever"; he wants no more "riotous" glimpses into the human heart. We should be too hasty if we condemned Nick for an unhealthy curiosity or for pompous self-righteousness. The tone of his narrative is never offensively positive, and we shall see that what may appear to be a peculiar form of pride is actually a serious kind of candor. Nick considers not only his friends, but himself as well. He tells us plainly what should interest us in his tale, and he introduces us to a period of his own life in which he is not entirely blameless and neutral. The quality of plainness, the device of direct revelation, has appeared to R. W. Stallman as the mask of the hypocrite, who is betrayed, symbolically, by his "irregular lawn."[7] To the contrary, Nick's irregularities of behavior, his carelessness, do not escape his judgment; he does not grow more confused but learns to see more clearly what Eastern society and morality are and how he has been corrupted by them.

Nick prepares us for his personal involvement in the action by his next words, when he reveals his own origins, or his reasons for thinking that he had "advantages." He came from a family of "prominent, well-to-do people" who have lived in "this Middle Western city for three generations." They have enjoyed commercial success, act together as a family, and regard the decisions and conduct of their relatives with grave concern. They have in-

[7] Ibid.

herited the moral seriousness of their Scottish ancestors, sustain their business and social position as a manifestation of their moral superiority, and have passed down to their heirs a strong "sense of the fundamental decencies."

The narrator's part complicates the action. We are expected to realize that what we are told comes to us through his peculiar agency, and therefore—to complete an obvious matter—our knowledge of the narrator will establish the limits of our knowledge of the whole action. Fitzgerald understood these limitations and in the direct, economical way of *The Great Gatsby* engages the reader at once in the particular interests which the novel should arouse. Immediately after his introductory remarks, Carraway narrates his first visit to the Buchanan household, where he delivers an exact description of a moneyed and corrupt Eastern society in Daisy's despair and in Tom's adulteries.

Here Nick meets Jordan Baker, a professional tennis player who has succumbed to the ennui of the frantic search for novelty and excitement to which she and others of her post-war generation had devoted themselves. She is also a persistent and obvious liar, and Nick soon perceives this fault. Yet he is interested in her, though exactly how intimate they become is only suggested by a scene in which Jordan easily accepts Nick's first attentions. Her unconcern for any standards beyond those of a frank self-indulgence is evidence enough that the two have become lovers. This relationship is Nick's most personal involvement in the dissolution which Jordan represents, and the perception of his share in a common guilt comes with his initial revulsion to his summer's experience, directly after Myrtle Wilson's death. He is suddenly disgusted by the vicious and now violent life about him, but even in his new wisdom, his passion for Jordan has not been completely destroyed. In his last conversation with her, he can feel that he might be "making a mistake" by ending their affair and finally that he is "half in love with her." We learn most about them at this point in Jordan's accusation that Nick is a "bad driver." He

is not the person she thought—not what he pretended to be—
and she says, "It was careless of me to make such a wrong guess.
I thought you were rather an honest, straightforward person. I
thought it was your secret pride." Nick answers: "I'm thirty. I'm
five years too old to lie to myself and call it honor." It was Nick's
pride to feel that he could accept Jordan on her own terms, with
her cynicism and her irresponsibility, and yet that he could escape
the consequences of that acceptance. But what was subdued or
ignored has now erupted, with Gatsby murdered and with Daisy
and Tom exposed in their terrible selfishness. It can no longer be
honorable for Nick to maintain the pretense that nothing serious
is involved in his affair with Jordan. Nick was dishonest because
he acted as though he brought no other standards of conduct to
judge their liaison with than those which Jordan's hedonism im-
pose; and it is now plain, in his disgust and self-recrimination, that
Nick has in fact deceived Jordan. She accuses him of having
thought of her all along as he does now, when he has given her
up. She is right, of course, and Nick, who is (he tells us) the most
honest man he knows, admits his twice-compounded duplicity, a
duplicity analyzed in a similar way by R. W. Stallman. But he
does not accept Nick's understanding of his personal responsibility.
When Jordan "calls his bluff," as Stallman puts it, the effect is to
make public Nick's own shame, so that, far from being "identified"
with Jordan,[8] Nick is separated from her and from her society. He
can no longer lie, and he leaves the East, without honor perhaps,
but with a new-found vision of his own guilt.

There is another complication in Nick's discovery of his error.
Even Jordan Baker, he says, came from the West. All the Westerners—Tom, Daisy, Gatsby, Jordan, and Nick—"possessed some
deficiency in common which made us subtly unadaptable to Eastern
life." Though the rest may have become more acclimated to the
atmosphere of Eastern society than Nick, none is entirely at ease.
None can rid himself of that "sense of the fundamental decencies,"

[8] *Ibid.,* p. 8.

however attenuated it may have become, which their origins have given them. None can finally be comfortable in the hedonism cultivated by the Eastern representatives of his generation, or at least by those with money and enough intelligence to be disillusioned by the war. After his revulsion, Nick returns to the comparatively rigid morality of his ancestral West and to its embodiment in the manners of Western society. He alone of all the Westerners can return, since the others have suffered, apparently beyond any conceivable redemption, a moral degeneration brought on by their meeting with that form of Eastern society which developed during the twenties.

Nick makes another commitment to the life he at last rejects, a commitment that includes what we should ordinarily take to be his humiliating part in the affair between Gatsby and Daisy. Nick is used and knows it, but his attachment to Gatsby leads him to make another important discovery, however vague it may remain in some respects, about the nature of morality itself. We should ask: What does Nick think of Gatsby? And why? And again a passage at the beginning of the novel will reveal the essential information.

After Nick has explained that there must be limits to his toleration, he excepts Gatsby from his general reaction, "Gatsby, who represented everything for which I have an unaffected scorn." "There was something gorgeous about him, some heightened sensitivity to the promises of life. . . ." Gatsby had "an extraordinary gift for hope, a romantic readiness." Gatsby, Nick says, "turned out all right at the end," and it was not he who drew Nick's scorn, but the "foul dust" which "floated in the wake of his dreams." We learn gradually about Gatsby's dream: about the events of his early life and his peculiar training, about his obsession, about his impersonal—indeed, royal—view of his own personality, about the reality which his vision of the perfect life must have seemed to him. Now, the capacities which Nick admires are the capacities of will: a tremendous energy to accomplish certain purposes, and a self-imposed delusion which makes those purposes meaningful. The delusion is the vision of Gatsby's life with Daisy, and the purposes are his need for money and social position to make himself worthy of her. Gatsby differs from the others of his time by virtue of these capacities. Whereas the behavior of the Eastern rich, the racketeers, and the Westerners who adopt Eastern ways is restricted and debased by the selfish motives of personal and sensual gratification, Gatsby acts for a good which he conceives, almost absurdly, as being beyond personal interest. Gatsby's last heroism in protection of the mistress of his dream confirms Nick's judgment. Gatsby does turn out all right, while Tom and Daisy sit comfortably at their family table, bound in their private safety. If Gatsby, as Nick says at the end, "felt that he had lost the old warm world, paid a high price for living too long with a single dream," his sacrifice has already been made and his life consummated. He had found a way to live as men had once lived, with a purpose and a meaning which transcended personal fate.

Nick accepts the probability that Gatsby himself realized the insufficiency of his dream. The vision was only Gatsby's and his goal only a personal one, if somehow ennobled, as Nick sees it, by Gatsby's strength of will. Further, Gatsby is a fraud. The structure of appearance erected to impress Daisy is founded on some kind of illegal traffic which only repels her, so that she is lost to Gatsby even before the accident of Myrtle's death. Nor is Nick ever in any doubt that Gatsby has valued only the tawdry and the vain. He is left at last with Gatsby's morality, or rather Gatsby's capacity to live according to a morality, his "romantic readiness." It is this ability which Nick feels that he and the others lack, presumably because of historical circumstance.

That, at least, is what I take to be the meaning of the last words of the novel, on the night when Nick left West Egg forever, and the "inessential houses began to melt away until gradually I became aware of the old island here that flowered once for Dutch sailors' eyes—a fresh green breast of the new world. Its vanished trees, the trees that had made way for Gatsby's house, had once pandered in whispers to the last and greatest of all human dreams. . . ." In Nick's day, I conclude, such dreams no longer correspond to any reality.[9] They present no real challenges, and only disillusion, even for a man like Gatsby, can ensue, if a lesser dream like Gatsby's is accepted. When Gatsby "picked out the green light at the end of Daisy's dock," Nick continues, "he did not know that it [his dream] was already behind him." A last contrast may now be made clear between Gatsby and Nick, Gatsby who thought he could remake the past and Nick who knew that it was irretrievably lost and that more than Gatsby's dream had gone with it.

Nick's discovery is that the power of will without the direction of intelligence is a destructive power, that there must be some real end beyond the satisfaction of private desire—however desire may be exalted—to justify the expenditure of life. But he believes too that, except for the anachronistic and fatal instance of Gatsby, the time when such ends could have existed is now done. We can only "beat on, boats against the current, borne back ceaselessly into the past."

Fitzgerald represents the past both as a loss and as a source of strength. It is the record of such deeds springing from such dedication as cannot now be expected, and in the Carraway family tradition, it confers a discipline and standards which, even as survivals of an old morality, may still produce better conduct than Nick witnesses on Long Island. Nick's honesty and his conception of a good existing beyond selfish ends may be only heirlooms, he realizes, honored for sentimental reasons, but they have been given a contemporary, limited reality in his own life. Nick includes

[9] Edwin S. Fussell suggests that the dream of the Dutch sailors was also "unreal" and relies on the associations of the word *pandered* to develop this theme of the failure of romantic wonder, the quest for youth and success. "Fitzgerald's Brave New World," ELH, XIX (1952), p. 298. The interpretation may be allowed, but only, I think, if the old dream be regarded as the "last and greatest." Gatsby's dream was, to repeat, an illusion.

his morality in his description of a graceless modern age and re-
duces his claims on it to the satisfaction of individual conscience.
He has no real alternative—in the sense that it may be said to be
available to other men—to the selfishness he condemns in Tom or
Jordan. He does not speak authoritatively. But while his voice is
subdued, it is never unsure. Nick's judgments are firm because he
assumes that evil may be clearly enough determined. His hopes
are modest because he regards the good only as a private, incom-
municable possession. He can assert his criticism and judgment of
Eastern society, including the revelation of his own guilt, but he
affirms no morality of his own, accepting the circumstances of his
birthright rather than affirming its permanent values. That Nick
proposes to "save the world by regimenting it,"[10] as R. W. Stallman
has it, because he wants the world to be at a "sort of moral attention forever" is a reading which attributes this understandable
reaction, this moral inertia, to a rigidity which Nick's private convictions could not support. Fitzgerald—so far as we can discern
from the tenor of his narration—expects to meet no disagreement
with his perception of evil, but assumes that he and his readers
will all be perplexed to find a common good. This combination of
conviction and diffidence produces the extraordinary contrast between the effects of cryptic description (as in Gatsby's youthful
regimen) and of ideographic device (as in Dr. Eckleburg's eyes)
and the quiet and deprecated role of the narrator.

Such an interpretation credits Fitzgerald with a moral seriousness which has, with reason, been challenged. With R. W. Stallman, W. M. Frohock finds Nick "short on moral perspective"[11]
and Fitzgerald's style catching the "feeling of things" but combined with a "romantic inability to interpret them."[12] Edwin S.
Fussell, on the other hand, defines the story of The Great Gatsby
and other works as "the work of the imagination in the New

[10] "Gatsby and the Hole in Time," p. 7.
[11] "Morals, Manners, and Scott Fitzgerald," p. 227.
[12] Ibid., p. 228.

World";[13] its failure to discover an objective for the romantic capacity is an American tragedy.[14] Failure, of course, attends Gatsby's career as inexorably as the current which sweeps the boats back into the past, but the failure must be experienced through Nick's moral sense, and his difficulties must be judged not as a lack of moral perspective but as the occasion for moral action of a peculiarly limited sort. Such a reading of Nick's role restores the emphasis which Fitzgerald gave to that moral judgment (developing awkwardly, it is true) which gives the novel its very form. And it may cast some light on the question of what Fitzgerald's early Catholic training may have meant to him:[15] a training which left him with the means to analyze and judge post-war American society even while he had lost the convictions which might have produced something more positive than Nick's retreat to the West.

The Great Gatsby is not a melodrama about Jay Gatsby, but a definition of the senses in which Nick understands the word "great." Its subject is an American morality. It is explored historically through the conflict between the surviving Puritan morality of the West and the post-war hedonism of the East; topically, through characteristic manifestations of American money values; formally and most significantly, through the personal history of a young American provincial whose moral intelligence is the proper source of our understanding and whose career, in the passage from innocence to revaluation, dramatizes the possibility and mode of a moral sanction in contemporary America.

[13] "Fitzgerald's Brave New World," p. 291.
[14] Ibid., p. 297.
[15] See the query by Professor H. W. Hausermann in Modern Fiction Studies, II, 2 (May, 1956), pp. 81-82.

THE GREAT GATSBY*
Richard Chase

Lionel Trilling speaks of *Gatsby* as follows: "To the world it is anomalous in America, as in the novel it is anomalous in Gatsby, that so much raw power should be haunted by envisioned romance. Yet in that anomaly lies, for good and bad, much of the truth of our national life, as, at the present moment, we think about it." The special charm of *Gatsby* rests in its odd combination of romance with a realistic picture of raw power—the raw power of the money that has made a plutocracy and the raw power the self-protective conventions of this plutocracy assume when they close in a united front against an intruder.

Gatsby gives us an unforgettable, even though rather sketchy, sense of the 1920's and what the people were like who lived in them. We know what the people were like because we are shown the publicly recognized gestures and attitudes by which they declare themselves as belonging to a certain ambiance at a certain time. Their manners (perhaps one should say their mannered lack of manners) are a clearly minted currency as readily negotiable as the money they all have such a lot of. At the same time the hero who comes to his spectacular grief is not only a man of

* Richard Chase, "The Great Gatsby," The American Novel and Its Traditions (New York: Doubleday and Co., 1957), pp. 162-67. Copyright © 1957 by Richard Chase. Reprinted by permission of Doubleday & Company, Inc.

the 1920's but a figure of legend. No one can doubt that the legend engaged the imagination of the author more deeply than the society in which the legend is played out.

Mr. Trilling attributes the continuing freshness and significance of *Gatsby* to "Fitzgerald's grasp—both in the sense of awareness and appropriation—of the traditional resources available to him." And this will apply whether we are thinking of the book as a romance or as a novel of manners. The story of Jay Gatsby is in origin an archetype of European legend and it is fascinating to observe how, in Fitzgerald's hands, this legend is modified and in some ways fundamentally changed in accordance with American ideas.

The European (perhaps universal) archetype has been memorably described, in relation to the novel, by Mr. Trilling himself. In his Introduction to *The Princess Casamassima*, Mr. Trilling refers to the legend of "the Young Man from the Provinces" which finds expression in certain great novels, such as Stendhal's *The Red and the Black*, Dickens's *Great Expectations*, and Balzac's *Père Goriot*. The young hero of the legend is likely to come from obscure or mean beginnings. There is some mystery about his birth; perhaps he is really a foundling prince. He is "equipped with poverty, pride and intelligence" and he passes through a series of adventures which resemble the "tests" that confront the would-be knight in Arthurian legend. He has an enormous sense of his own destiny. The purpose of his quest is to "enter life," which he does by launching a campaign to conquer and subdue to his own purposes the great world that regards him as an insignificant outsider "He is concerned to know how the political and social world are run and enjoyed," as Mr. Trilling writes; "he wants a share of power and pleasure and in consequence he takes real risks, often of his life."

At this point one begins to see how much and how little Gatsby belongs to the tradition of the Young Man from the Provinces. He has the necessary obscure beginning, born Gatz somewhere in the

Middle West. He has come to the more socially advanced East and made his way to a position of wealth and influence. He is more or less a mythic figure; he seems to have sprung from "a Platonic conception of himself" rather than from any real place; he is rumored to be the nephew of the Kaiser; he pretends to be an Oxford man and to have lived like a young rajah in all the capitals of Europe; he has committed himself "to the following of a grail." A good deal of this legendary build-up is comic in tone and satiric in intent. But Arthur Mizener, Fitzgerald's biographer, is correct in saying that the ironies of *The Great Gatsby* are never allowed to destroy the credence and respect given by the author to the legend of his hero. The life and death of Gatsby inevitably call to the mind of Nick Carraway, the narrator, the ideal meaning of America itself. Gatsby somehow invokes the poetic appeal of the frontier and his pursuit of the ideal recalls once again the "transitory enchanted moment when man must first have held his breath in the presence of this continent, compelled into an aesthetic contemplation he neither understood nor desired, face to face for the last time in history with something commensurate to his capacity for wonder."

These concluding lines are so impassioned and impressive, even if a little overopulent in the Conradian manner, that we feel the whole book has been driving toward this moment of ecstatic contemplation, toward this final moment of transcendence. What, at the end, has been affirmed? Apparently it is not the "power and pleasure" derived from knowing and mastering "the political and social world." At the end of *Père Goriot* what is affirmed by Eugene Rastignac's challenge to Paris *is* this "power and pleasure." And whereas it is true that Julien Sorel in *The Red and the Black* seeks an ideal transcendence, in the manner of many French heroes, from those of Racine to those of Malraux, his field of operations is social to a far greater degree than Gatsby's is ever shown to be.

Gatsby does not seek to understand and master society as an

end; and we have to take it on faith that he has understood and mastered it at all—was he *really* a bootlegger and a dealer in dubious stocks? Of course he was, but neither he nor his author nor his author's narrator, himself a bond salesman, shows any interest in these activities. Nor has Gatsby's shadowy battle with the world been, as it is for his European counterparts, a process of education and disillusion. *He* does not pass from innocence to experience—if anything it is the other way around, the youth who climbed aboard the millionaire's yacht being more worldly than the man who gazes longingly at the green light across the bay. In *The Great Gatsby* society and its ways, so far as the hero knows them, are not ends but means to a transcendent ideal. Finally, as Nick Carraway thinks, the ideal is so little connected with reality that it consists merely in *having* an ideal. Ideality, the longing for transcendence, these are good in themselves. So Nick Carraway implies when he shouts across the lawn to Gatsby, "They're a rotten crowd. You're worth the whole damn bunch put together." For even though Carraway "disapproved of him from beginning to end," he is forced thus to pay tribute to Gatsby's "incorruptible dream." Nor is the abstractness of Gatsby's dream modified by the fact that it centers around Daisy Buchanan, whom he has loved and lost. He does not see her as she is; he does not seem to have a sexual passion for her. He sees her merely as beauty and innocence —a flower, indeed, growing natively on the "fresh green breast of the new world."

Fitzgerald suggests near the end of the book that Gatsby is in the legendary line of Benjamin Franklin or Poor Richard. So we see from the self-disciplinary schedule Gatsby had written down as a boy and had always kept with him:

```
Rise from bed ....................... 6:00      a.m.
Dumbbell exercise and wall scaling ...... 6:15-6:30  " "
Study electricity, etc. ................. 7:15-8:15  " "
```

and so on down to:

```
Study  needed  inventions  .............. 7:00-9:00 p.m.
```

But he is also of the company of Natty Bumppo, Huck Finn, and Melville's Ishmael. For although he is treated with more irony than they, as befits a later worldliness, he shares their ideal of innocence, escape, and the purely personal code of conduct. Like them he derives his values not from the way of the world but from an earlier pastoral ideal.

But Gatsby lived too late. He is made to die sordidly in his swimming pool, shot by a garage proprietor. He cannot, like Huck Finn, light out for the territory. He cannot achieve even the dubious rebirth of Ishmael in the far Pacific. He cannot die full of years, facing the setting sun and attended by the primeval prairie gods, like Natty Bumppo.

None of these earlier heroes makes an assault on a plutocracy that has settled into a position of power and prestige. That was not an option in their time and place. When Gatsby does this he becomes what his predecessors never were: a tragicomic figure in a social comedy. He does not know how to conform to the class to which Daisy belongs and to this class he seems ridiculous, with his "gorgeous pink rag of a suit," his preposterous mansion, and his chaotic parties—parties at which ordinary people seem somehow to become themselves fantastic and to assume names like Miss Claudia Hip and the Dancies (I refer here to the inspired list of names, itself a great comic achievement, at the beginning of Chapter 4—there is an only somewhat less brilliant collection of comic names in the description of the masquerade at the beginning of Cable's *Grandissimes*). In Gatsby, that is, we have a figure who is from one point of view a hero of romance but from another is related to the gulls and fops of high comedy.

No one seems to know what T. S. Eliot meant when he wrote Fitzgerald that *Gatsby* was the first step forward the American novel had made since Henry James. The statement seems meaningful, however, if we compare *Gatsby* with James's only novel of similar theme, *The American*. Christopher Newman is a more relaxed, less willful, and less self-destined figure than Gatsby, but he comes of a similarly legendary America, makes a great deal of money, and vainly pursues a woman who is the flower of a high world forever closed to him. James, however, is content with his pleasure in the odd angularities of the legend of the successful American. And he sends Newman home, baffled and saddened by his rejection but not mortally hurt. It is a part of the fate of both Newman and Gatsby that they have information with which they could avenge themselves on their highly placed antagonists and that out of magnanimity they both refuse to do so.

But Fitzgerald has made more of the legend. For whereas Newman remains an odd though appealing stick of a man Gatsby has a tragic recklessness about him, an inescapably vivid and memorable destiny. He has something of that almost divine insanity we find in Hamlet or Julien Sorel or Don Quixote. Fitzgerald's great feat was to have opened out this possibility and to have made his American hero act in a drama where none had acted before. For although there had been reckless and doomed semilegendary heroes in American fiction, none had been made to play his part in a realistically presented *social* situation. Fitzgerald opened out the possibility, but scarcely more. It was not in him to emulate except for a brilliant moment the greatest art.

FITZGERALD'S TRIUMPH

Gale H. Carrithers, Jr.

Gale Carrithers is a young instructor at Duke University. This essay, which is published here for the first time, is used as an illustration of the kind of analysis that comes directly from the classroom experience of teaching The Great Gatsby.

The Great Gatsby dramatizes much that is true about the human situation. That is, by means of concrete and particular things, including structures, it communicates something about more general and even abstract things and therefore about the concrete and particular situations we each live with.

Whatever else we might want to say about any novel, we would agree at the start, I think, that it is a lengthy prose fiction involving men, in settings, in a structure of action and experience. The emphasis on any of these elements may vary, and the action may shift between extremes of the external and physical, Hemingway's retreat from Caporetto, for example, and the internal and psychological, the heart beating in the gathering darkness aboard Joseph Conrad's "Nellie." Obviously Fitzgerald will exploit all these resources, as even the first two pages show. He makes Nick Carraway speak of the fatherly advice he has taken with him, and of the world at, or not at, "moral attention," of coming West, and of people in the East.

304 Gale H. Carrithers, Jr.

Consider the characters, what sort they are, and the characterization, the ways we are made to know what sort they are. Fitzgerald quickly poses one of the novel's central questions, the question, in effect, of whether "By their gestures ye shall know them"; the word "if" in the novel's third paragraph seems ambiguous; it suggests that maybe we will not know them, or perhaps will know them only partially. But gestures, considered broadly, do take us some distance in the world of this novel. The novel could be illustrated but does not really need to be. Gestures are objective, precise, public, arguable—the exact opposite, Nick says, of Daisy's emotion, which is subjective, vague, personal, inarguable.[1]

One notices first that gestures show us many kinds of men. First Gatsby, "who represented everything for which I have an unaffected scorn. If personality is an unbroken series of successful gestures, then there was something gorgeous about him, some heightened sensitivity to the promises of life," like a seismograph, says Nick (p. 2). And he calls this seismographic responsiveness to destructive shock, which Gatsby's partly unmoved and partly moved life registers and dramatizes—Nick calls the responsiveness "an extraordinary gift for hope, a romantic readiness . . . which it is not likely I shall find again." Gatsby's smile (p. 48), is an overwhelmingly successful gesture in its "quality of eternal reassurance" and its "irresistible prejudice in your favor"—that is, in its transcendent hope and charity. Nick, with characteristic good faith and precision claims, however, only that it *seemed* to face the whole world. We learn later that Gatsby was tragically mistaken about his external world. He is, moreover, seen to be "an elegant young roughneck" as soon as the smile fades, and his "formality of speech," his "picking his words with care," "just missed being absurd." So his utterances, his verbal gestures, are not perfectly successful.

[1] F. Scott Fitzgerald, *The Great Gatsby*, The Scribner Library Edition, (New York: Charles Scribner's Sons, 1960), p. 108. All page references are to this edition.

We see his smile again (pp. 53, 154), and on p. 56, we see him, endowed with rich and admirable isolation: Gatsby stands as "the figure of the host . . . his hand up in a formal gesture of farewell." He makes this formal gesture in the midst of chaos, to guests mostly too drunk to recognize even the broken physical bond between wheel and car, much less the broken spiritual bond between host and guest. Tom Buchanan (p. 75) appears; Gatsby disappears: a discriminating gesture. But he places himself between Nick and Meyer Wolfsheim (p. 70), and the worlds they represent. And he continually makes unconscious gestures of restlessness (p. 64). Like a seismograph, he registers many of the forces shaking his society, and does so by being both moved and unmoved, in a sense conscious and unconscious of them. He is always conscious of the seriousness of personal falsehood, so he never lies quite successfully (p. 65). And he does have one brilliantly successful verbal gesture: of Daisy and Tom, he says: "Of course she might have loved him just for a minute. . . . In any case . . . it was just personal" (p. 152). This successfully implies, as Nick ironically hints, a willful and colossal conception of the self and of one's destiny.

Other characters, without being any more conscious, and without revealing as much of their society, reveal just as much about themselves by their gestures. Tom, the big-rich, high-ivy football and polo bum, that "national figure," that pack of muscle, is a horse. He travels with a string of polo ponies, has straw-hair, a hard mouth; he nibbles at ideas but is capable of enormous leverage, and he reverses the national trend in that he makes a stable out of a garage (p. 119), or probably we should say two garages. His typical gesture is to propel someone in whatever direction he wants the play to go: Nick into the house; Nick off the train, or to the apartment. But he's often unsuccessful: he presses Daisy unsuccessfully toward Gatsby's car. Later, even less successfully (p. 119), his mouth drops open in response to Daisy's one greatly successful vocal gesture, her exclamation which proclaims her love for Gatsby: "Ah . . . you look so cool." Ordinarily her verbal style is to speak—softly and thrillingly, therefore invitingly—things which are incomplete or inconclusive or incoherent or untrue, as when she irritates Nick by telling him irresponsibly that he is a rose (p. 15).

So, too, "Tom's voice groped unsuccessfully for the paternal note," as he tries to regain her from Gatsby (p. 131). He does regain her with a vocal gesture that recalls, with "a husky tenderness in his tone," his strength: he carried her down from the Punch Bowl.

Tom and Nick had been members of the same secret society in Nick's "solemn and obvious" college days, but in Chapter One, it is Tom and Daisy who are members of a secret society together. Their gestures and postures of arrogant indolence, and of vocal and intellectual irresponsibility dramatize this. Even at their best they are framed together—in a square of light—as they congenially inquire about Nick's engagement. Of course there is no engagement; they are characteristically equating an unchecked rumor with truth because three people reported it, and in the atmosphere of their house even Nick and Jordan have drifted into eavesdropping, deceit, and studied meaninglessness, but we do see a momentary tableau of good will.

Neither the good will at the end of Chapter One, nor Jordan's later criticism of Nick should obscure from us Jordan's membership in the Buchanan secret society—characterization abundantly given by her gestures and postures in relation to people and truth. Like Daisy, she has the position of the golden girl, the King's daughter in a white palace (p. 120), secure and inviolate above struggles and criticism, except that the status fits her just a whit uneasily, like a teacup on the chin. She lacks Daisy's thrilling sexuality—which she vaguely and indifferently recognizes, thinking that Daisy's voice is full of sex (p. 79)—but her "jauntiness" is a kind of not-very-feminine counterpart to Tom's athleticism. She's better than Tom and Daisy, of course: they both have injurious car-wrecks while pursuing adultery; she merely necks a little, and carelessly nudges a pedestrian. And, she would not carry well-forgotten dreams from age to age (p. 136). Nevertheless, if a partner of Daisy's must be disastrously committed to being a "gold-hatted, high-bouncing lover," Jordan's partner would be equally committed, as one of my students suggested, to being little more than a caddy.

Nick's gestures are characteristically vocal ones. Notice how often from the very beginning his witty imagery or his diction place him in a dual position: inside an event, enjoying it or victimized by it, and at the same time outside the event, emotionally detached and analytical or critical. He images World War I as a barbarian invasion and countermovement which, ironically, he "enjoyed so thoroughly" that home wasn't home anymore. Tom Buchanan came East in a fashion "that *rather* took your breath away"—but not quite. The Buchanans served "corky but rather impressive claret." Nick's style, with all its wit and variety and vitality from understatement to extravagance is completely meaningful (as style always should be). It is the very face of a man who describes himself as "within and without, simultaneously enchanted and repelled by the inexhaustible variety of life" (p. 36).

So in considering characterization by gesture, the reader may begin to see something of the variety of Fitzgerald's individuals. It is always necessary in a discussion of characterization to turn quickly to the characters' actions—as indeed the whole matter of gesture insists. But first another point needs to be made about individuality, namely, the way *degrees* of individuality vary in this book. This more-or-less stylistic matter of degree of individuality is made to body forth part of a theme running through the whole novel (and a problem running through modern life)—the problem of identity: "what am I?" "what is the essence of my self?" And only a step beyond these concerns looms the problem of "what is real?" "what is the nature of the world?" As in all the literature that we honor, resourcefulness of style is extension in meaning; form is content; the two can be looked at from different angles, but (as John Henry Newman argued) are not to be separated any more than the convex and the concave of a curve.

To return abruptly from the very general and abstract to the very specific and concrete, we may recall the butler's nose. It's red from too much silver polish. That is virtually the entirety of the butler's identity. Compare the shaggy, quivering, "tragic nose" of Meyer Wolfsheim, the repellently ludicrous figure who fixed the World's Series in 1919. Most striking of all, notice the catalogue of Gatsby's guests (beginning on p. 61), wherein all the identifying formulas of the news and society pages either fail to identify, or else identify damningly, or else are totally disregarded. "A prince of something, whom we called Duke, and whose name, if I ever knew it, I have forgotten." The catalogue is written, significantly, in the scattered empty spaces, and empty spaces of a railway time-table, a symbolic grouping pointing toward what is least permanent and least valuable in human life. The paper is bad, and therefore now disintegrating; and railway schedules are subject to change without notice.[2] Looking down the list, we notice the repetitious Chester Beckers and the incongruous Willie Voltaires, the Black-bucks, not quite tamed, and the Chrysties. With a graceful gesture of fidelity to fact, Nick makes clear the relationships Mrs. Chrystie and Hubert Auerbach appeared to have, and really had—the confusion of marital status common among people Nick observes. We probably doubt that Edgar Beaver's pelt turned white for no reason at all, and we must wonder about the real status of that displaced-person turned professional Southerner, Stonewall Jackson Abrams; we wonder who is preying on whom as between the Fishguards and the Whitebaits; are we given a family or the summary of an I. Q. test in the Hammerheads? Beluga the tobacco importer and Beluga's girls—also imported merchandise? What about "Don S.

[2] See the fine article by W. J. Harvey, "Theme and Texture in *The Great Gatsby*," *English Studies*, XXXVIII (1957), 19.

Schwartze (the son)," since we can't recognize Don S. Schwartze or anyone else as the father? And what about those rural families the Duckweeds and the Bulls? that modern family the Chromes? the not-so-modern family the Backhyssons?

That all this is sketchy characterization is exactly the point. We know all there is to know about these people: there isn't much; and significantly in some cases there is nothing: G. Earl Muldoon is brother to a known wife-strangler, therefore presumably without a brother now, and therefore nothing; "the young Quinns, divorced now," are no longer so young or any longer the Quinns; "Miss Claudia Hip, with a man reputed to be her chauffeur," but perhaps not even that, whatever his usefulness around the house may be; and Henry L. Palmetto, who achieved identity only upon getting planted.

West Egg, we are told, is an unprecedented place that Broadway begat on a Long Island fishing village, animated by raw vigor, chafing under the old euphemisms, shaped by the "too obtrusive fate that herded its inhabitants along a short-cut from nothing to nothing" (p. 108). The phrase "obtrusive fate" sounds mysterious, but we see that context defines fate as anything from fire and flood to a curious Tom Buchanan. The briefness of the short-cut permits the catalogue-crowd only the slightest individuality before nothingness and meaninglessness swallow up their identity. "Sometimes a shadow moved against a dressing-room blind above, gave way to another shadow, an indefinite procession of shadows, that rouged and powdered in an invisible glass" (p. 109). We recognize not only the terrible limitations of this individuality, but an echo, in the shadowy figures and the powder, of the valley of ashes. That valley is an earthly counterpart of Hell; the powdery figures all through Chapter Two, and in Chapter Eight, make little hells around themselves (hence the startling word *holocaust* on p. 163).

But we have pondered identity and lack of identity without yet agreeing about what is, in this book's terms, the principle of distinction. If lack of identity is nothingness and/or Hell, where is Heaven? What is a real man? What, in fact, is real? Simple substantiality is not enough to make something real for Nick Carraway, obviously. He theorizes that at the last, Gatsby must have recognized a "new world . . . material without being real" (p. 162). We might be puzzled by that and by such remarks as "the unreality of reality, a promise that the rock of the world is founded securely on a fairy's wing" if there were not other remarks on the same subject. One key passage describes Nick's reaction when Jordan tells how Gatsby has followed Daisy to Long Island: "He came alive to me, delivered suddenly from the womb of his purposeless splendor" (p. 79). Gatsby is a newborn man to Nick; man achieves identity, a fact achieves reality, when it becomes understood by another human being, and understood, significantly, partly in terms of purpose, hence of design, of life-structure.

In this case the immediate and larger contexts suggests that Gatsby's purpose has been to make himself into a kind of combination Sheik of Araby, and bright package under the Christmas-tree splendor of his garden—to make himself the kind of "gold-hatted, high-bouncing lover" that a Daisy Buchanan would feel she must have. Conduct, we remember from Nick's opening statement, may be founded on the wet marsh or on the rock; but the rock of the world, insofar as it is order and not chaos, is founded on that fairy's wing, imagination. As the whole novel insists, and as the metaphoric vehicle *wing* urges, imagination is a purposeful, structuring instrument. That is why Nick is sympathetic toward Daisy at one point: "Her voice struggled on through the heat, beating against it, molding its senselessness into forms" (p. 119).

The power of the shaping imagination and the fearful resistance of the brute material world are the twin focusses of much in the novel, and of the really central passage about reality (p. 99). Notice that Gatsby's reality was not the mere legal entity James Gatz, nor the mere physical existence of his hard, brown body. "The truth was that Jay Gatsby . . . sprang from his Platonic conception of himself. He was a son of God—a phrase which [I venture to gloss the pronouns here], if 'the phrase Son of God' means anything, means 'that he sprang from his Platonic conception of himself.' " A Platonic "conception," or ideal is, roughly, an utterly transcendent, spiritual, abstract entity more perfect than any material embodiment on earth. But a Platonically-conceived God might have an earthly son. Gatsby had, in effect utterly committed himself to the concept that "There is no god but Super-Gatsby, and Jay Gatsby is His Prophet." In worshiping a god created in his own image, he, like George Wilson, merely did to an extraordinary degree what any of us may tend to do. So there is appropriately a certain compassion in the ironic description of him being about "His Father's business," because this seventeen-year-old boy was (like all of us) insufficiently sophisticated intellectually, aesthetically, emotionally, and morally to make a very good god. On the other hand, no compassion can blunt the mockery imposed by natural disorder and the inhuman order of time on young Gatsby's god-like will, as his will spins a gaudy universe out of chaos. The clock ticks on, and fatigue "closed down upon" him, amid his tangled clothes.

So reality is, within certain limits, what you imaginatively recognize it to be and make it be. That is, you see the here and now and imaginatively recognize a structure of relationships that you want to develop with the not-here and not-now. The "unusual quality of wonder" which Nick admires in Gatsby, and in the owl-eyed man, and perhaps even a little in Chester McKee, is evidently aptitude for taking the imaginative, aesthetic view. On the other hand, the catalogue-people have limited reality because they are predators with limited imaginations. But this novel has always the double awareness—to a degree unexcelled in modern fiction— of the vitality of the moment, and of the clock ticking on the mantel, signalling the passage of all moments, and nature's tendency toward what must be seen in human terms as decay and disorder. Gatsby juggles the clock on Nick's mantel (p. 88), and they think he has broken it, but he has not.

The glance at nature and natural disorder can provide a kind of transition to the matter of setting, obviously of the liveliest concern to Fitzgerald in this novel. Nick alludes to Europe—to "tapestry scenes of Versailles," for example—a Europe which contrasts with a raw America; he often speaks of Eastern America and raw West, of East Egg condescending to raw West Egg, and of the frontier. But beware!

Fitzgerald does in fact dramatize the ideas of glorious frontier on the one hand and of the elegant East on the other hand as mush-minded, outdated clichés which have been knocked out of Nick Carraway, and knocked out painfully. East Egg and West Egg have a double importance. They are East and West in miniature, and "to the wingless" exhibit marked differences, largely because of age and established position. The palaces in East Egg tend to be occupied by Eastern people with established incomes; although Demaine, who had a fortune in the Western commodity oil, has disappeared, to what oblivion of jail, death, or disgrace we can only guess, making way for the Buchanans of Chicago and the Riviera, with an inherited fortune equally large. The people in West Egg tend to have only salaries, or commissions, however large.[3] The "towns beyond the Ohio" Nick at one time saw as "bored, sprawling, swollen towns," rough creations by comparison with the more finished towns of the East, as West Egg to East Egg. But to the man who isn't wingless, the man who takes the soaring, imaginative view of structures, the vista must be confusing: East and West are alike as two eggs, slightly broken by twentieth-century life, "crushed flat at the contact end,"[4] just as

---

[3] For this point, but not the reservations about it, I am indebted to Malcolm Cowley, "The Romance of Money"—his introduction to *The Great Gatsby* in *Three Novels of F. Scott Fitzgerald* (New York: Charles Scribner's Sons, 1953), p. xix; see also Leslie Fiedler, *Love and Death in the American Novel* (New York: Criterion Books, Inc., 1960), p. 303: "There is no need for a symbolic Europe to complete the scene;" but Europe was the catalyst starting Nick's process of maturation.

[4] Cf. John Aldridge, "The Life of Gatsby" in *Twelve Original Essays on Great American Novels*, ed. Charles Shapiro (Detroit: Wayne State University Press, 1958), pp. 230-231.

the "fresh, green breast of the new world" is torn and defiled by the valley of ashes. It is pathetic for Myrtle Wilson with Tom, and George Wilson with Myrtle, to dream that they can escape failures and frustrations, responsibilities and irresponsibilities, by fleeing to a little gray home in the West (p. 123). They would carry the valley of ashes with them. The Buchanans behaved equally badly the world around, and Dan Cody, "the pioneer debauchée," who achieved an income of Eastern magnitude "brought back to the Eastern Seaboard the savage violence of the frontier brothel and saloon" (p. 101). His spiritual son Gatsby exports Meyer Wolfsheim's more sophisticated forms of antisocial action back to the West. There's no romantic nonsense here about the West being better than the East, or vice-versa. Life is difficult anywhere; the real distinction is between the place where home is, and all the world where home is not. Nick has slowly been learning that, as Rebecca West observes, "a hearth gives out warmth," —a truth so simple that he had forgotten it, so complex that he had not completely learned it.[5]

If we haven't come awake to this earlier, we must sense it as we recover from the bone-shaking juxtaposition on pages 176-177: Gatsby's funeral and Nick's Christmases. Looking at that, our eye quickly falls on the most compassionate and charitable statement made at the funeral. "The poor son-of-a-bitch," said the owl-eyed man. Of course the charitable book, to which Gatsby gave his name, is yet to come, but it has less geographical and thematic continuity with Gatsby's life than it has discontinuity. The funeral and following scene define each other by multiple contrasts. Those returning trains are not so much mechanical conveniences as communities on the move toward bright and charitable things. Those Chicagoans postponed their festivities a bit in order to say goodbye to the others. The chief pronoun in the passage is *we*; invitations are not compared, they are *matched*.

[5] See her brilliant book, *The Meaning of Treason* (New York: The Viking Press, 1947), especially "Epilogue."

The train is a vehicle for Christmas cheer and communal and geographical identity. It was even, with a kind of winning, poignant naiveté, "our snow."

Poignant and naïve because, as Nick learns, snow and rain fall alike on the just and the unjust, the dead and the living. It is the ironic Nick, refusing to wear his heart quite on his sleeve, who says of the five Westerners that "perhaps we possessed some deficiency in common which made us subtly unadaptable to Eastern life" (p. 177). In one sense, they tended to adapt themselves all too well, to the worst in the East. In another sense they did have a crucial lack; a home in the East.

At the very height of Gatsby's dream, Nick is made to signal the doomed and hollow nature of Gatsby's and Daisy's idyllic moment. It is only an "in the meantime, in between time" moment of extra-marital adventure for Daisy, and these rich will get neither richer nor children. "All the lights were going on in West Egg now," except at Gatsby's, where a "solitary lamp" enabled the repellent Klipspringer to fumble at the piano. "The electric trains, man-carrying, were plunging home through the rain. . . . It was the hour of profound human change. . . ." Hearth and warmth against the elements, against confusion, against mutability, and the loveless world of merely getting richer. Compare the profound human change at Gatsby's, where a deeply-loved ideal is being confronted by an ultimately devastating actuality.

Again (p. 178), when Nick presents his journey to a group of homes where generations of friends know and care, from the city where, as the symbolic truths of his dream-vision have it, "no one knows and no one cares," he announces the movement with the homeliest of images, an image which seems, in context, able to point toward both East and West: "So when the blue smoke of brittle leaves was in the air and the wind blew the wet laundry stiff on the line I decided to come back home."

His laundry, and his burning leaves, like his snow, are all in the West, his hearth and community. But home takes on symbolic weight in yet a second way, a way rather different from the pieties of the social communion. Whether in St. Paul, Chicago, New Haven, Dan Cody's yacht, New York City, or Louisville, home is the Eden-like place where each of these people experienced what everyone experiences: the first major discovery of self, and the first major failure or loss of self.

Gatsby's home in this sense should have been Louisville, where he makes the tragic error of letting his dream be "incarnate" in Daisy Fay (p. 112), a loss of innocence reminding Nick of something he himself had lost.[6] Gatsby's mind could never thereafter youthfully "romp like the mind of God;" he goes there after the war to walk the holy ground, but the golden goddess is gone. He later aspires to return there and marry her "from her house," but is denied, as much by time and human nature as by Daisy Buchanan.

Gatsby's real home was as much Dan Cody's yacht as it was the West. Fitzgerald rejected and published separately as a short story an episode originally meant to show a South Dakota boyhood for Gatsby;[7] in the book we have, Mr. Gatz comes East for the funeral; the funeral does not go to him. Gatsby's home remains, as one seemingly bizarre Long Island rumor claims, and as his death on the air-mattress ratifies, a floating habitat, Cody's yacht where he got "his singularly appropriate education." The yacht sailed "three times around the continent," so this busily but only half-purposefully moving home is really Anyplace, U.S.A.

In making such arbitrary divisions in the body of this novel as these opening remarks on realities of person and place, we have crept up on the matter of what happens among these people, in these settings, and how those happenings are presented to us, how they are structured.

This novel's exploration both of the nature of action, and of

---

[6] See also Aldridge, *op. cit.*, p. 234.
[7] "Absolution," reprinted in *The Stories of F. Scott Fitzgerald* ed. Malcolm Cowley (New York: Charles Scribner's Sons, 1951).

the degrees of meaningfulness that action can have, comes out of four interlocking structures: imagery, action, time, and an ironic relation between narrator and material.[8]

One of the patterns of imagery is wealth, underscored by both literal and metaphorical uses of words like *gold* and *silver*. This novel is akin to such works as Katherine Mansfield's fine story, "The Garden Party" in that it explores the bitter-sweet paradox of wealth. That very wealth which makes great imaginative achievement possible (both aesthetic and social achievement) may have damned the getter in the getting of it, or that wealth may at least in the having of it lead to sterile self-absorption and drift. The Buchanans "drifted here and there unrestfully wherever . . . people played polo and were rich together" (p. 6).

Imagery of drift, flutter, or rush, the figure of purposeless action, of meaningless activity, is another pattern running through the novel: "foul dust floated in the wake of Gatsby's dreams" (p. 2). "In his blue gardens men and girls came and went like moths among the whisperings and the champagne and [with telling contrast in order and permanence] the stars" (p. 39). Then, too, there is the rush to destruction by car.

A contrasting pattern of imagery helps to define purposeful and orderly action: winged flight; sailing toward a goal. "With fenders spread like wings, we scattered light through half Astoria" (p. 68). And, ahead of "the white wings of the boat . . . lay the scalloped ocean and the abounding blessed isles" (p. 118).

The novel is full of metaphorical wakes and waters and symbolic oceans: the green surf of Tom's lawn, his shadow-rippling sea of a rug, with anchored royal barge, sea-changes of faces, emptiness flowing, that "obliging and indifferent sea" (p. 178) which Nick would not trust to sweep his refuse away, the "blue lawn" of Long Island Sound near the end, and last of all, "boats against the current, borne back ceaselessly into the past." The ocean seems to be a symbol of undifferentiated humanity, or un-

[8] See also W. J. Harvey, *op. cit.*

differentiated time/space/activity, the figure of something to be not so much lived in as traversed as gracefully as possible. Boats make significant journeys across oceans, or drift; in either case they are affected by currents. Those powerful or subtle currents obey natural laws which are often very difficult to understand, and which are quite alien to the laws of the human community.

Like "The Garden Party," but much more resourcefully, *The Great Gatsby* uses the party or related social gathering as a symbol of human community in general. Every chapter has at least one party or social gathering, often two or three, which define each other by similarity or contrast. We can always judge a man in the novel's own terms by those with whom he breaks bread and the style with which he does it. The interior structure of the novel's action is a movement from party to party, always with the hope of finding satisfactory community. That hope is sordidly and brutally disappointed, first more, then less, then more disappointed. These people are mentally, spiritually, emotionally away from home, some of them hopelessly so. The ultimate profaning of community occurs when a final uninvited guest acts in confusion to murder the host and himself; and subsequently a boy whose identiity isn't even known writes an obscenity on the walk.

Meaningless death and meaningless action are nightmare, and this is the final note in a nightmarish breakdown in the orderly and proper and expected that first prompted Nick to want the police (in Chapter One), that afflicted him in Tom and Myrtle's love-nest (where Nick, the writer, is unable to read, like Salinger's writer, Sergeant X), that made him think the butler shouted "The master's body," that found Nick floundering in the symbolic ocean and falling at Gatsby with "a sort of splash upon the keys of a ghostly piano" (p. 147), and that found Gatsby looking at "an unfamiliar sky through frightening leaves" finding "what a grotesque thing a rose is" (p. 162).

318 Gale H. Carrithers, Jr.

The novel's great counter-movement, and its framing action, is the painful journey toward order and meaning and charitable responsibility.[9] Gatsby's gift for hope and romantic readiness are spiritual victories in the conflict between being and nothingness; his physical, aesthetic, imaginative vitality is a kind of gaudy triumph over that dark oblivion into which the lives and works of men all tend to sink. But he is said to be "all right at the end" because *at the end* he takes responsibility for his actions and in fact for Daisy's actions. He has imagined and he has loved, but the third inter-locking element the novel dramatizes as necessary in human action—responsibility, the bulwark against chaos—he has evaded until he takes his unconsciously ironic stand outside Daisy's house, pledging his body and his sinister career to protect her from Tom and a losing court trial.[10] Amid the dead leaves of the sterile swimming pool, his body even as a drifting thing seals and ratifies by the circle of its blood that he has ended where he began: by offering to save a drifter from the rocks.

Nick Carraway drifted East not having dreamed much, even of the Trinity of "Midas, Morgan, and Maecenas," and not having loved much; we remember that his tennis partner's perspiring upper lip is enough to disqualify her. Moreover, his moral tendency toward responsibility is undercut by his habit of reserving judgment. He honestly tells us of his moral low points that summer (pp. 57, 81, 136). He drifts into and out of an office affair, and follows the line of selfish convenience with the parasitic Jordan, as she does with him—she who is jaunty or lazy, or sceptical, never responsive.

But Nick learns to stop reserving judgment, and to take charitable responsibility. "You're worth the whole damn bunch put

[9] See also Aldridge, *op. cit.*, p. 230.
[10] See also Tom Burnam, "The Eyes of Dr. Eckleburg: A Re-examination of 'The Great Gatsby'," *College English*, XIV (1952), 11; Lionel Trilling, "F. Scott Fitzgerald" in *F. Scott Fitzgerald, the Man and his Work* (Cleveland & New York: The World Publishing Co., 1951), p. 197 (also in *The Liberal Imagination*). [The latter essay is reprinted on page 232.]

together," he shouts to Gatsby (p. 154). He rejects Jordan's deadly invitation to "come in" to the Buchanans' house (p. 143), and he arranges Gatsby's funeral. He painfully has things out with Jordan, the girl he wanted to love (p. 59), and half did love (pp. 178-179). He erases the obscene word.

Then he returns to the loves, commitments, and responsibilities of home to write the true word, to be a new-born man, guide to the 20th Century. His feeling (p. 4) that he could be an original settler, and be warmly at home in West Egg is indeed an accidental and a mistaken feeling, as a student recently suggested to me. But the feeling is nonetheless the warm reflection of constructive action and a hint of his final, valid realization. He can be a guide and pathfinder in earnest, with valid and lasting effect, once he gives up the "privileged excursion" which affords irresponsible glances out of many windows, and gives up childish dreams of infantile bliss, indulgence, or excitement. He returns to look steadily at life "from a single window after all." That window might be literally his study window; it is certainly symbolically the window of his hard-earned identity as guide, the window uniting things that are simultaneously within and without; the window is also the supporting and framing structure of his deeply-experienced hearth and community values.

On pages 105 and 178 Nick complains that his eyes' power of correction is exhausted or exceeded. But he thinks over the summer's events for some months in pursuit of that ideal of corrected vision symbolized by T. J. Eckleburg's Eyes;[11] then he begins to construct his guidebook, and does so with loving care for the reader's understanding, as his interruptions on pages 56 and 102 indicate.

After a year of writing he has produced his manuscript, an act of love not for all the readers in his society perhaps, but for the understanders. Ordinarily, as the last page indicates, only the

[11] The perfectly corrected vision which George Wilson mistakenly thought he possessed.

striking, overwhelming new thing compels men to aesthetic contemplation. But his pathfinder's style, bringing together his own emotional-intellectual involvements in the scenes and intellectual-emotional detachments from the scenes, will invite us to an aesthetic contemplation of the familiar, whatever the familiar may be to each of us.

His learning and intellectuality and ironic similes will engage our wits and sense of distinctions; his puns and metaphors, subtle or exaggerated, will engage with gayety our sense of unsuspected relationships or unsuspected irrelationships; his metaphors and dramatic conflicts will engage our emotions and our care: phrases like "suspects himself of at least one of the cardinal virtues," "slippers shuffled the shining dust," "a thinning briefcase of enthusiasm, thinning hair" (pp. 60, 151, 136).

For the structure of the whole book is focussed not on Gatsby's tragic world, but on Nick's world and ours. Someone we know may have made tragic decisions, and may have died for them. But we remain alive, trying like Nick to make sense out of the somber, El Grecoish distortions and proportions of our world.

THE UNTRIMMED CHRISTMAS TREE:
THE RELIGIOUS BACKGROUND OF
*THE GREAT GATSBY**

Henry Dan Piper

Scott Fitzgerald began planning his third novel, *The Great Gatsby*, sometime during the late spring of 1922. "I've been lazy this month trying to outline a new novel," he wrote Maxwell Perkins, his editor at Scribner's, in mid-June. Several months earlier Scribner's had published his second novel, *The Beautiful and Damned*; and although it was selling well, it was currently getting harsh treatment from the critics and reviewers—treatment Fitzgerald privately admitted that it deserved. When *The Beautiful* had started running as a serial in the *Metropolitan Magazine* the previous autumn, he had at first been so embarrassed by its obvious shortcomings that for a time he had considered delaying publication of the book version until he could rewrite it entirely. But, this proving impractical, he had reluctantly let it come out between hard covers with few major revisions of any kind. Nonetheless, he had learned a lesson and was determined that his next

* Condensed from *Chapter VI of F. Scott Fitzgerald: A Candid Portrait* by Henry Dan Piper. Copyright © 1962 by Henry Dan Piper. Reprinted by permission of Holt, Rinehart and Winston, Inc.
Permission to quote from the unpublished writings of F. Scott Fitzgerald has been granted by Mrs. Samuel J. Lanahan.

novel, unlike *The Beautiful and Damned*, should be written slowly and with care. "I want to write something new," he had written Max Perkins that summer of 1922, "—something extraordinary and beautiful and simple and intricately patterned."[1]

This next novel, he told Perkins, would differ from his previous fiction in several other respects. "It's locale will be the Middle West and New York of 1885, I think. It will contain less superlative beauties than I run to usually and will be centered in a smaller period of time. It will have a Catholic element." As things turned out, however, he was to make little headway with it for the next two years. Instead, spurred on by the encouragement of Edmund Wilson and George Jean Nathan, and by his own hope of making a financial killing on Broadway, he spent the next eighteen months trying to write a successful play for the New York stage. Although Nathan openly predicted a promising future for him in the theatre, and Wilson called *The Vegetable* "the best American comedy ever written," it flopped deservedly during its Atlantic City tryout in November, 1923, leaving Fitzgerald $5000 in debt. Again the manuscript of his novel was put aside while he spent the next six months grinding out a total of eighteen short stories and articles for the slick magazines. It was discouraging work, especially since none of these pieces amounted to anything, and it left him exhausted. But by April, 1924, he had paid off all his debts and had enough cash on hand so that he could take his wife and daughter to the south of France and devote the next ten months to finishing his novel.[2]

By now, however, his conception of that novel had altered radically. Back in 1922 when he had first begun thinking about *The Great Gatsby*, he had been living in St. Paul, Minnesota, the

[1] Two letters to Max Perkins, no date (ca. mid-June, and July, 1922), files of Charles Scribner's Sons Inc. All material from these files quoted with Scribner's permission.
[2] To Perkins, n.d. (ca. June 20, 1922), Scribner files; E. Wilson to FSF, May 26, 1922 (Fitzgerald Papers, Princeton University Library); George Jean Nathan, *The Theatre, The Drama, The Girls* (New York, 1921), 16, 72.

Middle Western city in which he had been born and where he had spent his early childhood. Actually, after his departure from St. Paul for boarding school in 1911 at the age of fourteen, he had lived the greater part of the next ten years in the East. But in 1921, after the success of his first novel, *This Side of Paradise*, and his marriage to Zelda Sayre, he had felt a compulsion to return, a triumphant celebrity, to the scene of so many childhood frustrations and disappointments. Zelda was expecting their first child, and Fitzgerald felt it was important that it should be born where he had been born.

But after a year in St. Paul they had moved East again in the autumn of 1922. This time they rented a house in Great Neck, Long Island, in hopes this proximity to Broadway would help in the search for a producer for *The Vegetable*. By April, 1924, when Fitzgerald was again in a position to work on *The Great Gatsby*, he had decided to shift its setting from the 1880's to the immediate present, and from the Middle West to the vicinity of Great Neck. At this time he also decided to abandon the conventional third-person method of narration he had used in his preceding two novels, and to adopt instead the device of a first-person narrator named Nick Carraway.

Just before he sailed to France he wrote Max Perkins explaining some of these new intentions. "Much of what I wrote last summer is good," he said, "but it was so interrupted that it was ragged and in approaching it from a new angle I've had to discard a lot of it—in one case 18,000 [words] (part of which will appear in the *Mercury* as a short story)." The story mentioned was "Absolution," which his friend H. L. Mencken published in the June issue of the *American Mercury*. "I'm glad you like it," Fitzgerald wrote Perkins after it appeared. "As you know it was to have been the prologue of the novel but it interfered with the neatness of my plan."[3]

Ten years later, in a letter to one of *The Great Gatsby's* ad-

[3] To Perkins, n.d. (ca. April 16, 1924) Scribner files.

324   Henry Dan Piper

mirers, Fitzgerald again mentioned the connection between his novel and "Absolution," saying this time that the latter had been "intended to be a picture of his [i.e., Gatsby's] early life, but . . . I cut it because I preferred to preserve the sense of mystery." Any attempt to come to terms with *The Great Gatsby*, therefore, cannot afford to overlook its relationship to "Absolution." The short story is especially important because it makes explicit the religious considerations that served its author as the basis for the moral judgments that he made so conspicuously in its sequel, *The Great Gatsby*.[4]

"Absolution" is the story of a ten-year-old boy's first encounter with evil, whereas *The Great Gatsby* is the story of the consequences of that boyhood encounter. Rudolph Miller, the hero of the short story, is the son of pious, hard-working Roman Catholic immigrants living in a drab farm community on the Middle Western prairie. A lonely child endowed with a lively imagination, his closest playmate is a companion of his imagination with the elegant name of Blatchford Sarnemington. Blatchford is Rudolph's alter ego, the romantic superman he would like to be. Where Rudolph is expected to mind his parents, school teachers, and parish priest, Blatchford soars above such mundane obligations. He is beyond good and evil, responsible only to his own imagination. When Rudolph does something he shouldn't, his first impulse is to pretend that it is not himself, Rudolph, who has done wrong, but Blatchford. Unfortunately, however, his well-developed conscience will not allow him to indulge this fiction for very long.[5]

The story commences one Saturday afternoon when Rudolph impulsively tells a lie to his priest during confession. He has been reciting his usual catalogue of petty sins, and wishing that he could liven up the occasion by confessing something really spectacular, when the priest unexpectedly asks if he hasn't some lies

[4] To John Jamieson, April 15, 1934, quoted in Arthur Mizener, *The Far Side of Paradise* (Boston: Houghton Mifflin and Co., 1951), p. 172.
[5] *The Short Stories of F. Scott Fitzgerald*, ed., Malcolm Cowley, (New York: Charles Scribner's Sons, 1951), pp. 159-172.

to confess, too. Of course, he tells lies. But instead, Rudolph un-
thinkingly seizes the opportunity to make a dramatic gesture.
Drawing himself up to his full height, he proudly assures the
priest that he *never* tells lies. It is a convincing performance, and
afterwards, walking home, Rudolph savors to the full the esthetic
satisfaction of a dramatic action brilliantly executed. But before
long his conscience reminds him of the terrible thing he has
done. Not only has he lied to the priest but, by telling a lie during
confession, he has nullified the value of the priest's subsequent
act of absolution. He has trouble convincing himself, however,
that an action which has been so unpremeditated and the source
of such intense pleasure could be displeasing to God. His first
thought is to excuse the lie by pretending that Blatchford said it,
for it is the kind of performance of which Blatchford would have
approved. But eventually his religious training reasserts itself.
After several unhappy days during which he expects momentarily
to be stricken down by the hand of an angry God, Rudolph finally
seeks out the priest and confesses everything.

At this point, however, the priest fails him. Father Schwartz
is also an incurable romantic. In Rudolph's actions he sees mir-
rored his own frustrated desires for a fuller, more esthetically
satisfying life. Instead of disciplining the child, exacting the pen-
ance he expects as his punishment, and then absolving him,
Father Schwartz offhandedly excuses his conduct by mumbling
a technical expiatory formula over Rudolph's head. Then the
priest launches out into a crazy speech that Rudolph understands as justification of what he has done. Leaving the unhappy
old man, Rudolph now believes that all his previous suspicions
about God and His Church have been confirmed. Somewhere
there is a glittering world where he can exist apart from God and
his priests, morally responsible only to the promptings of his own
imagination. This is the world of Blatchford Sarnemington, a
world that he can enter merely by shedding his everyday identity
and becoming Blatchford. Henceforth, as Blatchford Sarnemington, he would dwell "in that small corner of his mind where he

was safe from God, where he prepared the subterfuges with which he often tricked God."[6]

In *The Great Gatsby* Rudolph Miller reappears as Jimmie Gatz while Blatchford Sarnemington has been renamed Jay Gatsby. Jimmie's decision to change his name, Fitzgerald tells us, was "the specific moment that witnessed the beginning of his career." And that career began, as we know from "Absolution," when ten-year-old Jimmie Gatz decided to commit himself to the moral world of his private imagination "where he was safe from God." "The truth was," Fitzgerald says, "that Jay Gatsby of West Egg, Long Island, sprang from his Platonic conception of himself. He was a Son of God—a phrase which, if it means anything, means just that—and he must be about His Father's business, the service of a vast, vulgar, and meretricious beauty."[7]

The source of "Absolution," as we might expect, was its author's own childhood. At the age of eleven Fitzgerald had told a lie during confession and endured several subsequent days of terror before he finally mustered up the courage to tell the priest what he had done. Many years later he still remembered it distinctly as having been "a very chilling experience." Moreover, although he never went so far as to formally change his name, he had gone around the neighborhood as a child claiming that he was not the son of his parents but had been found on the Fitzgerald doorstep one cold morning wrapped in a blanket to which was pinned a paper bearing on it the regal name of "Stuart." These were merely manifestations of his passionate desire to escape from the drab, everyday world into the more exciting one of his imagination. He was convinced that the latter was a better world, esthetically as well as morally. But when he told grown-ups about the adventures he had in that other world they merely scolded him and accused him of "telling lies."[8]

[6] *Ibid.*, p. 163.
[7] F. Scott Fitzgerald, *The Great Gatsby*, The Scribner Library Edition (New York: Charles Scribner's Sons, 1960), p. 99.
[8] See unpublished ms. of Chap. I of "The Romantic Egotist," and Fitzgerald's unpublished autobiographical Ledger, Princeton Library.

By the time Fitzgerald was twenty-two, that is, by the time he had decided to become a professional writer and had begun to write his first novel, he had renounced his moral responsibility both to his parents and to their church—the Church of Rome—and had committed himself to the realization of his own romantic dreams. In his Ledger opposite September, 1917, (his twenty-first birthday) he noted "last year as a Catholic." For the next several years this new philosophy paid off handsome dividends. He completed the autobiographical novel, "The Romantic Egotist," which, rewritten and retitled *This Side of Paradise*, made him rich and famous. He married the elusive, much-sought-after Alabama girl, Zelda Sayre, who (as he proudly noted in his Ledger) had been voted "prettiest and most attractive" by her high school graduating class.[9]

But by 1922, when Fitzgerald began to plan his third novel, *The Great Gatsby*, the romantic idealism which had supported him so well at the beginning of his career was beginning to wear thin. By hard work and single-minded devotion to his adolescent dreams, he had made every single one of them come true: fame, money, success, marriage to a popular girl. Yet one by one as he had reached out and seized them, they had literally turned to ashes in his grasp. Now looking back from a more mature vantage point, he saw how much he had enthralled himself in the service of a spurious set of ideals. In "Absolution," we find Fitzgerald scrutinizing his own past, trying to locate where it was that he had gone wrong. He was by no means ready to discount completely the value of his romantic egotism. "That's the whole burden of this novel," he would write Ludlow Fowler while he was still working on it during the summer of 1924, "—the loss of those illusions that give such color to the world that you don't care whether things are true or false so long as they partake of the imagined glory." But he was nonetheless keenly aware of the limitations of this philosophy as a guide to what was actually "true and false." In "Absolution" we see Fitzgerald struggling awk-

[9] Ledger, Princeton University Library.

wardly to judge it from the only other moral point of view at his disposal, that of the childhood religious faith in which he had been reared.[10]

The trouble with "Absolution", however, is that Fitzgerald's personal history so muddied up the narrative that the story failed to make its point effectively. Fitzgerald was so sentimentally involved in his private dislike for Father Schwartz (probably based on someone he had once known) that the reader easily misses the point that Rudolph, who is a much more attractive character, is being judged by the standards of the church served so badly by its crazy priest. To Fitzgerald's chagrin, after "Absolution" appeared in the *American Mercury*, he was accused by some of his Catholic friends of having written a sacrilegious story. We can see from its sequel, *The Great Gatsby*, however, that Rudolph by his choice is irretrieveably damned.

One of the things that saved Fitzgerald, in *Gatsby*, from the subjective pitfalls of "Absolution," was his decision to approach his material "from a new angle" by presenting it through the eyes of a narrator, Nick Carraway. Nick is a marked improvement over Father Schwartz because although, like the priest, he both sympathizes with and judges the hero, he is capable of a much wider sympathy as well as a more universal and less dogmatic kind of judgment. Fortunately Fitzgerald saved the first draft of *The Great Gatsby* that was written from this new approach. And from it we can see that at the beginning Fitzgerald was almost as confused and uncertain about Nick's relationship to Gatsby as he had been about that of Father Schwartz to Rudolph Miller. This is especially true of the opening chapter, in which Nick is first introduced. But as the new version of *Gatsby* took shape, especially after the first draft was finished and Fitzgerald had gone back and carefully revised it, Nick gradually developed a clear relationship to the hero as well as a definite personality all his own.[11]

[10] To Ludlow Fowler, n.d. (ca. August 1924), Princeton Library.
[11] Pencil draft, *Gatsby* ms., Princeton, Chap. I.

During this process the specifically Catholic framework of "Absolution" disappeared and Nick's judgment of his neighbor, Gatsby, was established on other terms. Nick and Gatsby, like Rudolph Miller and Blatchford Sarnemington, were originally doubles—projections of two different aspects of Fitzgerald's own personality. How much Nick and Gatsby at first were almost identical characters we can see by turning back to this first draft of the novel; but gradually, after extensive revision, they assumed separate identities. What distinguishes Nick from Gatsby most conspicuously, of course, is the fact that despite his deeply-rooted self-identification with Gatsby, Nick is capable of judging him— and so is saved from a similar fate.

What is it that saves Nick from following in his gaudy neighbor's footsteps? What has taken the place of the Catholic framework that served for "Absolution"? Nick survives because he possesses two kinds of knowledge that Gatsby lacks. The first is that heritage of traditional moral values that he has learned from his father. He is indebted to Mr. Carraway, he says at the beginning, both for that "habit of reserving all judgments" which allows him (alone of all of Gatsby's acquaintances) to value his neighbor's romantic idealism, and for that "sense of the fundamental decencies of life" which makes it possible for him to see the shabby limitations of Gatsby's dreams. At the start of the story, you recall, Nick was ready to reject this moral heritage, along with the Carraway name. That is, Nick refused to take the job awaiting him in the Middle Western wholesale hardware business that had been in his family for three generations. Instead he left the "bored, sprawling, swollen towns beyond the Ohio" and came East to take a job in a Wall Street brokerage firm. But by the end of the novel it is the values represented for Nick by the image of his father that have saved him from Gatsby's terrible mistake. Realizing this, Nick is ready at last to come home.

The second kind of knowledge that Nick possesses, in contrast to his neighbor, is his ever-present awareness of man's mortality.

For Nick the fact of death stands inexorably between man's dreams and the chances of realizing them during his brief lifetime. Not only is Nick continually aware of death, and his narrative strewn with death images, but the entire novel seems to have been conceived by Fitzgerald as the expression of a death wish— a wish that, in his first draft, he actually has Nick express at the conclusion of Chapter I. At this initial stage of his conception of *The Great Gatsby*, Nick resembled Gatsby not only in his Mid-Western origins and his romantic setting off for the East, but by the fact that Nick had also been in love with Daisy Buchanan before her marriage to Tom. In this earliest version that we have of Chapter I, Nick has not yet seen Daisy since her marriage. So, when he learns the facts about that marriage he is profoundly disturbed. It is bad enough to find Tom having an affair with another woman. What shocks Nick even more is Daisy's amoral attitude toward her situation, her "basic insincerity," as he calls it. Discovering this, it is as though the virginal Daisy of Nick's dreams has been contaminated by an evil so palpable that everything surrounding him has been corrupted by it—not only Long Island, but the whole American continent stretching out to the Western sea. Indeed so intense is Nick's mood of disillusion in this earliest version of Chapter I that Fitzgerald was inspired at this point to write the long, oft-quoted threnody to the memory of the continent's lost innocence (that "fresh, green breast of the new world . . .") that he eventually made the coda-like conclusion to the entire novel.

At this point also, in this earliest version that we have of Chapter I, Nick also said (in a passage later altered):[12]

> It was already deep summer on roadhouse roofs and on the dark murmurous little porches and around the garages where new red gas-pumps sat out in pools of light—and summer always promised fulfillment of my old childish dreams. I wanted something definite to happen to *me*, something that would wear me out a little—for

[12] The quoted passage will be found in the pencil draft, *Gatsby* ms., at a point corresponding to line 19, p. 25, of the 1925 pub. text.

I suppose the urge to adventure is one and the same with the obscure craving of our bodies for a certain death.

Then, looking out across the bay, Nick notices for the first time
the shadowy silhouette of his mysterious neighbor, Gatsby, standing on the beach nearby. Thus, everything that is still to happen—
all of Gatsby's subsequent history—is to serve Nick as a kind of
moral exemplum, a cautionary tale illustrating the kind of fate
Nick himself might have suffered if his love for Daisy had blinded
him, as it did Gatsby, to the evil that is as much a part of her
nature as it is of any other mortal being.

But Nick, unlike Gatsby, is continually aware of the fact that
man must die. Indeed the odor of mortality is everywhere in the
novel, even more in the early drafts than in the published version
of the text. In one draft, when Gatsby proudly shows Nick his
oversized yellow sports car ("the death car," as the New York
newspapers will later call it after Myrtle's death), Nick is automatically reminded of a hearse. Indeed, a few paragraphs further
on, when Nick is riding in Gatsby's car to New York, he actually
passes a funeral and is confronted with the image of "a dead man
. . . in a hearse heaped full of flowers." Undoubtedly the most
conspicuous death image in the novel is that of the waste land
of dust and ashes over which Gatsby and his neighbors must pass
every time they go to New York. From this limbo blows that
"foul dust" that, Nick reminds us, "floated in the wake of Gatsby's
dreams." It is typical of Tom Buchanan's inverted sense of values
that, after having helped to contrive Gatsby's murder, he arrogantly tells Nick "He [Gatsby] threw dust in your eyes just
like he did Daisy's." At one time Fitzgerald even planned to call
his novel "Among the Ash-Heaps and Millionaires."[18]

Over this portentous waste land brood the sightless eyes of Dr.
T. J. Eckleburg—rooted (as Fitzgerald says in another deleted

[18] The deleted reference to the hearse (pencil draft) comes at line 6, p. 77,
of the 1925 text; see letter of Maxwell Perkins to FSF, April 4, 1924 (Princeton).

passage) "in a spot that reeks of death." Nearby stands the squalid, ash-covered garage of George Wilson, the insane agent of Gatsby's doom. (In his manuscript Fitzgerald carefully changed the color of Wilson's hair from "yellow" to the more deathly hue of "pale.")[14]

At the end, the simple fact of Gatsby's death is quickly stated in a sentence. But the implications of that death necessitate a long, concluding chapter. No one besides Nick is willing to confront those implications. Gatsby's fatuous father, (an obvious contrast to Nick's father) consoles himself with the sordid lie of his dead son's "success." Gatsby's other friends all stay away presumably following the corrupt Wolfshiem's maxim that in matters connected with death "it is better to leave everything alone." Only Nick is incapable of letting things alone. The fact of his neighbor's death rouses Nick—the hitherto passive onlooker— to one of the few positive actions of his career.

> As he lay in his house and didn't move or breathe or speak, hour upon hour, it grew upon me that I was responsible because no one else was interested—interested, I mean, with that intense personal interest to which every one has some vague right at the end.

Whereupon Nick sees that his dead friend has a decent funeral and then, taking up one more responsibility, goes back home.[15]

Nick's vicarious involvement in Gatsby's destiny, in other words, has permitted him to see the world for a brief space through the glasses of Dr. T. J. Eckleburg. What he sees is a waste land without moral sanctions of any kind, an anarchy in which romantic idealists like Gatsby are the most vulnerable of all. "After Gatsby's death," Nick says, "the East was haunted for me . . . distorted beyond my eyes' power of correction. So . . . I decided to come back home." Dr. Eckleburg is the symbol of a world without the idea of God, a kind of anti-God. When George Wil-

---

[14] The deleted reference to Dr. Eckleburg's eyes (pencil draft) comes at line 3, p. 28, of the 1925 text.
[15] *Gatsby*, 178 (Scribner Library Edition).

son discovers that his wife has been unfaithful he drags her to the window of his garage and there, in front of the eyes of Dr. Eckleburg, tells her: "God knows what you've been doing. You may fool me but you can't fool God." "God sees everything," the vengeance-crazed husband tells Michaelis after Myrtle's death, just before setting off on his quest for vengeance. As we might expect, he only succeeds in killing the wrong man.[16]

The evidence of "Absolution" thus serves to emphasize the crucial role played by Nick Carraway in *The Great Gatsby*. Nick is one aspect of Fitzgerald judging another aspect of himself. To do this Nick must possess not only sympathy but also the capacity for moral judgment. As the basis for this judgment, Fitzgerald initially tried to draw upon the framework of his own Catholic childhood; but his feelings about the Church of Rome had become so confused that he was unable to make objective use of them. In one sense his first novel, *This Side of Paradise*, had been the chronicle of his loss of religious faith. His subsequent feelings about the Church probably had not changed materially from those he attributed to his hero, Amory Blaine, at the end of that novel:

> The idea was strong in him that there was an intrinsic lack in those to whom religion was necessary, and religion to Amory meant the Church of Rome. Quite conceivably it was an empty ritual, but it was seemingly the only assimilitative traditionary bulwark against the decay of morals. . . . Yet, acceptance was, for the present, impossible. He wanted time and the absence of pressure. He wanted to keep the tree without the ornaments.[17]

Fitzgerald's solution, in *The Great Gatsby*, was to retain the tree—the residual tradition of moral values represented by the advice given Nick by his father—without the sectarian dogma. Underlying this was his profound, perhaps, unconscious, awareness of death.

The result was a moral position that permitted Fitzgerald to

[16] *Ibid.*, 178, 160.
[17] F. Scott Fitzgerald, *This Side of Paradise* (New York: Charles Scribner's Sons, 1920, 1948), p. 281.

value the romantic impulse he shared in common with Nick and Gatsby (a "heightened sensitivity to the promises of life"), as well as to see its limitations. Thus, *The Great Gatsby* became a criticism of the romantic egotism Fitzgerald had celebrated in *This Side of Paradise*. It was a retreat toward, though by no means into, the bosom of Mother Church. How desperately Nick longed for such a moral absolute by the end of *Gatsby* is suggested by his remark, "When I came back from the East last summer I wanted the world to be in uniform and at a sort of moral attention forever." The closest Nick can come to such an absolute, however, is to go back home and take up his responsibilities as a member of the Carraway clan.[18]

Several months after *Gatsby* was published, Fitzgerald complained in letters to both Edmund Wilson and John Peale Bishop that (as he wrote Wilson) "of all the reviews, even the most enthusiastic, no one has the slightest idea what the book is about." What it was about, he told Bishop, was himself. To this Bishop objected strenuously. "I can't undertand your resentment of the critics' failure to perceive your countenance behind Gatsby's mask. . . . It seems to me to be interesting, if at all, privately only." What Fitzgerald meant, however, was not his literal, but rather his moral countenance. Like T. S. Eliot's *The Waste Land*, *The Great Gatsby* is a religious work because it has as its source a deeply felt religious emotion. This, perhaps, was what Mr. Eliot had in mind when, soon after it was published, he called it "the first step the American novel has taken since Henry James."[19]

[18] *Gatsby*, 2.
[19] FSF to Edmund Wilson, n.d. (ca. autumn, 1925) reprinted in *The Crack-Up*, ed. by Wilson, (New York 1945), 270; Bishop to FSF, n.d. (ca. Jan. 1926) Princeton University; T. S. Eliot to FSF, Dec. 31, 1925, reprinted in *The Crack-Up*, 310.

BIBLIOGRAPHY

A Selective, Annotated Checklist of Works Useful to a Study of
The Great Gatsby

For a much more elaborate checklist, the reader is referred to that
compiled by Maurice Beebe and Jackson R. Bryer, in the Spring,
1961 issue of *Modern Fiction Studies*.

I. Books

Katcher, Leo. *The Big Bankroll: The Life and Times of Arnold
Rothstein.* New York: Harper's, 1959.

Useful for portrait of New York underworld of the 1920's.

Kazin, Alfred, editor. *F. Scott Fitzgerald: The Man and His Work.*
Cleveland & New York: World, 1951.

An intelligently edited collection, containing essays or letters on *The Great Gatsby* by H. L. Mencken, Maxwell
Perkins, T. S. Eliot.

Miller, James E. Jr. *The Fictional Technique of Scott Fitzgerald.*
The Hague: Martinus Nijhoff, 1957.

A brilliant analysis of Fitzgerald's growth to maturity as
an artist, concentrating upon *The Great Gatsby* as the
great achievement.

Mizener, Arthur. *The Far Side of Paradise.* Boston: Houghton,
Mifflin, 1951.

Not only the best biographical and critical study of Fitz-gerald, but one of the best of its kind in recent years.

Mizener, Arthur, editor. *The Afternoon of an Author: A Selection of Uncollected Stories and Essays.* New York: Charles Scrib-ner's Sons, 1958.

Especially useful for Fitzgerald's journalistic pieces of the 1920's, bearing upon social phenomena of the decade.

Wilson, Edmund, editor. *The Crack-Up.* New York: New Direc-tions, 1945.

An indispensable collection of essays by and about Fitz-gerald, excerpts from his Note-Books, letters to and from him. Of special value to a study of *The Great Gatsby* are the Note-Books and Fitzgerald's reminiscent essays about the 1920's.

II. *Essays*

Aldridge, John W. "The Life of Gatsby," in *Twelve Original Essays on Great American Novels,* edited by Charles Shapiro, 210-37. Detroit: Wayne State University Press, 1958.

An indecisive and even inept reading of the novel.

Bewley, Marius. "Scott Fitzgerald's Criticism of America," *Se-wanee Review,* 62 (Spring, 1954), 223-46; slightly en-larged version in *The Eccentric Design,* 259-87. New York: Columbia University Press, 1959.

Early version reprinted in this book.

Bicknell, John W. "The Wasteland of F. Scott Fitzgerald," *Virginia Quarterly Review,* 30 (Autumn, 1954), 556-72.

The more obvious suggestions of Eliot's influence in Fitz-gerald's work.

Chase, Richard. *"The Great Gatsby,"* in *The Modern Novel and Its Tradition,* 162-67. New York: Doubleday Anchor Books, 1957.

Reprinted in this book.

Frohock, W. M., "Morals, Manners, and Scott Fitzgerald," *Southwest Review*, 40 (Summer, 1955), 220-28.

Fussell, Edwin. "Fitzgerald's Brave New World," *English Literary History*, 19 (December, 1952), 291-306.
A revised version printed in this book.

Geismar, Maxwell. "Orestes at the Ritz," in *The Last of the Provincials*, 287-352. Boston: Houghton, Mifflin, 1947.
Pages 313-22 discuss *The Great Gatsby*.

Hanzo, Thomas A. "The Theme and the Narrator of 'The Great Gatsby,'" *Modern Fiction Studies*, 2 (Winter, 1956-57), 183-90.
Reprinted in this book.

Hindus, Milton. "The Eyes of Dr. T. J. Eckleburg," *Boston University Studies in English*, 3 (Spring, 1957), 22-31.

Hoffman, Frederick J. "*The Great Gatsby*," in *The Twenties*, 111-19. New York: Viking, 1955.

Ornstein, Robert. "Scott Fitzgerald's Fable of East and West," *College English*, 18 (December, 1956), 139-43.
East-West contrast in *The Great Gatsby*, its effect on Carraway and Gatsby.

Raleigh, John Henry. "Fitzgerald's 'The Great Gatsby': Legendary Bases and Allegorical Significances," *University of Kansas City Review*, 23 (June, 1957), 283-91.

Stallman, Robert W. "Conrad and *The Great Gatsby*," *Twentieth Century Literature*, 1 (April, 1955), 5-12.
A useful study of Conrad's influence.

——. "Gatsby and the Hole in Time," *Modern Fiction Studies*, 1 (November, 1955), 1-16.
Major emphasis on implausibility of Carraway as judge of Gatsby's world, because of dishonesty, immorality; an exaggerated and often incorrect interpretation.

Thale, Jerome. "The Narrator as Hero," *Twentieth Century Literature*, 3 (July, 1957), 69-73.

Conrad's Marlow and Fitzgerald's Carraway compared; Carraway the real hero of *The Great Gatsby*.

Trilling, Lionel. "F. Scott Fitzgerald," in *The Liberal Imagination*, 243-54. New York: Viking, 1950.
Reprinted in this book.

Troy, William. "The Authority of Failure," *Accent*, 6 (Autumn, 1945), 56-60.
Reprinted in this book.

Wescott, Glenway. "The Moral of Scott Fitzgerald," in *The Crack-Up*, 323-37. New York, New Directions, 1945.
Reprinted in this book.